STRATEGIC SUPPLY MANAGEMENT REVISITED

Competing in an Era of Rapid Change and Disruption

Robert J. Trent

J.ROSS PUBLISHING

Copyright © 2018 by J. Ross Publishing

ISBN-13: 978-1-60427-150-8

Printed and bound in the U.S.A. Printed on acid-free paper.

10 9 8 7 6 5 4 3 2 1

Library of Congress Cataloging-in-Publication Data

Names: Trent, Robert J., author.
Title: Strategic supply management revisited : competing in an era of rapid
  change and disruption / by Robert J. Trent, Ph.D.
Description: Plantation, FL : J. Ross Publishing, [2018] | Includes
  bibliographical references and index.
Identifiers: LCCN 2017060794 | ISBN 9781604271508 (hardcover : alk. paper)
Subjects: LCSH: Business logistics—Management. | Strategic planning. |
  Materials management. | Industrial procurement—Management.
Classification: LCC HD38.5 .T7425 2018 | DDC 658.7—dc23 LC record available
  at https://lccn.loc.gov/2017060794

Direct all inquiries to J. Ross Publishing, Inc., 300 S. Pine Island Rd., Suite
305, Plantation, FL 33324.

Phone: (954) 727-9333
Fax: (561) 892-0700
Web: www.jrosspub.com

CONTENTS

This book is dedicated to my wife, our two children and their spouses, and our five grandchildren.

PREFACE

Welcome to the exciting and sometimes frustrating world of supply management. It's a world where the legacy function called *purchasing* is replaced with a forward looking and progressive approach to sourcing called *strategic supply management*. It's a world where a reactive focus on transactions, arm's-length relationships, and price is replaced by the development of leading-edge supply strategies. It's a world where the contributions that are made by supply managers are continuously refreshed through new and exciting initiatives. And it's a world that features rapid change and disruption.

In 2007, I authored a book titled *Strategic Supply Management: Creating the Next Source of Competitive Advantage*. That book provided a framework for creating a supply management organization that provides a reliable source of supply and, eventually, competitive advantage. It was targeted to supply managers and executive leaders across all industries and firms of all sizes. The book also targeted non-supply leaders who wanted a deeper understanding of the supply management process.

That book presented a systematic journey through the world of supply management that is still relevant today. Each chapter presented information about concepts, processes, tools, and best practices that relate to a specific topic. The contents were supported by extensive research, experience with leading companies, and information available from objective sources. The chapters presented what we needed to know about each topic in order for the reader to gain a holistic perspective that focused on breadth rather than depth. The objective was to appreciate how the elements that comprise strategic supply management come together to create a hard-to-duplicate source of competitive advantage. That objective is still important today.

While the body of knowledge presented in the 2007 book is largely still relevant, the world has changed in ways that require an appreciation of a new set of topics. As Chapter 1 will explain, there is no denying that over the last decade or so, some interesting things have happened (and continue to happen) that affect the management of supply networks and supply chains. What are those things?

- Entrance of new competitors and the introduction of disruptive technology (such as 3-D printing)
- Increased commodity market volatility
- Supply chains that have become riskier
- Demographic workforce changes and an exodus of experienced employees
- Emergence of big data and predictive analytics
- Customer requirements that are progressively more demanding
- Supply chains that are increasingly complex and global
- An ever-expanding list of government regulations
- Relentless and severe pressure to reduce cost and cycle times

While this is not an exhaustive listing of what makes a supply manager's life interesting, we should appreciate that the supply world can be a tough place. How does *Strategic Supply Management Revisited: Competing in an Era of Rapid Change and Disruption* help us better understand how to survive and even thrive in this environment?

This book consists of 15 chapters that are organized into three parts. Part I includes two chapters that set the stage for the remainder of the book. Chapter 1 provides a concise explanation of strategic supply management, addresses the changing competitive landscape, and identifies the characteristics of a leading supply organization. Chapter 2 explains the true meaning of overused and misused terms and concepts in supply management. The chapter could easily have been titled: *How Not to Sound Dumb When You Are Trying to Sound Smart.* When using buzzwords, it is important to at least use them correctly.

Part II focuses on the four areas that enable strategic supply management to become a reality. Chapter 3 explores the shift from human resource management to talent management; Chapter 4 explores evolving organizational designs; Chapter 5 highlights new directions in supply measurement; and Chapter 6 deals with the information-enabled supply organization. Do not minimize the role that these four areas play when crafting supply management strategies.

Part III consists of nine chapters that explore a set of current topics in supply management. Most of these topics failed to make it onto the radar screen back in 2007. Chapter 7 addresses the importance of developing well-crafted supply strategies (with company examples), while Chapter 8 deals with linking supply management success to corporate financial success. Chapter 9 explains how to gain competitive advantage through true collaborative relationships, while Chapter 10 helps us understand how to become the customer of choice to suppliers. Chapter 11 deals with the inevitability of risk, while Chapter 12 presents over a dozen types of flexibility that help reduce risk and increase corporate resilience. Chapter 13 discusses the importance of global supply management and explores in detail the topic of reshoring. This chapter will explain why reshoring work back to a home country, such as the United States, is not as easy as it sounds. Chapter 14 makes the case for becoming a process-driven organization and identifies a set of best practices associated with four critical processes. The book concludes with a comprehensive coverage of complexity, including why we have it and how to overcome it.

Creating a supply organization that can be counted on to deliver a steady stream of performance improvements does not happen by chance. This book will strengthen your knowledge about what it takes to compete in an era of rapid change and disruption. Certain words capture well the current state of supply management—risky, exciting, and dynamic. These descriptors can work in your favor—or they can completely overwhelm you. Understanding the topics presented throughout this book will help ensure that the former rather than the latter is the case.

ABOUT THE AUTHOR

Dr. Robert J. Trent, Ph.D., is the supply chain management program director and professor of supply chain management at Lehigh University. He holds a B.S. degree in materials logistics management from Michigan State University, an M.B.A. degree from Wayne State University, and a Ph.D. in purchasing/operations management from Michigan State University.

Prior to his return to academia, Bob worked for the Chrysler Corporation in the company's aftermarket division. His industrial experience includes assignments in production scheduling, packaging engineering with responsibility for new part packaging set-up, and the management of nonproductive materials, distribution planning, and operations management at the Boston regional distribution facility. He also worked on numerous special projects. Bob has provided consulting services, educational services, and presentations to almost 60 corporations, government agencies, and associations and has worked directly with dozens of other companies during research visits. He is also extensively involved with executive education.

Bob has authored or coauthored eight books and 50 articles that have appeared in a range of publications. He has also coauthored eight major research monographs published by *CAPS Research* and has made presentations at dozens of conferences and seminars.

Bob has been awarded the *MBA Core Curriculum Teacher of the Year*, the *MBA Elective Teacher of the Year*, and the *Staub Award for Excellence* in undergraduate teaching at Lehigh University. He has also been awarded the *Mercy Professorship* and the *Beckwith Professorship* at Lehigh.

He and his family reside in Lopatcong Township, New Jersey. He can be reached at rjt2@lehigh.edu.

Web
Added
Value™

At J. Ross Publishing we are committed to providing today's professional with practical, hands-on tools that enhance the learning experience and give readers an opportunity to apply what they have learned. That is why we offer free ancillary materials available for download on this book and all participating Web Added Value™ publications. These online resources may include interactive versions of material that appears in the book or supplemental templates, worksheets, models, plans, case studies, proposals, spreadsheets and assessment tools, among other things. Whenever you see the WAV™ symbol in any of our publications, it means bonus materials accompany the book and are available from the Web Added Value Download Resource Center at www.jrosspub.com.

Downloads for *Strategic Supply Management Revisited: Competing in an Era of Rapid Change and Disruption* include total landed cost and DuPont financial models, research findings, a supplier relation and trust analysis, and a supplier satisfaction survey.

Part I

Setting the Stage

1

THE CHANGING COMPETITIVE LANDSCAPE

Over the last 30 years, large North American and European multi-national corporations have enjoyed one of the strongest periods of prosperity in modern economic history.[1] From 1980 to 2013, after-tax operating profits for larger firms grew 30% faster than global GDP, and corporate net income grew 50% faster than global GDP. Furthermore, large North American and Western European companies captured more than half of all global profits.

While the last 30 years has been a remarkable era, it is also an era that appears to be ending. New rivals, including technology disruptors and nongovernmental firms in emerging markets are putting established incumbents on notice.[2] These new entrants often play by different rules and demonstrate an agility and aggressiveness that many larger Western companies will struggle to match. At a minimum the new entrants represent a new and troubling source of competition. Welcome to the era of rapid change and disruption.

Market success will increasingly require firms to bring a *total package* to the table—a package that must include a set of progressive supply management activities and practices. The supply package can be broad, involving a set of expected activities that includes integrated global sourcing, early supplier involvement, commodity management teams, and supplier development. But, disruptions and market changes are causing firms to ramp up their supply management prowess and stress an emerging set of strategies that address supply chain complexity, financial management, collaboration, and risk. A common feature of these emerging strategies is that they have the ability to make contributions well beyond the functional level—they can affect corporate performance.

As companies search for ways to grow, they cannot ignore the changes affecting supply management. This chapter refreshes our understanding of what strategic supply management is about and explores the changes that have been affecting, and will continue to affect, supply markets and supply chains. This chapter concludes with a set of characteristics that define a supply management leader—characteristics that later chapters will build upon.

WHAT IS STRATEGIC SUPPLY MANAGEMENT? A FAST REFRESHER

My earlier book, *Strategic Supply Management*, defined supply management in great detail. Since it is safe to assume that a number of the readers of this book may not have read *Strategic Supply Management*, this chapter will provide a refresher regarding what supply management is all about. First, fundamental differences exist between purchasing and supply management. Purchasing is a functional group (a formal entity on the organizational chart) as well as a functional activity (buying goods and services). The purchasing group traditionally performs many of the activities that support an organization's operations, including negotiating with suppliers, buying, contracting, and research.

Supply management, on the other hand, is a cross-functional, proactive process for obtaining goods and services that features the active management and involvement of suppliers. The supply management process involves identifying a company's total requirements, developing supply strategies, evaluating and selecting suppliers, and then managing and developing those suppliers to achieve performance advantages at a level higher than what competitors realize.

A key part of the supply management process is its cross-functional nature, meaning it involves purchasing, engineering, supplier quality assurance, suppliers, and other related functional groups working together as one team, early on, to further mutual goals.[3] It involves internal groups and external suppliers working together to achieve advantages in cost, innovation, product development, risk and financial management, delivery, supply chain responsiveness, technology, cycle time, and quality.

Supply management features longer term win-win relationships between a buying company and a carefully selected set of suppliers (Chapter 2 explains the concept of win-win). At times, supply management provides support directly to a supplier in exchange for continuous performance improvements, such as price reductions. Critical suppliers become almost an extension of the buying company.

Supply management processes and approaches are remarkably robust as we move across industries. It's surprising how well the language of supply management translates across industry sectors. Every industry evaluates, selects, and measures suppliers; enters into contracts; pursues supplier development initiatives; and sources at least part of their purchase requirements worldwide. The good news is that laggard industries can learn from those industries that are

Table 1.1   Factors affecting the need for strategic supply management

Less Need	Greater Need
Buyer controls most production requirements internally	Outsourcing is a major part of the business model
New product development cycle times are stable	New product development cycle times are shortening rapidly
Suppliers are primarily domestic	Suppliers are primarily global
Competitors are slow to improve their performance	Competitors are rapidly improving their performance
Customers exert minimal pressure to improve	Customers exert intense pressure to improve
Competitors are primarily domestic	Competitors are primarily global
Your industry features a slower rate of technological change	Your industry features a rapid rate of technological change
Suppliers minimally impact your ability to compete	Suppliers extensively impact your ability to compete
Purchases make up a small portion of revenues	Purchases make up an extensive portion of revenues

at the forefront of supply management. Do not discount the value of someone else's lessons learned, especially when those lessons are learned the hard way.

It is misleading to think that all companies should endorse this thing called strategic supply management. Some competitive environments demand that sourcing and supply activities take place at a sophisticated level. Other environments may only require a purchasing group to have functional competence to be successful. Table 1.1 identifies a set of factors that affect the need for pursuing more sophisticated levels of supply management. All industries and companies are not created equal, either in their need or their desire for strategic supply management.

Keeping in mind that not all companies need to endorse strategic supply management at the same rate or level, a set of general principles also underlies strategic supply management. These principles further define strategic supply management as a concept:

- Not all supplier relationships matter equally
- Supply chain improvement is a never-ending journey and supply managers play a primary role
- Processes are critical to supply management success
- Measurement is an essential enabler of supply management success
- Becoming a strategic supply organization does not happen overnight
- Supply managers can be creative

- Strategic supply management involves more than just achieving the lowest price
- Risk is the new supply chain wildcard
- Strategic supply management is organizational rather than functional
- Supply management activity does not necessarily lead to accomplishment
- Industries pursue strategic supply management at different rates
- Strategic supply management won't happen without the right people, systems, and organizational support structure

No longer simply a transactional activity, supply management is about creating new areas of competitive advantage. This can involve the attainment of better quality, lower costs, faster responsiveness to end-customer needs, and incorporating supplier-provided technologies and features into new product designs. Supply managers should envision the domain of advantages they bring to the table as being broad rather than narrow.

WHAT HAS CHANGED?

Almost all of the ideas and the body of knowledge that appeared in the predecessor to this book are still relevant today. But, there is no denying that over the last decade or so changes and disruptions of many kinds have occurred (and are still occurring) that affect supply networks and supply chains. The following information presents some of the noteworthy changes that affect our discussion of strategic supply management.

New Disruptors and Game-Changing Technology

Without question we have entered an age of economic disruption. Airbnb, a company with no physical hotel properties or assets has had a higher market capitalization than Hilton and Hyatt hotels combined (although this can change as the stock market changes). In what universe is it possible that a company with no significant assets to speak of can be worth more than companies with physical properties located all over the world? Uber, at least before it suffered a host of self-inflicted problems, had a market value greater than GM, Ford, and Honda. And, who does not wish that he or she had purchased Amazon stock 15 years ago? Welcome to the age of disruption.

Table 1.2 provides examples of game-changing market disruptions. Some of these disruptions are due to technology changes; some are due to changing customer and consumer preferences or tastes. All can have the effect of disrupting someone's business model, perhaps irreparably (Chapter 2 explains the concept of a business model). Market disruptions also make supply chain planning increasingly difficult.

Table 1.2 Examples of market threats and disruptors

Victim	Threat or Disruptor
Steel	Aluminum, plastics, composites
Calculators, watches, landline phones, cameras	Smartphones
Suits and ties	Business casual
Toll booth collectors	EZ Pass, Fast Pass
Brick and mortar retailers	Online retailers, especially Amazon
Bank tellers	ATMs, online banking
Service jobs, such as fast food and airline check in	Self-service kiosks
Dial-up Internet modem	High speed fiber optic Internet
Cable TV	Satellite and Internet TV
On-campus education	Online education
Manual and repetitive jobs	Robotics, automation
Vinyl records	8-track, cassette, CDs, digital music
Traditional surgery	Robotic surgery
Cab and truck drivers	Self-driving vehicles
AM/FM radio	Satellite radio; Internet radio
Myspace	Facebook and Instagram
Traditional job shops	3-D printing
Cab service	Uber and other services
Minivans	SUVs
Boxing	Mixed martial arts
Gas powered engines	Electric/hybrid vehicles
Server sales to companies	Cloud computing
Restaurants	Home meal kit services; prepared supermarket meals
Photographic film	Digital photography
Vehicle sales	Fewer teenagers getting a driver's license; ride-sharing services
Coal	Natural gas
Established consumer food product companies	Shift toward organic foods, new brand entrants, store brands
Integrated steel producers	Mini mills
Legacy airlines	Low-cost airlines; new airlines
Caskets	Cremation
OPEC	U.S. energy industry and fracking; renewable energy sources

Travel agents	Online travel sites such as Expedia, Travelocity, Hotels.com, Kayak
Hotels	Airbnb
Book and magazine printers	Electronic books and magazines
GPS add-on units in vehicles	Factory installed GPS; smartphone apps
Major beer brands	Craft brewers
Port crane operators	Automated ports

It was not long ago that a major question facing supply chain professionals was how best to leverage RFID technology as they marveled at their Nokia or Blackberry phone. Today, we are witnessing rapid disruptions that have major supply and supply chain implications. These disruptions include the creation of omni-channel distribution channels to support online retailing, autonomous vehicles, nanotechnology, artificial intelligence applications, expanded use of drone technology, robotics, blockchain data technology, small satellites, new rocket launch providers, alternative energy vehicles, a revamped Panama Canal that promises to alter trade routes, new composite materials, and predictive analytic tools and techniques. Widespread change and disruption are the order of the day.

One area featuring game-changing technology involves 3-D printing. Boeing, as well as other aerospace companies, expects to build satellites more quickly through new production practices that rely more on 3-D printing with fewer workers, which the company expects will transform the company's traditional way of building high-end commercial and military satellites and spacecraft.[4] Chapter 7 will examine Lockheed Martin's use of 3-D printing and how this fits within its supply management strategy development framework.

Increased Financial and Market Volatility

Financial and market volatility is such an important supply topic that it deserves extended treatment here. The volatile nature of commodity markets has introduced higher levels of financial and supply risk. The bottom line is that finance and supply chain professionals share something in common—both do not like commodity volatility. Volatility makes everyone's ability to plan more difficult, if not impossible. As an example: a news report noted that cotton future prices increased 12% over a three-day period! This price surge disrupted the industry during a crucial time in the crop cycle for U.S. cotton.[5]

A study by the International Monetary Fund confirmed that the size of fluctuations in commodity prices has more than tripled since 2005, compared to the period from 1980–2005. Those who follow supply markets know that when demand exceeds supply, the results are the allocation of supply, a shifting of power from buyers to sellers, and financial risk due to higher prices. And, when supply exceeds demand, we often experience a sudden drop in prices. While market speculators might see volatility as a way to capture trading profits quickly, supply chain and financial managers see it as something to manage and even avoid, if possible.

Why do we have such serious fluctuations today? Unlike previous waves of volatility, the current period of fluctuating commodity prices is not driven by a fundamental crisis such as a world war or a great depression. The volatility appears to be a structural change in the way the global economy has organized itself as only eight countries produce the majority of the world's commodities. Also, one cannot discount the impact that the economic rise of China has had on commodity markets. As demand keeps rising, prices are prone to fluctuations and this, rather than outright scarcity, is the major challenge. Other challenges facing commodity markets include a willingness of countries to manipulate the supply of certain resources to their advantage (think of OPEC)—water scarcity, climate change, and energy constraints that limit output. Mining projects in Chile and Mongolia have been delayed over the last several years due to energy and water shortages—something that has affected world prices. Nationalization of commodity companies and the confiscation of foreign-owned assets (such as in Venezuela) are also factors in an era of fluctuating prices.[6] It has also become evident that industrial buyers are not only competing with other companies for commodities, they are competing with investors and speculators who look to commodity markets for financial returns. The manipulation of commodity markets has also become a concern.

We can also have volatility because of the abrupt changes or shocks that occur in the demand or supply side of the commodity equation. We are all familiar with stories involving a facility that explodes and takes with it a disproportionate amount of the world's supply of whatever it is that facility produces. At times we cannot even pronounce what that facility makes. We quickly come to realize, however, that the item that just disappeared is important to many industries that rely on it to make their products.

Abrupt shifts can also affect the supply side of commodity markets. When a large player or even an entire industry enters a commodity market, sometimes for the first time, the result is often a dramatic shift in the demand curve with a lagging shift in the supply curve. The inevitable result of this scenario is higher commodity prices.

Supply Chains Are Becoming Riskier

Each year Allianz Insurance conducts a survey to identify the top risks faced by corporations based on responses from more than 1,300 risk experts in over 50 countries.[7] At least from a supply chain perspective, the Allianz risk barometer indicates the world has indeed become a riskier place. Table 1.3 identifies the percentage of firms that indicate a particular item represents a top three risk from a much larger list of choices. Supply chain risks clearly are now at the forefront of business risks. Supply chain risk, unfortunately, has made it to the big leagues.

While natural disasters like hurricanes and floods capture the headlines, the reality is that supply chains face an abundance of risks that most observers believe only to be increasing. A survey by APQC revealed that 75% of responding companies indicated that they were hit by a major supply chain disruption over the last two years from the date of the survey. These firms know all too well that supply chain risk is real. IBM has identified a set of factors that are affecting the riskiness of supply chains:

Table 1.3   Top 10 global business risks

Risk Category	2017 Score and Rank	2016 Score and Rank
Business interruption (incl. supply chain disruption and vulnerability)	37% (1)	38% (1)
Market developments (volatility, intensified competition/new entrants, M&A, market stagnation, market fluctuation)	31% (2)	34% (2)
Cyber incidents (cybercrime, IT failure, data breaches, etc.)	30% (3)	28% (3)
Natural catastrophes (such as storms, floods, earthquakes)	24% (4)	24% (4)
Changes in legislation and regulation (government change, economic sanctions, protectionism, etc.)	24% (5)	24% (5)
Macroeconomic developments (austerity programs, commodity price increase, deflation, inflation)	22% (6)	22% (6)
Fire, explosion	16% (7)	16% (8)
Political risks and violence (war, terrorism, etc.)	14% (8)	11% (9)
Loss of reputation or brand value	13% (9)	18% (7)
New technologies (such as impact of increasing interconnectivity, nanotechnology, artificial intelligence, 3-D printing, drones, etc.)	12% (10)	10% (11)

Percent value equals the percent of firms indicating the item is a top three business risk.

- Increased globalization and outsourcing, which stretches end-to-end supply chains
- Additional regulatory compliance imposed by government entities, further complicating international trade (such as the Customs Trade Partnership Against Terrorism and conflict mineral reporting requirements)
- Increased levels of economic uncertainty and market volatility, which create variability in demand and supply and make it more difficult to plan
- Shorter product life cycles and rapid rates of technology change, which increases the risk of obsolescence
- Demanding customers who require better on-time delivery, higher order fill rates, improved service levels, and shorter cycle times
- Supply capacity constraints, making it more difficult to meet demand requirements
- Natural disasters and external environmental events, which affect global supply chains
- Complex networks of suppliers and third-party service providers, as well as large interdependencies among multiple firms, which increase the need to coordinate risk

Some factors expose a company to heightened supply chain risk through indirect effects. These include just-in-time delivery and lean systems that result in little to no buffer inventory; a trend toward centralized decision making that may reduce response times and flexibility at local levels; continuous cost reductions that may affect a company's ability to plan and respond to risk events; greater use of single sourcing, which often leaves a company with fewer supply options and higher supplier switching costs; and widespread outsourcing, potentially leading to a loss of supply chain control. Sometimes our worst risks are self-inflicted.

While we can debate whether or not the world has actually become a riskier place, there is no debate that many firms are more aware and even better able to anticipate and manage the risks they face on a worldwide basis. The subject of risk management will be addressed in Chapter 11.

Demographic Workforce Changes

For some powerful reasons, the need to manage supply chain talent is becoming a strategic necessity. Beginning over five years ago, the first of the baby boomer generation (Americans born between 1946 and 1964) began to turn 65 years old. What this means is that we are witnessing a large exodus of experienced employees from the workforce. Almost 80% of top HR and IT executives at midsize to large U.S.-based companies say that the threat of losing critical expertise is more of an issue than it was five years ago. And, 84% say they sometimes or frequently do not have a successor in place when a top manager leaves.[8]

Other workforce changes are occurring. Two changes in particular include the growth in the Hispanic population in the United States and the pressure to increase the diversity of the workforce. Without question the purchasing and supply management profession continues to feature white males. According to Data USA, graduates of supply chain-related programs in the United States are over 65% male, with white males comprising the vast majority of the male segment. White males and females combined earned 2,800 supply chain-related bachelor's degrees during a recent academic period, black males and females combined earned 350 bachelor's degrees, and Hispanic males and females combined to earn just over 300 bachelor's degrees.[9] If the academic pipeline is any indication, the profession will continue to be heavily influenced by white males. Companies will need to think about this as they craft their diversity and talent recruitment strategies. Talent management will be addressed in greater depth in Chapter 3.

Emergence of Big Data and Predictive Analytic Tools

The big deal today involves something called *big data* or *predictive analytics*, which includes the sophisticated tools, techniques, and models that analyze the reams of data generated every second of every day. A predictive model is simply a mathematical function using algorithms that use input data. Predictive analytics is the branch of advanced analytics that uses data to make predictions about unknown future events. It uses many techniques from data mining, statistics, modeling, machine learning, and artificial intelligence to analyze current data to make predictions about the future.[10] Other names associated with predictive analytics include business intelligence, data analytics, and business analytics. Predictive analytics will be explored in further detail in Chapter 6.

Changing Customer Requirements

It is safe to conclude that, over time, customer demands steadily increase rather than decrease. And, it is also safe to conclude that once a customer receives something of value, he or she will not be too appreciative when a provider attempts to take it away. A shift occurs as characteristics that win orders at some point become qualifiers for future business as competitors converge on those same characteristics. Eventually almost every product or service migrates toward a commodity, or nondifferentiated status. Customer requirements are constantly shifting as order winners become qualifiers and new order winners emerge—at least until they become qualifiers.

This brings us to the main point: consumers are increasingly basing their purchase decisions, particularly for consumed products, on attributes such as being organic, non-genetically modified, and ethically sourced. This has created a tremendous strain on supply chains, as a growing number of buyers chase a relatively small, but growing group of suppliers. These suppliers include farms, ingredient providers, production and distribution sites, and transportation providers.

According to a TechSci Research report, the global organic food market is projected to register an annual growth rate globally of over 16%. This growth can be attributed, among other factors, to growing health concerns among consumers and increased awareness regarding the potential health benefits of organic food.[11] This growth is relatively recent, and it promises to make the lives of supply managers ever more challenging as the demand for natural and organic outstrips the supply of natural and organic. The ability to develop and deliver organic products is increasingly becoming an order-winning characteristic.

Supply Chains Are Becoming Increasingly Complex

As a concept, complexity is difficult to quantify or even define since no one seems to agree on exactly what comprises complexity. Supply chain complexity exists in many shapes and forms and has many causes. Something we do know is that most CEOs expect the internal and external complexity faced by their organizations to increase. A study cited in Chapter 15 reveals that almost 80% of CEOs say that they expect to see high or very high complexity as they look out over a five-year horizon. More than half of CEOs have concerns about their company's ability to manage complexity.

Increased business or supply chain complexity is not necessarily bad. Some researchers have argued persuasively that organizations that learn how to manage and exploit complexity can generate additional sources of profit and gain competitive advantage. Few would question that FedEx's mastery of global logistics, an area that is woefully complex, has enabled it to expand its locations, services, customer base, and profitability.

Here is an illustration of how supply networks quickly become complex, even for a seemingly simple item. Zady's, an online retailer based in New York, wanted to develop a new line of sweaters that were made entirely of U.S. materials. The *Made-in-America* label would feature prominently in its marketing campaign. What could be so hard about that? After an extensive search, the company finally located a wool supplier in Oregon who agreed (grudgingly) to provide the much-needed wool. Obtaining the wool, however, was only the first part of a complex journey that progressed from raw material to finished sweater. Figure 1.1 illustrates the travels of a Made-in-America sweater. Notice

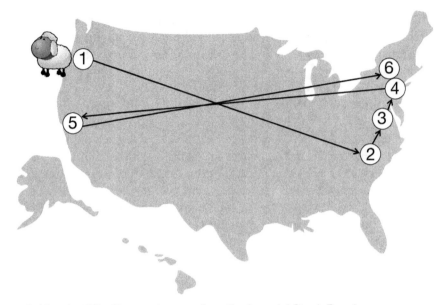

1. Maupin, OR—The wool comes from the Imperial Stock Ranch
2. Jamestown, SC—The wool is washed to remove dirt and greases
3. Philadelphia, PA—The wool is dyed by a company operating in the same location since 1869
4. Nazareth, PA—Kraemer Yarns spins the dyed wool into a fine soft yarn
5. Commerce, CA—Ball of Cotton knits the yarn into pullover sweaters
6. NYC—The sweaters arrive in New York to be packaged and shipped from Zady's distribution

Figure 1.1   Travels of a sweater

how many suppliers and logistics providers are involved in the production of something as simple as a sweater made entirely in one country!

Complexity is something that, if not managed well, can consume your business. Conversely, if managed well, new and profitable opportunities may be available that are not available to less competent competitors. You will find a more extensive discussion of this subject in Chapter 15.

Regulations, Regulations, and More Regulations

The last decade witnessed a newfound love between government regulators and new regulations. Many of these regulations directly affect the supply and supply chain community, including the Food Safety Modernization Act, Importer Security Filing (ISF) rule, and conflict mineral rules, which addressed the sourcing of tungsten, tin, tantalum, and gold from certain regions of Africa.

The ISF rule, more commonly called 10+2, requires containerized cargo information to be transmitted to U.S. Customs and Border Protection (CBP) at least 24 hours before goods are loaded onto an ocean vessel headed to the U.S. It requires importers to provide ten data elements to CBP, as well as two more data documents from the carrier.[12] The United States alone issued well over 20,000 new regulations in the period between 2009–2016. Somewhere in the depths of government bureaucracy must be a reward system that encourages government regulators to increasingly regulate. The topic of supply chain complexity is examined in more detail in Chapter 15.

Pressure to Shorten Cycle Times

The pressure to reduce cycle times across virtually every major industry continues unabated. Nowhere is this more pronounced than during new product and process development. In the mid-1980s, U.S. producers required 60 months to take a vehicle from concept to customer. Today the cycle time is 18 to 24 months. Supply managers have played a major role in shortening development times through the use of early supplier involvement.

There are some powerful reasons for wanting to reduce product development cycle times. The quality of information only deteriorates as we look further into the future. Who can really understand customer wants and needs five years into the future? And, let's not forget that product development is clearly an expense for firms. It would be nice to more quickly generate revenue from products that are actually introduced. We also know that firms that excel at developing new products quickly can create legal barriers to entry for competitors as they capitalize on their speed to market. While other good reasons exist for wanting to compress development times, you get the idea.

Of course, product development is not the only process under time reduction pressures. Other supply chain processes under time reduction pressures include supplier evaluation and selection, customer order fulfillment (witness SpaceX's efforts to launch rockets more quickly than competitors), demand estimation, and planning and implementing capital projects. One thing is certain—the pressure to reduce cycle times will continue across all parts of the supply chain. This is a topic that is explored further in Chapters 9, 10, and 15.

THEMES UNDERLYING THIS BOOK

A number of themes underlie this book, particularly the second half. These themes influence the kinds of topics presented and the way they are presented. The following are six important suppositions that affect supply management today and for the foreseeable future.

Supply Management Is an Embedded and Important Part of Supply Chain Management

It is difficult to talk about supply management without overlapping into areas that are traditionally associated with supply chain management. Supply management and supply chain management have what can be described as a symbiotic relationship. It is difficult, if not impossible, for one to exist without the other.

Supply management plays a critical role within the supply chain, especially the upstream portion. Topics that are featured predominantly in this book—including financial management, risk management, flexibility, and complexity management—all relate to the end-to-end supply chain. And, since supply management is an important part of supply chain management, these topics are relevant to supply managers. Something that needs to occur is for supply managers to gain a better understanding regarding how they fit into the bigger picture. The supply chain is that bigger picture. Supply managers must operate within the context of an integrated supply chain.

Supply Management Can Be Strategic

The word *strategic* is one of the most overused and, surprisingly, least understood words in business. When asked to explain the term, most individuals struggle to describe the concept. As Chapter 2 will explain, something is strategic if it has great importance within an integrated entity or whole. This means that strategic activities, plans, or decisions have the ability to affect a firm's overall competitive or market success. This typically excludes day-to-day or tactical activities that are part of traditional purchasing and supply chain responsibilities. Developing a collaborative relationship with a supplier that results in the attainment of a new technology that is not available to competitors, for example, can clearly have strategic implications. It is important to understand what can make a difference at the corporate level. Without question, supply initiatives can strategically affect the success of the firm. Closely related to this is strategy development, which is explored in Chapter 7.

It's Difficult to Automate Supply Management

Hardly a day goes by without hearing about a bold new technology that is automating some part of the supply chain. One area where this automation is proving to be elusive is within supply management. Supply management continues to remain a knowledge business that has not yet been fertile ground for the development of artificial intelligence or other applications that are designed to replace humans. The same is not true within finance, which has witnessed thousands of job losses as new software executes trades within nanoseconds. In reality, the floor of the New York stock exchange is not even needed. What is left of the trading floor makes a nice backdrop for television and tourists. While basic functional or clerical duties within purchasing will continue to be streamlined through the use of new tools and techniques, the crafting of worldwide supply strategies and managing intensely collaborative relationships should remain a people business, at least for a while.

The Domain of Supply Management Continues to Expand

Some of the more seasoned employees at your firm may remember when:

1. Supply management was simply called purchasing;
2. Crafting strategies and managing relationships were not a normal part of the work process;
3. The purchasing job was essentially a lower-level function offering limited career growth;
4. Components and other direct material requirements were obtained from a supply base that was primarily local or domestic; and
5. Being reactive was the nature of the job.

Some of these seasoned employees may actually think of this as the good old days. How the times have changed. Today's supply manager is not only involved with sourcing direct materials but also capital items like plant and equipment, indirect items including MRO supplies, and services of all kinds. And, a worldwide supply base is now the norm, not the exception. Wherever a meaningful pool of money is involved, we should expect the supply management group to be involved directly.

Instead of managing items from a price perspective, supply managers must now perform sophisticated cost modeling and analysis. Instead of managing arm's-length relationships, supply managers must understand when, where, and how to apply an appropriate relationship. And, the supply management group must be at the forefront of risk management. Over the last decade or so, the domain of supply management has evolved to the point where today's supply professionals must be cost, financial, relationship, and risk managers. This is the new normal, and it will only get more demanding rather than less. For those longing for the good old days, give it up. Those days are not coming back.

We Live in a *What Have You Done for Me Lately?* World

At one point in my career at Chrysler, I reported to a manager who had an interesting social style. When the manager would see one of his direct reports, instead of saying good morning or hello he would ask, "What have you done for me lately?" While initially thinking this manager may have failed his social etiquette course in high school, this manager's true intent soon became apparent. This manager was conveying a message about:

1. Being in an environment where results matter,
2. How relying on the past will not go far when looking toward the future, and
3. How complacency and resting on one's laurels is not an option.

In the academic world it is not unusual for a faculty member to expect a promotion in rank because he or she published an article five years earlier in a premier journal. While that publication may have been impressive at the time, what has this person done lately?

It is apparent the *what-have-you-done-for-me-lately* mindset is only accelerating. The CEO of Ford, Marc Fields, is widely credited for the successful introduction of the new F-Series aluminum trucks, a challenge that was a massive undertaking from a supply, technical, and marketing perspective. Because of his efforts, Mr. Fields, at least for a while, was widely hailed as *the man*! Fast forward several years and Ford's Board of Directors pressed Mr. Fields to sharpen his strategy as the company races to introduce electric cars, reverse its shrinking market share in the U.S., and address its languishing stock price.[13] The board then abruptly announced that Mr. Fields was being replaced as CEO. Apparently the distinction of being *the man* is not a permanent one. The supply implications of the all-new aluminum F-Series trucks at Ford will be discussed in a later chapter.

The bottom line is that any good things you have done last year, last quarter, or even last month tend to fade quickly. The shelf life for achievements is shortening; the shelf life for failures remains longer than the shelf life of plutonium. The challenge becomes one of being able to answer the question, "What have you done for me lately?" The details of how to translate supply accomplishments into financial accomplishments are examined in Chapter 8. Supply managers must understand how to thrive in a *what-have-you-done-for-me-lately* world.

Change, Risk, and Disruption Are the Only Certainties

As mentioned previously, we are living in an era where constant change, heightened risk, and economic and market disruption seem to be the new normal. A key part of this book is designed specifically to better understand and manage the wildcards that are just over the horizon. Virtually all the topics presented through-out this book are intended to help the reader survive in this unpredictable era.

PROFILE OF SUPPLY LEADERS AND EXCELLENCE

Research by A. T. Kearney, as well as other sources, has resulted in the development of a profile of what a leading supply management organization looks like. The following list presents a profile of supply management leaders. Each of these traits or characteristics is explored more fully in subsequent chapters. A primary objective of this book is to identify and then build upon the traits that define supply management excellence.

- *Supply management objectives and goals align with business needs.* Supply management is considered a support function within Michael Porter's value chain model. This means that in addition to its own goals and objectives, supply management objectives and goals must align with and support the attainment of business needs as well as the needs of other internal groups. Supply leaders understand their corporate responsibility as a support function. They work to align their goals with other groups through participation on joint strategy development or planning teams, early involvement in new product development, strategy review sessions with corporate leaders, and colocation of personnel. A research report by Ardent Partner revealed that 63% of chief procurement officers (CPOs) at best-in-class firms say their procurement objectives and goals are tightly aligned with overall business objectives. Only 29% of CPOs at all other firms indicate a tight alignment.[14] Organizational design and alignment topics are addressed in Chapter 4.
- *Supply groups contribute to the top and bottom line.* The world of the purchasing or supply manager has historically focused on cost reductions that enhance bottom line results. Increasingly, leading supply organizations are also active in taking steps to grow the top line, which means revenue growth. This is not an environment where most supply managers feel overly comfortable given their historical focus on managing costs rather than growing revenues. Top-line revenue growth is addressed in various chapters, but particularly in Chapters 9 and 10.
- *Supply leaders address risk systematically.* A recurring theme throughout this book concerns the growth in supply chain risk. Supply leaders understand the financial, operational, and even strategic impact of risk, and manage it systematically. Risk management is the focus of Chapter 11.
- *Supply leaders develop supplier relationships that create differential advantage.* Supplier relationships supported by trust are essential to supply

management success. While seemingly a simple sounding concept, the trust that underlies relationships is actually an intricate topic. The importance of trust-based relationships is explored in Chapter 10.

- *Supply leaders develop well-crafted category strategies.* The essence of strategic supply management remains the development and implementation of well-thought-out supply strategies. These strategies can address commodities, or they can deal with any area where supply managers are looking to add value. Strategies could be in place for obtaining supplier technology, managing risk, developing supplier performance capabilities, or global outsourcing, to name a few areas. The research by Ardent Partners mentioned earlier concluded that best-in-class firms have an average of 87% of their expenditures under managed contracts while all others have an average of 58% of their spend under contracts. The development of supply strategies is discussed in greater depth in Chapter 7.

- *Supply leaders seek out and adopt technology.* Supply leaders are early adopters of technology—particularly information technology. The information-enabled supply chain supports better effectiveness and efficiency, data transparency, and decision making. Some of the emerging information technology that supports supply managers today is reviewed in Chapter 6.

- *The supply organization wins the battle for talent.* This trait refers to the growing need to manage an organization's human talent. Talent or people management is the process through which employers anticipate and meet their needs for human capital in an era of change. Fortunately, various ways are available for ensuring that an organization is a talent management leader rather than follower. The shift from traditional human resources to talent management is explored in Chapter 3.

- *Supply leaders quantify the value they provide to their organization.* The need to engage in supply chain financial management has never been greater. Supply and supply chain managers must understand how to frame their accomplishments in terms of their impact on corporate-level indicators. They must speak the language of finance and show the value they create in terms that corporate leaders understand. Insight into this important leadership trait is provided in Chapters 5 and 8.

CONCLUDING THOUGHTS

A constant need to improve and ever-increasing global pressures have combined to create a need to search for new sources of competitive advantage. Market success requires that firms bring a total package to the table—a package that includes a set of progressive supply management activities, approaches, and strategies. For most firms, this means endorsing new ways to manage their supply base and supply chain. Supply managers must present a vision; compete for resources that are on par with other major groups; and develop the talent, systems, measures, and processes that will make supply management a hard-to-duplicate source of value creation.

REFERENCES

1. R. Dobbs, T. Koller, and S. Ramaswamy, "The Future and How to Survive It," *Harvard Business Review*, October 1, 2015, from https://hbr.org/2015/10/the-future-and-how-to-survive-it.
2. ibid.
3. K. R. Bhote, *Strategic Supply Management: A Blueprint for Revitalizing the Manufacturing-Supplier Partnership* (New York: American Management Association, New York, 1989): 13.
4. A. Pasztor, "Boeing Looks to Build Satellites More Quickly, With Fewer Workers," *The Wall Street Journal*, February 21, 2017, from https://www.wsj.com/articles/boeing-looks-to-build-satellites-more-quickly-with-fewer-workers-1487692416.
5. J. Wernau, "Cotton-Price Surge Jolts Mills, Merchants," *The Wall Street Journal*, May 16, 2017, B11.
6. S. Eisenhammer, "Governments Must Tackle Sharp Commodity Price Swings," *Reuters*, from www.reuters.com.
7. From http://www.agcs.allianz.com/assets/PDFs/Reports/Allianz_Risk_Barometer_2017_APPENDIX.pdf.
8. J. Green, "Chowing Down on Boomers' Brains," *Business Week*, (January 25, 2016): 20.
9. From https://datausa.io/profile/cip/520203/#demographics.
10. From http://www.predictiveanalyticstoday.com/what-is-predictive-analytics/.
11. From http://www.prnewswire.com/news-releases/global-organic-food-market-to-grow-at-over-16-by-2020-concludes-techsci-research-523104261.html.
12. From www.wikipedia.com.
13. C. Rogers and J. Lubin, "Ford's Board Turns Up Heat on CEO Mark Fields," May 9, 2017, from http://www.foxbusiness.com/features/2017/05/09/fords-board-turns-up-heat-on-ceo-mark-fields.html.
14. A. Bartolini, *CPO Rising 2017: Tools of the Trade*, a white paper by Ardent Partners, 2017.

2

OVERUSED AND MISUSED TERMS IN SUPPLY MANAGEMENT

Almost 70 years ago a series of films were made that featured a New York City gang called The Bowery Boys. The lead character in the series, Slip, was notorious for trying to sound smart but coming across as much less so. He was noteworthy for his Brooklyn accent and his misuse of the English language. He would say, for example, "a clever seduction" instead of "a clever deduction," "I depreciate it!" instead of "I appreciate it!", and "I regurgitate" instead of "I reiterate." And why would anyone examine a situation when he could "exampitate" it instead?

Today we often hear the executive business version of the Bowery Boys when managers and executives attempt to dazzle us with their language. Imagine you are at a presentation conducted by a high-level supply chain executive and hear the following:

> *"Relying on empowered individuals and work teams to pursue strategic initiatives, we will work collaboratively, innovatively, and synergistically with our value chain partners to leverage our core competencies in a sustainable fashion to achieve a paradigm shift, leading to significant win-win opportunities that optimize our global supply chain."*

Most of us have no idea what that paragraph says, although it sounds impressive. Is there anything not to like here? If you were keeping score, you probably realized this paragraph just won the Bingo Buzzwords competition. Bingo Buzzwords is an informal event that is held anytime someone who is standing in front of a group tries to sound smart but comes across much differently. At any moment, as a television commercial made light of some years ago, someone might feel the urge to yell, "bingo!" after hearing the eighth or ninth buzzword. Most of us know at least one person who could qualify as a Bingo Buzzword champion.

This chapter presents a collection of some of the most misused, overused, and trendy terms in our business vocabulary today. This discussion is important for several reasons. First, many of the terms presented here are used throughout this book, making a working knowledge of them essential. Second, most of these terms and concepts are relevant to supply and supply chain managers. Using them incorrectly can negatively affect your reputation. And finally, it might be enjoyable to see a perspective that differs from our normal frame of reference.

AN UNSCIENTIFIC LISTING OF OVERUSED AND MISUSED TERMS

The listing of terms and concepts presented here are the result of years of experience working with business leaders as well as insights from the popular press. This list is not based on any scientific research or evidence. And, I readily admit to personally abusing most, if not all, of these terms myself. With that confession out of the way, let's explore, in no particular order, some common but often misused or overused business terms, many of which are an essential part of supply management. Some of these terms will be explained more fully in later chapters.

Collaboration

Few people in the civilized world would likely admit to being against collaboration. Unfortunately, the overuse of this term has resulted in a bit of a dumbing down of the concept. A number of years ago, researchers for the Center for Advanced Purchasing Studies conducted research that focused explicitly on collaboration within the supply chain. As interviews were being conducted with executives at leading companies, something became apparent—most individuals were using the words collaborative or collaboration to describe relationships that were actually cooperative. A word that is meant to represent something that is special and unique was being used in a way that represents something that is more common.

What, then, is the primary difference between cooperation and collaboration? The primary feature of cooperative relationships is the open sharing of information. This includes information on product design, costs, or any other area that one party might be reluctant to share with another. Collaboration involves two or more enterprises working together to achieve shared strategic goals that produce greater value for all parties than could be gained by acting alone or by operating in a noncollaborative environment. While collaborative relationships also feature the open sharing of information, they are noteworthy because they usually feature the sharing of risk, rewards, and/or resources. And, of course, even when sharing takes place, it will occur at varying degrees. Collaboration is not simply a yes or no proposition (yes it occurs or no it does not). The real question is: to what degree does this sharing and collaboration occur?

While many observers freely interchange the terms cooperate and collaborate, others will argue that a collaborative relationship is the most intensive and highest form of supply chain relationship. An appropriate analogy applies that involves best friends. While an individual can have many friends (i.e., supplier relationships), how many are truly best friends? A true collaborative relationship, like a best friend, is special and unique. The next time you hear an individual say he has 30 best friends, you can safely assume that is a cry for help. And the next time you hear a supply manager say his company has 30 collaborative relationships with suppliers, you can safely assume that individual does not fully understand what defines a collaborative relationship. Collaboration is addressed extensively in Chapter 9.

Win-Win

Have you ever heard someone say something to the effect, "This will be a win-win for everyone involved?" It is safe to conclude that few individuals can define precisely the concept of win-win and win-lose beyond vague generalities. Win-win means much more than you win and I win. What, then, does it actually mean?

Like most of the terms and concepts presented in this chapter, win-win does not come with a universally accepted definition. Win-win relationships or interactions mean that the amount of value that is available to different parties through their relationship is variable rather than fixed. By working together, parties can grow the amount of value they derive from their relationship. As value grows, each party has the opportunity to capture ever increasing amounts of that value.

Win-lose relationships feature a fixed amount of value that the parties compete over. No appreciable attempt is made to alter the size of the value pie through cooperative or collaborative efforts—any gain by one party must come at the expense of the other. Win-lose relationships are essentially a zero-sum game. Win-win relationships are about expanding the value pie; win-lose relationships are about dividing the value pie. Lose-lose relationships mean the parties are actively working against the interests of each other. The proverbial value pie is, in all likelihood, shrinking rather than remaining constant. Perhaps the best way to describe a lose-lose relationship is to say, "I may be going down, but I am going to take you with me." The differences between win-win, win-lose, and lose-lose are meaningful within strategic supply management.

Figure 2.1 presents a figure that is also discussed later in this book. It provides an important way for linking the concepts of win-win, win-lose, and lose-lose to specific types of relationships. It is also a relatively easy continuum to remember, since each of the relationships begins with the letter C. As this figure shows, cooperative and collaborative relationships are, by definition, win-win relationships. Conversely, competitive relationships are, by definition, win-lose. Counterproductive relationships are described as lose-lose relationships.

Negotiation sessions and strategies can also be categorized as being win-win or win-lose. When an individual is taking a win-win negotiating position, we say this person is practicing integrative bargaining. When that individual assumes a win-lose position, we say this person is engaging in distributive bargaining. In reality, few individuals enter into a negotiation and ask, "Do you want to practice win-win bargaining?" The other party will likely respond in the affirmative, although they may not know exactly what they just agreed to. It is highly unlikely that the party would respond by saying, "No, we do not believe in win-win. We would rather negotiate to the point where you are crying for mercy."

A win-win negotiation strategy applies to certain situations. This includes when the items or services under consideration are critically or strategically important, a high level of trust exists between parties, and both parties endorse a win-win approach. An important, although counterintuitive, point is that all win-win negotiations and relationships also feature a win-lose component.

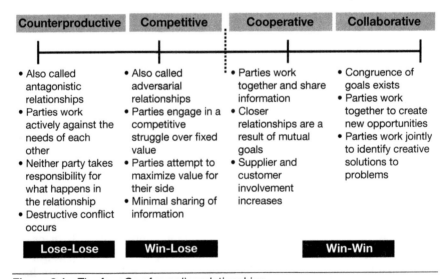

Figure 2.1 The four Cs of supplier relationships

Even when the parties to an agreement are able to expand the value pie, they must still divide that pie.

How a negotiator determines whether his or her counterpart is taking a win-win versus win-lose approach is usually determined by behavior. Character-istics of win-lose negotiations include rigid negotiating positions, arguments over a fixed amount of value, strict use of power by one party over another, and adversarial competition played out at the negotiating table. Conversely, win-win negotiations feature the participants trying to understand each other's needs and wants, building on common ground and working together to develop cre-ative solutions that provide new or additional value, and an environment that features the open sharing of information. The differences between a win-win and win-lose approach to relationships are important to understand.

Significant or Significance

Let's take a reality check here. Who is not impressed, at least a little, by the word *significant*? Doesn't this word sound so . . . well, significant? And therein lies the problem. It is an important sounding word that is often used to add emphasis to what is being said. A standard dictionary defines significant as something that is sufficiently great or important to be worthy of attention. In many cases, the word is used correctly. It is also a word that when it is applied within a statistical context (i.e., this is a significant finding), connotes something that is often far more important than what the reality of the situation warrants. Within statistics the word significant has a precise meaning.

When a statistic is significant, it simply means that with a certain level of confidence (say, 95%), the observed statistic is reliable. It does not provide any insight or judgment into whether the finding is important in terms of its magni-tude. Significance is calculated and reported for a variety of statistics, including correlations, t-test differences of means, multiple regression variables, and the coefficient of determination (also called R^2).

Perhaps the most misleading usage of this word arises when a researcher presents the R^2 statistic. It is not an understatement to say that R^2, the value of which ranges between 0 and 1, is one of the most powerful statistics in existence. So, how is it misused? For simplicity, let's say we have created a multiple regres-sion model where some independent variables (called X variables) are used to predict the outcome of a dependent variable (called the Y variable). R^2 indicates how much of the change in the independent variable(s) explains the change in the dependent variable. R^2 is a ratio that considers total explained variation (the numerator of the R^2 formula) compared to the total variation in a data set (the denominator of the R^2 formula). An R^2 of .70, for example, means that the observed changes in the independent variable(s) explain 70% of the change in the dependent variable. It also means that 30% of the change in what we are observing is not explained statistically by the model.

Why is saying something is significant often misleading? R^2 is always calculated with an accompanying significance level. We might say, for example, that an R^2 value in a study is significant at the .05 level. This simply means that with 95% confidence the value of R^2 is not zero. If we calculate a confidence interval around the R^2 value using a standard error of estimate, the confidence interval does not include zero. But, with a large enough sample, just about any R^2 value will be *significant*, or non-zero. A graduate statistics professor of mine once commented to his class, "God rewards large sample sizes." That reward comes in the form of progressively narrower rather than wider confidence intervals around the true R^2 value due to larger sample sizes. And, as a confidence interval becomes narrower, it is less likely to include zero. The width of a confidence interval is partly a function of the sample size of the data set. God rewards large sample sizes.

A researcher who studied the performance impact of board of director gender diversity was quite proud of her *significant* research results that claimed that board diversity significantly affected corporate performance. What was not so proudly stated was the R^2 value (.02) of her main finding. Her model could only explain 2% of what she was studying with 98% left unexplained. As the great Shania Twain once declared in a song, "That don't impress me much." Working in the researcher's favor was a sample size that exceeded 20,000 observations. In this case a significant finding simply means that the confidence interval constructed around the R^2 value of .02 did not include zero, due primarily to the large sample. Reporting proudly about a non-zero finding does not sound quite as impressive as reporting proudly about a significant finding. Do not be fooled by the deception that is wrapped around the word *significant*.

Global and Globalization

Several challenges arise when using the terms global and globalization. First, different groups define these terms differently based on their frame of reference. Marketing, finance, and procurement all have different interpretations of globalization. Second, it is the one term in this chapter that can evoke raw emotions outside of the business community. At a World Trade Organization meeting in Seattle, a face-covered anarchist was smashing a Starbucks window. When a reporter asked what this individual was protesting, he replied, "Globalization." When the reporter asked why he was against globalization, he replied, "Because it is bad." (At least the anarchist answered this question with an insightful explanation that listeners surely wrote down for future reference.) To some individuals, globalization represents exploitation, child and slave labor, environmental damage, and a host of other evils that you would not be proud to tell your mother about if you worked for a global corporation. To some politicians, globalization means unfair rather than fair trade, along with a loss of jobs. Just as our enlightened anarchist explained—globalization is bad.

In the supply community, globalization is often carried out through a process called global sourcing. The terms *international purchasing* and *global sourcing or supply* are often interchanged. Technically, they should not be. Using definitions developed by Monczka and Trent (definitions that could be subject to debate), fundamental differences exist between international purchasing and global sourcing. International purchasing is the process of buying goods and services from suppliers outside of your firm or business unit's country of operation. Global sourcing and supply management refers to the proactive integration and coordination of material and service requirements across worldwide business units, looking at common items, processes, technologies, designs, sourcing practices, and suppliers. Fundamental differences exist between these terms— and the definition of globalization within the supply management domain will not at all resemble the definition from other business domains. A global supply management continuum is presented in Chapter 13, where the topic is explored in greater depth.

Strategic

Imagine a scenario where you are making a presentation to your senior management. While you try to resist the urge to do so, in a moment of weakness you mention how the project that you are working on is strategic. Not only that (after all, you are on a roll at this point), project failure will have strategic implications for your firm. The probability exists that someone in your audience has heard this before from others who were also convinced of their strategic importance.

What is the risk here? The *uh-oh* moment comes when someone in the audience challenges you to defend your statement about being strategic. This is not the time to look down at your shoes and mumble some answer simply to fill the void. A cynic will say that when so many things are called strategic, how can we truly know what is strategic? The term is overused.

What does the term strategic actually mean? One perspective argues that something is strategic if it has great importance within an integrated entity or whole. This means that strategic activities, plans, or decisions are those that have the ability to affect a firm's overall competitive or market success. This normally excludes day-to-day decisions or tactical activities that are part of traditional purchasing and supply chain responsibilities.

Several examples will help clarify this concept. It is hard to imagine that a procurement card program that simplifies the ordering of lower value items—while ideal for reducing transaction costs—has strategic implications. No one buys a product because the seller's company has an awesome employee procurement card program. Conversely, developing a collaborative relationship with a supplier that provides your company with leading-edge technology before competitors even hear about that technology is a different story.

Make sure that you understand what makes a difference at the corporate level. More often than not, this will require drawing a link between any change or initiative and its subsequent impact on key corporate indicators. The subject of how to link supply management success to corporate financial success is addressed in Chapter 8. This will help the reader to better articulate the strategic implications of a supply management initiative.

Core Competency

Perhaps the most misunderstood and overused business concept today is the notion of core competencies. Core competency is another one of those buzzwords that the reader wishes he or she had a dollar for every time the term was used. When asked to explain what a core competency is, most respondents reply that it is something they or their firm does well. The concept of core competencies is increasingly being applied at the individual level. Doing something well is not the defining characteristic of a core competency.

C. K. Prahalad and Gary Hamel originally put forth the idea of core competencies in their *Harvard Business Review* (HBR) article titled, "The Core Competence of the Corporation."[1] The article is still regarded as one of the most influential ever to appear in the HBR. Prahalad and Hamel define a core competency as collective learning in an organization—especially how to coordinate diverse skills and integrate multiple streams of technologies. They further refined this concept by saying that in the long run, "competitiveness derives from an ability to build, at lower cost and faster than competitors, the core competencies that spawn unanticipated products and services." Conceiving of a corporation in terms of core competencies widens the domain of innovation. A company that organizes around competencies does not envision itself as a group of unrelated businesses, divisions, or product lines.

Prahalad and Hamel offered three basic, yet powerful, tests for determining if a collective learning may qualify as a core competency. The core competency must provide access to a wide variety of markets; the competency should make a significant contribution to the perceived customer benefit of end products or services; and the core competency should be difficult to imitate.

Let's illustrate this concept with several examples. Many employees at FedEx will argue that the company's ability to deliver packages overnight is a core competency. While FedEx's ability to deliver packages overnight is valued by customers and provides access to a wide variety of markets, it is no longer difficult to duplicate. A host of other companies, even the U.S. postal service, offer overnight package delivery service. Overnight delivery, while important to FedEx's business model, has shifted from being a core competency to a core capability. Referring to something as a core competency when in fact it is actually a core capability is the most common mistake when misusing this term.

Let's consider several companies that have a true core competency. Casio makes hundreds of products including calculators, watches, and musical instruments. While its product line appears diverse, each shares a core competency or collective learning that is difficult to imitate, is valued by customers, and provides access to a wide variety of markets. That competency is the ability to miniaturize electronic components. Yoplait is known for its ability to develop probiotics that then become part of the company's varied yogurt products. Probiotics are live bacteria cultures that stabilize and balance the intestinal system and are beneficial to digestive health.

During the strategic planning process, core capabilities and competencies are something to be protected and nurtured. Areas that are not core to the business become candidates for outsourcing or divestment. At the highest planning levels, the concepts of core competencies and capabilities influence the development of supply strategies and relationships.

One misperception regarding core competencies is the belief that if a company has a true core competency, it guarantees its success. We have to look no farther than a once-proud company called Polaroid to realize this is not the case. A true core competency at Polaroid was the company's ability to acquire images instantly—a competency it shared with only one other company (Fuji). The collective knowledge about how to acquire images using instant film technology was incorporated into all of the company's product lines; it was valued by customers; and it was difficult to imitate. Instant image acquisition qualified as a true core competency.

Then why is Polaroid no longer a viable company? The rapid transition from instant image acquisition through film to digital was cruel. Polaroid had nothing distinctive to offer in the digital arena. In this case the competence proved to be a liability since it was designed into every product developed by Polaroid. It also caused the company to become myopic, something that blinded it to the rapid shift toward digital technology. The harsh reality is that core competencies are subject to the same destructive forces of creativity and competition that affect all parts of a business. The economist Joseph Schumpeter once said that capitalism is a process of creative destruction. At Polaroid, the creative destruction was complete.

Teams

It is safe to say that the use of teams across most industries and corporations has become widespread. It is common, but often wrong, to refer to any assembled group of people as a team. Although it may appear that we are splitting hairs or getting caught up in minutia, real differences exist between groups and teams. While all teams are groups, not all groups are teams. An analogy is to say that while all dogs are animals, not all animals are dogs.

What defines a group versus a team? A group consists of two or more people working in an arrangement that permits some degree of interaction among members who share a sense of identity. Conversely, teams are real, self-managed or self-regulated groups that have an intact social system, one or more tasks to perform for which the members are held mutually accountable, output that others external to the team receive or review, and operate within a formal organizational context. The characteristics that define a team do not apply to a group.

Let's use this discussion to further enhance our understanding of teams. Without question, teams can yield the kinds of benefits envisioned by their creators, such as better decisions and the ability to bring greater knowledge and skills to bear at the same time. And, as more and more work crosses functional boundaries, the use of cross-functional teams becomes an attractive way to organize work. But, do not be lulled into thinking that teams bring with them an inherent goodness. Teams can waste the time and energy of members, enforce lower performance norms, create patterns of destructive conflict within and between groups, and make notoriously bad decisions. They can also exploit, stress, and frustrate members—sometimes all at the same time. Using teams comes with no guarantee of success.

There is no shortage of teams or groups within the supply chain space. What this means is that the odds are good that most individuals will be assigned to some sort of team or group during their career. It makes sense to become familiar with the nuances of working in a team since they are so prevalent today. Consider some of these groups and teams that are often part of the supply chain:

- Buyer-supplier councils
- Customer advisory boards
- Commodity management teams
- Demand and supply planning teams
- Value analysis/value engineering teams
- Customer order fulfillment teams

- Supply chain project teams
- New product development teams
- Customer relationship management teams
- Global sourcing steering committees
- Supplier development teams

Three primary features characterize effective teams—features that are not typically associated with groups. First, the productive output of the team meets or exceeds the performance standards of those who receive and/or review the team's output. Next, the team's experience maintains or enhances the capability of members to work together on future assignments. Finally, the team experience, on balance, satisfies rather than frustrates the personal needs of team members. The next time someone assembles a group of people, at least recognize whether they are being assembled as a group or a team. If nothing else, you can amaze your colleagues as you explain the differences.

Empowerment

We all know that empowerment is such a good thing that it can only bring positive results. Go forth and empower your people! When an executive tells you that you are empowered, your immediate response should be, "Empowered to do what?" Empowerment is something that always has boundaries or limits. And, empowering people who do not deserve to be empowered can be dangerous. One article that argued for true employee empowerment began by saying, "Employee empowerment is one of those phrases that tends to make people groan."[2]

Basic dictionary definitions of empowerment say it represents the authority or power given to someone to do something, often without any required permission to act. The reality is that empowerment is simply about giving an individual or team the authority to make decisions or to take actions. Granting authority, however, does not sound as sexy as empowerment.

Various kinds of authority (i.e., empowerment) relate to self-directed and self-managed work teams. Figure 2.2 defines four kinds of work team authority. After reviewing these dimensions, it should come as no surprise that granting certain kinds of authority to individuals and work teams should streamline the decision-making process, something that supports reduced complexity.

The bottom line is that when someone is told that he or she is empowered to act, this person should ask for more detail about what this includes. The corporate landscape is littered with examples of misunderstood and misused authority. Empowerment needs to be more than a vaguely defined term or buzzword.

Scheduling Authority

Ability of a team to schedule its meeting without others approving the decision.

Selection Authority

Ability of a team to select its leader(s) and/or new team members as required to complete assigned tasks.

Internal Authority

Ability of a team to control internal activities, such as allocating budget and material resources to support team activities, determining team performance goals and objectives, making timing decisions regarding the completion of specific activities, and requesting non-team members to support assignments as required.

External Decision-Making Authority

Ability of the team to make decisions that bind or commit an organization. This is conceptually the highest authority dimension because it allows a team to operate independently of external managers.

Figure 2.2   Four kinds of team authority

Learning Curve

Oftentimes we hear broad references to moving up and down the learning curve. Or, perhaps we have to shift the learning curve. In reality, the most basic type of learning curve (there are different ways to apply learning curve analysis) is a relatively narrow concept that applies to improvements in the average direct labor required to perform a task. It is based on the principle that as individuals become more familiar with a task, the average amount of direct labor to perform that task declines by a predictable rate. This predictable rate is the learning rate that defines the learning curve.

Learning rates represent the predictable reduction in direct labor requirements as production doubles from one level to another. If, for example, an item has a learning curve of 95 percent, it means that as production doubles from one level to another, the average direct labor hours required to produce that next quantity declines by 5%. If the learning rate is 85 percent, the average direct labor required for the doubled quantity declines by 15% (100% − 85% = 15% learning rate).

Learning curves come with an important caveat: learning curves do not apply to simple items or items where a supplier has extensive experience. While an item may be new to a buyer, the supplier may have produced many thousands for other customers. When referring to the improvement that occurs at an organizational level, the term *experience curve* is more applicable. Performing learning curve calculations is demonstrated in Chapter 12 of my previous book titled *Strategic Supply Management* (doing so here is beyond the scope of this chapter).

Benchmarking

Benchmarking appears to be a straightforward word. How could it possibly be part of a listing of overused and misused words? Unfortunately, it seems as if any comparison made between two things today is called benchmarking, when in reality, it is merely a comparison. Years ago, when a supply chain professional got in a car to make a one-time visit to another company, she said she was jumping in the car to go make a visit. Today we would say it is a benchmarking visit. Many years ago, I drove a truck as a summer job. On my college resume, I noted that I was a truck driver. Today, you can be sure that resume would read *logistics specialist*. Some terms simply carry more cachet. Benchmarking is one of those terms.

Benchmarking is the continuous and systematic process of measuring products, services, processes, and practices of a firm against world-class competitors or those companies recognized as industry or functional leaders. Figure 2.3 presents a generic view of the benchmarking process. Central to benchmarking is an understanding of the processes that drive different performances rather than understanding only the outcome from a process.

All organizations can benefit from benchmarking, even industry leaders. First, no company is the best in every supply chain process or activity—room for improvement always exists. Second, just because an organization is best-in-class today is no guarantee that it will be the best tomorrow. Competitors may be improving at a rate faster than your company, meaning that at some point, performance curves will intersect and shift. Few good excuses exist for not engaging in true benchmarking, given the massive amounts of information that is available today. Identifying potential benchmark candidates or collecting secondary data is not the burden it was previously.

It is hard to argue against the reasons for pursuing true benchmarking. Benchmarking offers the opportunity to incorporate best practices from any industry. The process also stimulates and motivates those who must implement benchmarking findings—something that can break down resistance to change. Other reasons to benchmark include identifying technological breakthroughs from other industries, developing professional contacts, and supporting the growth and development of personnel. Perhaps most important, benchmarking can reduce the probability of committing two mortal sins—corporate complacency and arrogance. The landscape is littered with the corpses of companies that believed it was their birthright to stay in business forever.

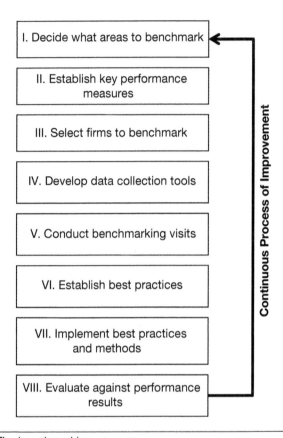

I. Decide what areas to benchmark

II. Establish key performance measures

III. Select firms to benchmark

IV. Develop data collection tools

V. Conduct benchmarking visits

VI. Establish best practices

VII. Implement best practices and methods

VIII. Evaluate against performance results

Continuous Process of Improvement

Figure 2.3   The benchmarking process

Engaging in true benchmarking, rather than the watered down version we often see today, can change a corporate culture. Table 2.1 describes the world with and without true benchmarking. On which side of this table do you want your company to be?

Partner and Partnership

The term *partnership* is used so freely that it becomes difficult to understand what it actually means. Unfortunately, a misunderstanding of this term can have legal implications. When the term is used loosely, it usually refers to a cooperative endeavor undertaken by multiple parties. This endeavor may or may not be covered by an agreement governing the partnership. It is generally a good idea to lay out specific terms and expectations at the outset of an arrangement

Table 2.1 Corporate cultures with and without benchmarking

With Systematic Benchmarking	Without Systematic Benchmarking
• Realism regarding strengths and weaknesses prevails • Decisions based on objective evaluation • Understanding of industry best practices exists • Proactive • Forward thinking • Constant search for new ideas • Higher commitment for changes • Breakthrough opportunities leading to superior performance	• Decisions based on historical data • Changes are reactive and lagging rather than proactive • Marketplace strengths and weaknesses not well understood • Internal, evolutionary change • Not invented here syndrome prevails among personnel • Average performance • Industry best practices not understood

with suppliers, so that disagreements can be settled according to predetermined rules. In some cases, such an agreement is legally required.

From a legal perspective, a partnership is an arrangement in which two or more individuals share the profits and liabilities of a business venture. Various arrangements are possible: all partners might share liabilities and profits equally or some partners may have limited liability. Not every partner is necessarily involved in the management and day-to-day operations of the venture. In some jurisdictions, partnerships enjoy favorable tax treatment relative to corporations. So, when this term is used, which version of partner and partnership applies?

A bit of cynicism often surrounds these terms. Buyers sometimes deal with a supplier that wants to become a partner so they can lock in their business and then raise prices. The seller perceives the sole aim of the partnership with buyers is to force the supplier's price lower. Some companies have gone so far as to prohibit employees from using the term partner or partnership unless a true legal arrangement is in place. Again, a partnership is a legal form of business operation between two or more individuals who share management and profits. This definition applies to few relationships with suppliers, particularly in the U.S. We should probably stop tossing these terms around so freely.

Talent Management

Without question, we are hearing the term *talent management* used more and more. For some, talent management is simply a new way to describe what human resource groups have done for generations. To some degree, there is some truth to that statement. It will not come as a surprise if human resource groups start to rename themselves as talent management groups. The increased use of this phrase is a bit trendy.

Formally speaking, talent management is the process through which employers anticipate and meet their needs for human capital. It is a continuous process that involves important activities, including identifying, recruiting, analyzing, developing, deploying/redeploying, and retaining human assets. The fundamental difference between human resources and talent management is that human resources is a functional group or activity while talent management represents a set of strategic processes.

For some powerful reasons, the need to manage supply chain talent is becoming a necessity that far transcends the typical responsibilities that are associated with human resources. One study revealed, for example, that having the right people involved when developing global supply strategies was the most important success factor out of several dozen factors. Unfortunately, this same study revealed that a lack of access to people with the right knowledge and skills when pursuing global initiatives was the most significant barrier affecting success.[3] This gap reveals the importance of managing human talent. Talent management is discussed in more detail in Chapter 3.

Optimize and Optimization

Optimization can denote something that is general or something that is quite specific (such as verifying mathematically that an optimal solution exists). In general, users of the terms perceive *optimize* and *optimization* as making the best or most effective use of a situation, opportunity, or resource, or to make something as good or as effective as possible. What we usually do not know is how much effort went into the as possible part. The 10-K report of a major U.S. food company states that the company's Supply Chain and Administrative Efficiency Plan includes steps to optimize the entire supply chain network. The report does not actually state how this optimization will occur. The challenge becomes one of understanding what optimization actually means.

A more specific approach argues that optimization is concerned with finding, usually through mathematical modeling, an alternative with the most cost effective or highest achievable performance given a set of constraints, either by maximizing desired factors or minimizing undesired ones. The question becomes whether we have actually taken steps to show something is the optimal alternative or choice. What often separates the different perspectives of optimization is the level of rigor applied when searching for an optimal solution or alternative. In all likelihood, many things that are called optimal lack the rigor that would prove they are, in fact, optimal. The term is often misused.

In supply chain modeling, optimization is achieved by using techniques such as linear programming (or Solver if using Excel). These techniques find an optimal solution, if one exists, given a cost or profit objective and a set of operating constraints. Other techniques, such as routing software, may identify the route that a delivery vehicle should take to minimize distance and time traveled throughout the course of a day. Purists will argue that optimization historically involves a mathematical model that seeks to arrive at an optimal answer given the objectives and constraints under which a system is operating. These purists will also likely argue that the more general uses or definitions of optimization dilute the concept to the point that one can never be certain that something described as optimal is even remotely optimal.

Paradigm Shift

Telling your friends that you are responsible for achieving a paradigm shift at your organization is almost too cool for words. Shifting an entire paradigm has to be right up there with a tectonic shift. It is a big deal.

But, is it really such a big deal? A paradigm represents a typical example or pattern of something—or a model. In a business setting, we might describe our business model as a paradigm. So, why is changing a business model in today's vernacular now a paradigm shift? This is the point where confusion and misuse starts to kick in. A paradigm shift, as originally conceptualized by American physicist and philosopher Thomas Kuhn, is a fundamental change in the basic concepts and experimental practices of a scientific discipline. Since the 1960s, the concept of a paradigm shift has migrated to nonscientific contexts to describe profound changes in a fundamental model or perception of events.

In 2015, the philosopher Martin Cohen described the notion of a paradigm shift as an intellectual virus spreading from the hard sciences to the social sciences, and then on to the arts, business, and even everyday political rhetoric.[4] Like so many of the terms and concepts presented here, a term that has a rich and insightful history has been watered down so much that it barely resembles its original meaning. Still, the term sounds impressive, which likely explains why there has been a paradigm shift in the use of the term paradigm shift.

Sustainable and Sustainability

We have all likely heard an executive proclaim, "This level of growth is not sustainable," or, "This strategy is sustainable." A search of definitions reveals a variety of perspectives on the word *sustainable*, ranging from capable of being maintained at a certain rate or level; relating to, or being a method of harvesting or using a resource so that the resource is not depleted or damaged permanently; or relating to a lifestyle involving the use of sustainable methods. Merriam-Webster alone provides eight perspectives of the word *sustain*. The following captures the true essence of this concept before business leaders commandeered it for other purposes:

> *When we hear the word sustainability, we usually think of renewable fuel sources, reducing carbon emissions, protecting environments, and a way of keeping the delicate ecosystems of our planet in balance. In short, sustainability looks to protect our natural environment along with human and ecological health while driving innovation and not compromising our way of life.*[5]

A parody posted on an environmental website highlighted the overuse of this term. It displayed a regression model that extrapolated the expected growth in the use of *sustainable* as it is used in written text. The analysis concluded that by 2036, *sustainable* will appear on average, one time per written page; by 2061, it will appear on average, one time per sentence; and by 2109, all sentences will contain just the word sustainable repeated over and over.[6] While this is a facetious, yet amusing example of an extended forecasting model, the question needs to be asked: "Why are the words *sustainable* and *sustainability* so blatantly overused and misused?"

Few would likely argue, at least publicly, against the merits of sustainability (whatever the word means). It has a goodness associated with it that is likely a function of its connection to being a good steward of the earth. And, who does not like the earth? Unfortunately, executives often use the word, not because what they are talking about has anything to do with the word's true meaning, but rather because of the goodness associated with it. The marketing materials at one consulting firm stated, "Consultants come. Consultants go. But do they really make a sustainable difference to your company?" This sounds good, although it drifts from the concept's historical roots. It is difficult to determine at this time whether or not the overuse of sustainable represents a sustainable condition.

Innovation

Innovation is one of today's hot topics. How hot is it? A major corporation referenced the term innovation over 400 times in its annual report! Unfortunately, moving beyond a hundred references likely reduces this term's impact. How can we tell when an innovation is meaningful when the word is so blatantly overused?

A misconception exists today that anything new must be innovative. While some might argue this to be the case, not all innovation is valuable or welcomed by the customer. In fact, oftentimes the customer does not see or experience any direct benefit from a so-called innovation. Modern dictionaries are not much help here, and in fact, often perpetuate the idea that anything new is an innovation. Merriam-Webster supports this perspective by defining an innovation as the introduction of something new; or a new idea, method, or device. The following perspective does a better job of capturing the true meaning of innovation:[7]

> *Innovation is the process of translating an idea or invention into a good or service that creates value or for which the customer will readily pay. In order to be called an innovation, an idea must be replicable at an economical cost and must satisfy a specific need. Innovation involves the deliberate application of information, imagination, and initiative to derive greater or different values from resources. It includes all processes by which new ideas are generated and converted into useful products or services. In business, innovation often results when ideas are applied by the company in order to further satisfy or exceed the needs and expectations of the customers. Innovation is synonymous with risk-taking, and organizations that create revolutionary products or technologies take on the greatest risk because they create new markets.*

Michael O'Bryan, a former intelligence analyst and founder of the innovation consulting firm *360 Thinking*, maintains that the term *innovation* is the most important and overused term in America today. He says the word has become the standard response of executives, politicians, and educators to the question: "What do we need to be successful?" The overuse and generalization of this term has led to a loss of understanding of what it is we need when we say we need more innovation. We also risk losing sight of the specific skills and behavior needed to be innovative.[8] Not everything new is an innovation, and not every innovation is a worthwhile innovation.

Laser Focused

This phrase has gained immense popularity over the last decade. It is generally used by executives to describe the pinpoint precision or accuracy of their company's business strategies. An executive at a large U.S. corporation commented while on a business news channel that his strategy was laser focused. He also said his attention to the customer and the marketplace was laser focused. Apparently, this guy had a bunch of lasers at his disposal. At a high school wrestling championship, a coach was asked to comment on his star wrestler. The coach responded that his wrestler was laser focused on his match. Unfortunately, this wrestler's laser battery must have run down because he lost his match. An article in *APICS Magazine* was titled *Targeting Continuous Improvement with Laser Focus*.[9] So, what is wrong with using this term? First, is anything we are talking about actually as focused as a highly concentrated beam of light? And second, this term is trendy and vastly overused—its use has become annoying.

CONCLUDING THOUGHTS

This chapter presented an unscientific listing of some of the most misused, overused, and trendy terms in business today. And, by no stretch of the imagination is this list comprehensive. Our discussion could also have included terms such as leverage, value-add, synergy, rightsizing, and integration. Many of the terms presented in this chapter appear elsewhere in this book.

It is possible, perhaps even likely, that some will argue with the interpretation of the terms presented here. Still, as we move forward, we can take comfort in knowing that while these words will continue to be used far too casually and even incorrectly, if forced to do so, we should at least have a working knowledge of their true meaning. Hopefully, no one will sound dumb when they are trying to sound smart.

REFERENCES

1. C. K. Prahalad and G. Hamel, "The Core Competence of the Corporation," *Harvard Business Review*, 68, no. 3 (May/June 1990): 79–91.
2. F. G. Annette, "Boost Productivity by Empowering Employees," *apics.org/magazine*, (March/April 2017): 21.
3. R. J. Trent and R. M. Monczka, "Achieving Excellence in Global Sourcing," *Sloan Management Review*, (Fall 2005), from http://sloanreview.mit.edu/article/achieving-excellence-in-global-sourcing/.
4. From https://en.wikipedia.org/wiki/Paradigm_shift.
5. From http://www.environmentalscience.org/sustainability.
6. From http://www.treehugger.com/culture/why-word-sustainable-becoming-unsustainable.html.
7. From http://www.businessdictionary.com/definition/innovation.html.
8. From https://www.wired.com/insights/2013/11/innovation-the-most-important-and-overused-word-in-america/.
9. I. Nielsen, "Targeting Continuous Improvement with Laser Focus," *apics.org/magazine*, (March/April 2017): 39.

PART II

Building the Foundation

3

SHIFTING FROM HUMAN RESOURCES TO TALENT MANAGEMENT

Supply managers have no shortage of concerns to occupy their thinking. Whether it is a concern about market shortages and disruptions, an abundance of supply chain risks, rising costs, or nonperforming suppliers, supply managers usually have no trouble finding something to consume their nervous energy. A study by Ardent Partners that identified the top challenges faced by supply executives revealed that one of the top challenges facing procurement is staff and talent constraints. This was the second highest-rated challenge with 44% of chief procurement officers (CPOs) indicating this to be a top procurement challenge.[1] Not surprisingly, the top-rated challenge or constraint facing supply managers involves budget constraints—cited by 46% of CPOs. It would be a challenge to find a procurement study that does not note the importance of human talent.

This chapter explores talent management as a critical supply management enabler. What used to be thought of primarily as human resources (HR), talent management has evolved to become a proactive process for anticipating and then satisfying an organization's human requirements. This chapter addresses the importance of talent management and employee engagement, presents a set of knowledge and skills necessary to achieve supply management excellence, identifies approaches for acquiring and developing talent, and concludes with a set of talent management trends.

UNDERSTANDING TALENT MANAGEMENT

A single, encompassing definition of talent management that all can agree upon does not appear to exist. Everyone seems to put their own spin on this somewhat trendy topic. Lewis and Heckman, two researchers who conducted an extensive literature review concluded that a clear lack of clarity or consensus exists regarding this term. Based on their work, they have identified three primary perspectives that relate to talent management.[2]

The first perspective says that talent management is nothing more than a trendy term that will change once a more fashionable term becomes available. Proponents of this perspective maintain that talent management is simply comprised of the practices associated with HR management, including employee recruiting, development, and retention. A second perspective focuses on modeling the flow of personnel throughout an organization based on factors such as skill development, growth, attrition, and the supply and demand for HR. A third perspective stresses the sourcing, development, and rewarding of human talent. This perspective argues for the differential treatment of employees based on their knowledge, skills, and expertise, and that certain employees have the ability to make a significant difference to the performance of an organization.[3] These three perspectives reveal the broad nature of talent management.

Another perspective of talent management, which is probably as good as any other, maintains that talent management is the process through which employers anticipate and meet their needs for human capital.[4] We can add further detail to this by saying that talent management is a continuous process that involves some primary objectives:

- *Anticipating* the human talent needs of the organization beyond the short term
- *Identifying* the specific knowledge and skills that a supply organization requires, both currently and in the future
- *Recruiting* qualified personnel into a group, function, or organization
- *Redeploying* HR to match tasks and jobs to employees in order to find the right professional fit for each employee and to reenergize employees through new assignments
- *Developing* talent continuously within the supply organization through formal training, coaching and mentoring, leadership roles, and continued education and professional certifications
- *Rotating* personnel into and out of the supply organization
- *Retaining* employees who are central to strategic supply management, including recognizing and rewarding superior performance at the individual level

It should come as no surprise that a variety of perspectives exists regarding talent management. While a degree of overlap exists among some of these perspectives, most provide their own interpretation of the topic.

Why Is Talent Management Becoming so Important?

For some powerful reasons, the need to manage supply talent is growing as a strategic necessity. As was noted in Chapter 2, one study revealed that having the right people involved when developing global sourcing strategies was the most important success factor of several dozen factors evaluated. This same study also found that a lack of access to people with the right knowledge and skills was the most significant barrier affecting the development of global strategies.[5] Few would argue against the notion that supply chains are becoming increasingly global and complex, something that affects the need for talent management.

While certain procurement tasks and activities have been automated, supply management is still an intellectual endeavor requiring human decision makers. Until the day comes when artificial intelligence eliminates the need for human decisions, effective supply management will continue to rely on human brainpower. Strategic supply management requires strong thinkers, making the acquisition, management, development, and retention of these thinkers an important pursuit.

Demographic trends are having a profound effect on the importance of talent management. Starting in 2011, the first of the baby boomer generation (Americans born between 1946 and 1964) began turning 65 years old. In fact, about every eight seconds, on average, a member of the 76-million baby boomer generation turns 65 years old. The next generation has 11 million fewer members to replace those who are departing.[6] What this means is that we are witnessing highly skilled and experienced employees exiting the workforce. Almost 80% of HR and information technology (IT) executives at midsize to large U.S.-based companies say that the threat of losing critical expertise is more of an issue than it was five years ago. And, 84% say they sometimes or frequently do not have a successor in place when a top manager leaves.[7]

The exodus of talent will result in the loss of something called *deep smarts*. Deep smarts represent organizational wisdom and knowledge that cannot be quickly replicated once it is gone.[8] Demographic shifts resulting in a major loss of knowledge are driving the need to elevate the importance of talent management.

Besides demographic changes, an expanding list of pressures faced by supply managers increases the need to manage talent. The transition from tactical purchasing to a more strategic and global model requires a major retooling of personnel capabilities. Supply managers are under growing pressure to better manage costs, engage in risk management, manage strategic supply chain relationships, and contribute to top-line revenue growth. The ever expanding domain of supply management responsibilities supports an obvious conclusion regarding the importance of human talent. And, let's not forget that corporations are also under intense pressure to increase the number of employees from historically underrepresented groups. This will also factor into the talent management equation.

How companies now administer pension plans will likely affect the need to manage talent. Companies are increasingly ending their defined pension plans in which employers manage an investment portfolio that guarantee set payments to retirees. Instead, they have shifted to contributory (401k) plans where workers are responsible for their own investment decisions. The number of Fortune 500 companies that offer only contributory plans increased to 401 from 333 over the last five years. New regulations governing defined pension plans, higher costs for employees who are living longer, and increasing fees charged by regulators have made the defined plans less attractive for corporations.[9] Contributory plans that are portable when an employee leaves an organization could have the unintended effect of encouraging job turnover since individuals will no longer risk losing accumulated pension years. The potential for increased turnover affects the importance of retaining human talent.

The need to secure and develop human talent is only going to grow in importance. Fortunately, various ways are available for ensuring that an organization is a leader rather than a follower in this regard. A later section presents approaches for acquiring and developing human assets.

The Importance of Engagement

Another factor affecting the importance of talent management, and one that deserves special attention, is to avoid an affliction that affects far too many organizations—poorly engaged employees. Engaged employees are those who are involved in, enthusiastic about, and committed to their work and workplace. Gallup, the leader in public opinion polls, has studied employee engagement probably more than any other organization. They concluded that employee engagement in the United States is somewhere around 35%, which surprisingly is near a record high since Gallup started tracking employee engagement in 2000.[10] Worldwide, Gallup has concluded that employee engagement is a mere 13%. This is troubling since research studies have revealed a clear linkage between employee engagement and organizational health.

Since teams are an integral part of supply management organizations, employee engagement with their teams should be of interest. According to Gallup, engaged teams have 24% to 59% less turnover, 10% higher customer ratings of their output, 21% greater profitability, 17% higher productivity, and 41% less absenteeism compared with disengaged teams. These findings clearly suggest that higher engagement translates into higher performance.[11]

Another in-depth perspective of engagement comes from Hewitt and Associates, who argues that engagement is a reflection of the energy and passion that employees have for their organization. Research by Hewitt and Associates has concluded that engaged employees take action to improve business results for their organization, say positive things about their workplace, and strive to go above and beyond to deliver extraordinary work.[12] Research by Towers and Perrin found that over 65% of highly engaged employees expect to remain with their employer, while only 12% of disengaged employees plan on staying.[13]

The value of engagement is clear. Improving employee engagement should be a primary objective associated with the talent management process. Gallup has identified five best practices for improving employee engagement and performance:[14]

1. *Incorporate engagement into the company's human capital strategies.* Successful companies have a clear purpose behind employee engagement strategies. This includes leadership involvement, clear communication strategies, systems that hold leaders and managers accountable for using engagement data, and learning and development that align with the engagement elements. The most effective approach to engagement is a continuous process that resides alongside regular business activities.

2. *Use validated surveys or instruments to measure engagement.* Just about every employee survey today is referred to as an engagement survey. Few surveys or instruments, however, are validated through rigorous statistical analysis or academic peer review. Many companies are attempting to increase engagement by focusing on problems that may not affect engagement or by measuring engagement incorrectly.

3. *Understand a company's current state and where it needs to be in the future.* After taking a baseline measurement, the development of a three-year road map is recommended for addressing improved engagement. The road map should address a company's need for improved engagement and include realistic milestones and actions.

4. *Look beyond engagement as a single measure or construct.* Some companies focus on moving the overall value of an engagement measure while overlooking the tactics that lead to improved performance. When companies focus largely on measuring engagement rather than improving engagement, they often fail to make the changes that will engage employees or meet employees' workplace needs. Improved engagement is the result of clarifying work expectations, providing people with the resources needed to perform their job, developing individual capabilities, and promoting positive coworker relationships.

5. *Align engagement with other workplace priorities.* Engagement should not be another task required of an employee or manager. It is about incorporating engagement concepts into the workflow, even as businesses change and adopt new initiatives.

Gallup concludes that creating a culture of engagement requires a company to examine the critical engagement elements that align with performance and with the organization's human capital strategy, keeping in mind that every interaction with employees potentially has an impact on engagement and organizational performance.

The Growth in Talent Analytics

Something that separates talent management from HR management is the use of sophisticated analytics. A large part of talent management increasingly involves something called talent analytics, which is part of a broader category of techniques called predictive analytics.

Talent analytics involves adopting sophisticated methods of analyzing employee data to ensure the highest productivity, engagement, and retention of talent. Kimberly-Clark, a company with a corporate culture where employees believed they had a job for life, now uses talent analytics software to track and evaluate salaried workers' progress. The use of sophisticated analytics has resulted in the career expectancy of laggards to become much shorter than in years past.[15] Figure 3.1 identifies various kinds of talent analytics.[16]

Talent Supply Chain Analytics

Address how workforce needs should adapt to changes in the business environment.

Talent Value Model Analytics

Analyze why employees choose to stay with or leave an organization.

Workforce Forecasts Analytics

Help identify when to increase or reduce staffing levels.

Human-Capital Analysis

Provides insight into which actions have the greatest impact on the workforce and the business.

Analytical Human Resources

Help identify which departments or individuals need attention.

Human-Capital Facts Analytics

Help identify the key human-related indicators that link to organizational performance.

Figure 3.1   Kinds of talent analytics

SUPPLY MANAGEMENT KNOWLEDGE AND SKILL REQUIREMENTS

Transitioning from traditional purchasing to strategic supply management has altered the knowledge and skill sets required of supply organizations. The knowledge and skills required to succeed today are quite different from those required in an era characterized by managing transactions. The challenge becomes one of identifying the knowledge and skills that supply organizations require now and in the future and then developing the human talent that meets that challenge.

We could identify hundreds of skills that could be part of the supply management skill set. If we ask 20 people what set of knowledge and skills a supply professional should have, we will likely receive 20 different responses. Some areas are mentioned so often that their importance is taken for granted. Who is willing to argue against the need for supply managers to demonstrate leadership, communicate and listen well, solve problems, manage change, and plan effectively? A recognized set of knowledge and skills will always be important.

Our interest here is not about what any one individual can master, but rather what a supply organization has mastered collectively. The following presents a set of knowledge and skill areas where supply organizations should demonstrate mastery. These areas have been identified through extensive research with leading firms and numerous discussions with supply management leaders. Still, this set of items is subject to interpretation and debate regarding its completeness and relevancy.

It might be worthwhile to note the differences between knowledge, skills, and competencies. Knowledge relates to knowing something with familiarity gained through experience, learning, or association. We often speak of a body of knowledge as it relates to different professional areas. Skills represent the ability to use one's knowledge effectively and readily during the execution of performance. Finally, competencies involve a measureable pattern of behavior and knowledge that cause or predict superior performance in a given role or set of responsibilities. Recall the discussion of core competencies from Chapter 2. Let's explore the knowledge and skills areas that supply organizations must master.

Ability to Understand the Corporate Business Model

A business model describes how an organization competes. Best-in-class companies should have clearly articulated the competitive model they must put in place to succeed. Imagine the problems that could result when a company's business model features speed to market with niche product offerings while supply managers select suppliers that provide lower costs through large volume runs and long lead times. Material costs will be low, but does that support a business model that requires responsiveness, speed, and flexibility?

According to the value chain model developed by Michael Porter, procurement and supply management is a support function. As such, it must understand how a company competes and creates value. Recall from Chapter 1 that a characteristic of a supply leader is the ability to develop strategies that align directly with a firm's competitive business model. To be effective they must understand and support that model. Alignment between supply management and corporate management is a strategic necessity.

Ability to Assume a Holistic Perspective

A holistic perspective means to emphasize the organic or functional relation between the parts and the whole. Within supply management, a holistic perspective means evolving from a narrow, functional perspective to one that understands how the different elements of a value chain interact to create value. It is about seeing how pieces of a puzzle interact to arrive at the *big picture*. Holistic thinking requires the development of supply strategies and tactics that support not only corporate objectives but also the objectives of supply management's internal customers, particularly operations and engineering.

Ability to Support Nontraditional Purchase Areas

Some readers may recall the good old days when the purchasing group involved itself primarily with the buying of components according to internally derived specifications. Instead of just buying components, today's supply managers are sourcing assemblies, systems, and even entire finished products. Instead of just sourcing direct materials, supply managers are involved with buying just about everything that an organization requires to operate. This includes services of all kinds, capital equipment, and even employee benefits. A note from a supply chain graduate to his former professor sums up well the scope of even this young buyer's expanding involvement into many different supply areas:

> "I started my career in spares purchasing, helping to outfit the Navy ships that we are building with everything from engine spares, toilet paper, to gun holsters. Everything that isn't bolted down, I have purchased. I've moved on to bigger things now. I'm in charge of several specs, including the rudder, hull castings, anchor, and anchor chain. I'm also the buyer for all labor subcontracts, whether it is for temporary welders or engineering consulting work. I also have all weld rods and some spare parts responsibility. Needless to say, they keep me busy here."

Anywhere there is a significant amount of money spent, we should expect supply management to assume a leading role. This means that supply management groups must expand their knowledge base to manage an ever growing list of purchase requirements.

Knowledge of Processes and Process Management

An organizational process consists of a set of interrelated tasks or activities designed to achieve a desired outcome or objective. Examples of objectives include the selection of world-class suppliers, the timely fulfillment of customer orders, or the development of innovative new products or services. Because they don't know better, organizational processes almost always cross functional boundaries. The ability to take a holistic view will come in handy when trying to understand organizational processes.

Because processes create the output that leads to desired outcomes, it is important to understand the processes that create value, both within and outside of supply management. Supply managers must be able to visualize these processes; articulate their objectives; and understand the role, either leading or supportive, that they play in making sure the process achieves its intended results. Assuming a process view also helps manage the conflict and trade-offs that inevitably occur across a supply chain. Developing supply personnel with strong process design and management skills supports nicely the goals of strategic supply management. Chapter 14 addresses developing a process-driven supply and supply chain organization.

Ability to Manage Supplier Relationships

Something all industries share is the importance of supplier relationships. Not surprisingly, the most common organizational design feature that medium and larger firms have in place is assigning specific individuals to manage supplier relationships. The need to manage relationships effectively, however, is not easy. Later chapters will address the importance of collaborating with suppliers, segmenting relationships based on importance, building trust with suppliers, and becoming the customer of choice.

Ability to Use IT Systems

Perhaps one of the most important reasons for developing information systems is to relieve supply personnel of mundane, time-consuming duties. Some of these systems support the separation of strategic and operational responsibilities, thereby allowing supply managers to focus their efforts in areas that will provide the greatest return. Supply managers must understand when, where, and how to develop and use a wide range of IT systems—something that Chapter 6 explores.

Ability to Perform Statistical Analyses and Make Fact-Based Decisions

The ability to perform statistical analyses and make fact-based decisions means that strategic supply management processes are supported by objective data. It also implies that measurement systems are in place to provide timely and objective information. What are some areas that benefit from statistical analyses and fact-based decisions? A partial list includes:

- Selecting suppliers
- Identifying candidates for supply-based reduction
- Identifying financial paybacks from supplier development efforts
- Calculating the impact of supplier nonconformance
- Evaluating supplier suggestions in terms of importance and feasibility
- Identifying suppliers for longer term agreements
- Identifying the impact of price concession strategies during negotiation planning
- Identifying the benefits of leveraging purchase volumes with suppliers
- Calculating bankruptcy probabilities based on supplier financial health
- Determining whether to insource or outsource

Knowledge of Cost, Quality, Risk, and Financial Management Techniques

Important differences exist between price and cost management. Knowing when and how to apply the different types of analyses is a critical part of strategic supply management. Cost analytic techniques focus primarily on the individual costs that are aggregated to create a price. While a price is technically a cost, it represents the total of various cost elements and drivers that are added together. Traditional purchasing has been largely price-focused, regardless of the item or service being considered for purchase. Chapter 7 addresses this topic within the context of strategy development.

The ability to manage supplier quality and supply chain risk is also an essential part of supply management. Never before have companies relied on suppliers for such a large portion of their final product value. Increasingly, supply organizations must have the ability to apply a range of financial tools and techniques. Chapter 8 deals with supply chain financial management.

Ability to Span Boundaries

While supply management is a boundary-spanning process, the degree of boundary spanning is increasing. Supply managers must increasingly work across a mix of boundaries:

- *Functional boundaries*: This relates to the growth in cross-functional interaction, often due to the use of cross-functional teams and organizing around supply chain processes.
- *Organizational or enterprise boundaries*: This relates to the need to work with suppliers and customers to manage product development, demand and supply planning, sourcing, customer order fulfillment, and continuous supply chain improvement.
- *Geographic boundaries*: This relates to the growth in working with internal suppliers and with suppliers that are geographically dispersed, sometimes around the world.
- *Cultural boundaries*: This relates to working internally and externally with different cultures. An extension of cultural boundaries is language boundaries. Supply managers increasingly work in a virtual and globally dispersed world.

Ability to Understand Ethics and Ethical Decision Making

Ethical decision making involves taking ethical considerations into account when selecting a logical choice from available options. Ethics deals with questions relating to the fairness, justness, rightness, or wrongness of an action and includes the set of moral principles or values guiding our behavior. When trying to arrive at an ethical decision, a person must weigh the positives and negatives of each option, and consider all the alternatives. It is important for supply managers to understand that legal compliance is usually regarded the minimum acceptable standard for ethical business behavior.

Ethical deficiency within a supply organization presents serious risks, both to individuals and to the entire organization. Part of the challenge when promoting ethical behavior is understanding that ethical principles or values can vary from person to person, business to business, culture to culture, and country to country. No perfect alignment of what constitutes ethical behavior exists across the world. Given the amount of money that supply managers control, it is no surprise that ethical issues can be a concern. Understanding ethics, ethical decision making and how to promote ethical behavior is something that all supply organizations should strive to attain.

Project Management Understanding

Virtually every talent survey that queries executives reports on the need for employees to understand project management. The next chapter presents work by Deloitte that indicates future organizations will be comprised of networks of teams working on projects. All kinds of work tasks can benefit from applying project management techniques as well as project thinking. Supply management personnel who are interested in gaining greater knowledge about project management should learn more about the Project Management Institute (PMI). PMI awards a certification in project management called the Project Management Professional.

It is reasonable to expect that an effective supply organization has gained proficiency within the areas just presented. It is not reasonable to expect any single individual to be an expert within each area. While this list contains some important knowledge and skill areas, there are certainly others that could be added to the list. The bottom line is that the kinds of knowledge and skills that are required to support supply management excellence affect the kind of human talent that supply organizations recruit.

APPROACHES FOR ACQUIRING AND DEVELOPING TALENT

A variety of traditional yet still effective approaches are available for acquiring and developing the talent required to support an organization's supply objectives. The objective of each approach is to gain access to leaders that will guide the supply organization into the future.

Approaches for Acquiring Talent

The following approaches are logical ways to acquire human talent. While not too glamorous, they have demonstrated their effectiveness over time.

Recruit from Other Functional Groups

It is increasingly common to see individuals without a procurement background, such as engineering or finance, working in supply management. Supply management is increasingly viewed as offering an attractive career path with solid job opportunities. When recruiting from other functional groups, it is probably a good idea not to blatantly poach talent from other internal groups, particularly since supply managers will likely have to work with those groups.

Develop Close Relationships with a Select Group of Colleges

Some companies develop close relationships with a select group of colleges and universities. These companies extensively recruit interns, co-op students, and recent college graduates from these institutions. They conduct *meet and greet* sessions with students, work with faculty to inform students about the company, attend career fairs, and interview students directly on campus. Many companies have identified six or so institutions where they recruit regularly for supply chain talent. This does not mean these companies ignore job candidates from other institutions. On-site recruiting, however, tends to occur at a limited set of schools.

Recruit Honorably Discharged Military Personnel

Some companies regularly tap into a pipeline that includes individuals who are honorably leaving the military. Consider the maturity, skills, and discipline these individuals bring to the workplace. Besides receiving training that is often highly technical, these individuals have worked under stressful conditions that require teamwork and commitment. This is a talent pipeline that many supply organizations should pursue more aggressively.

Recruit Management Consultants

Consulting firms hire some exceptional individuals who quickly take on demanding supply management projects for their clients. While consulting initially appears to be an exciting, perhaps even glamorous career, many individuals find that travel demands and time away from home can prove to be burdensome. After a period of time, some of these talented individuals are thinking about a more stable work environment. This may also be the case if an employee fails to become a partner in the firm.

Hire Talent Externally

Like sports teams, some companies go to the marketplace and recruit the talent they need. This approach requires a willingness to make attractive offers that will entice job prospects to leave their current employer. It is often worthwhile to work with a search firm to coordinate recruiting efforts. The demise of the defined pension plan mentioned earlier should remove some of the risk to the employee of changing employers.

Post Positions and Submit Applications Online

Any organization that does not have a way for potential job candidates to locate job openings easily from your organization's website probably should not be in business. And, these individuals should have an easy way to submit applications and resumes. A word of caution is in order here. Some companies are earning a poor reputation because of their lack of feedback or responsiveness to candidates who have submitted a resume online. The submission process is viewed as a black hole that sucks in matter but releases nothing out. Anecdotally, at times college students have advised other students to avoid certain companies that suffer from *black hole* syndrome.

Approaches for Developing Talent

Many ways exist for developing, engaging, and hopefully retaining personnel who are currently part of the supply organization.

Create Leadership Rotation Programs

Early on, progressive firms identify their most promising hires—perhaps during the college recruiting process—and then place them in a leadership training or rotational program. These programs, which generally last from one to two years, rotate new hires across different assignments. These individuals become highly visible as they move through their assignments. An analysis by *Business Week* revealed that just over 30 of the top 50 organizations identified as the best places for new graduates to work offered formal management training programs.

Create a Mentoring Program

Many companies have created mentoring programs to develop promising supply leaders. With these programs, a senior supply leader works directly with junior personnel to provide guidance and to share tribal knowledge and experience. The mentors meet with the mentee on a regular basis, introduce him or her to other executives, and include these individuals in any experiences that would further develop these prospective leaders.

Not all mentoring occurs at the executive or managerial level. Given the importance of teams it makes sense for qualified team leaders to mentor members who will eventually assume leadership roles. It also makes sense to assign a mentor to new college hires. A mentoring program assumes that mentors are qualified to assume the role and will be diligent in their duties. A poor mentor will be counterproductive to the objectives of the mentoring program.

Reward Personnel for Knowledge and Skill Advancement

This approach focuses on rewarding personnel for advancing their skills and knowledge through formal education. This includes earning degrees or certificates in supply or supply chain management. Each year the *Institute for Supply Management* (ISM) publishes a list of colleges and universities that offer procurement and supply chain management degree and certificate programs. Colleges and universities that do not have formal supply or supply chain programs often offer courses related to supply management. Supporting continuing education through tuition reimbursement further encourages the development of a firm's human talent.

Provide Leadership Training and Development

A shift toward strategic supply management almost always requires a major retooling of the workforce. This retooling or development often takes the form of continuous training programs and leadership development opportunities.

Interestingly, some companies have experienced some attrition after their employees complete a development program. Many younger employees, whose higher potential was a factor in being nominated for a development program, often find they are attractive to other companies after completing the development program. This is a risk that corporations need to understand and manage.

Make Training Courses Available on an On-Demand Basis

Most companies develop a generic menu of courses and then offer them to employees on a regular basis. It is not unusual for large groups of employees to receive virtually the same training. Best practice companies understand the necessity of offering general training to the masses. But, they also understand the importance of assessing the knowledge and skill needs of their personnel and then crafting training programs that are customized to each employee's needs. An employee who is assuming the role of commodity team leader, for example, might benefit from team leadership training. Another employee who is assigned to a supplier development team may benefit from Lean Six Sigma training. Ideally these training modules are for viewing asynchronously through web-based systems.

Assign Promising Personnel to Team Leadership Positions

Research reveals that the effectiveness of a team leader has a disproportionate effect on team success. For a variety of reasons, the role of formal team leader is one of the most demanding positions within organizations today. Most firms rely extensively on teams to manage various supply activities, including the development of supply management strategies. In some respects, team leadership roles are analogous to playing in the minor leagues before progressing to the major leagues. Effective team leaders become prime candidates for future supply leadership positions.

Develop Career Maps

Most employees would like some idea of the path their career may follow. These perspectives, called career maps or ladders, can be valuable aids when recruiting new talent into the supply organization. Career ladders illustrate various supply tracks or career paths. Employees usually appreciate a graphical representation of how their careers might advance.

Career ladders are important because most organizations have de-layered their organization from top to bottom.[17] Organizational levels have given way to broad groupings of positions within different bands. Job changes that were previously vertical, which usually meant a promotion, are now often lateral, within a certain band. This de-layering of the organizational structure has made career ladders an important part of retaining talent, as they help supply professionals visualize their professional growth.

TRENDS IN TALENT MANAGEMENT

It should come as no surprise that different perspectives exist regarding the trends that will affect talent management. An Internet search of *talent management trends* reveals a variety of sources that enlighten us about the future. Unfortunately, while a degree of overlap exists among these perspectives, most put their own spin on the topic.

Deloitte has performed some rigorous work in the area of talent management. Part of this work includes an annual survey of global managers. Based on this survey, Deloitte has identified ten trends to focus on in order to better organize, manage, develop, and align people at work.[18] The following elaborates on five of these trends. Table 3.1 summarizes all ten trends identified by Deloitte.

The Organization of the Future Is Arriving Now

Organizations face a growing need to redesign themselves to move faster, adapt quickly, learn rapidly, and embrace dynamic career demands. Leading organizations are moving past the design phase to actively build this new organization. Unfortunately, only 11 percent of respondents in Deloitte's survey indicate that they understand how to build the organization of the future. One promising technique for designing a future strategy is organizational network analysis (ONA). ONA uses specialized software and methodologies to study who is talking to whom. This analysis uses patterns in e-mails, instant messages, physical proximity, and other data, and allows leaders to see what networks are in place and identify the connectors and experts.[19] The insight gained from this analysis supports the creation of an organizational design.

Learning Is Becoming Real Time, All the Time

Few would question that continuous learning is critical for business success. Today's business environment calls for delivering learning that is always on and

Table 3.1 Top global human capital trends

Trend	Description
The organization of the future—its arriving now	Organizations are being redesigned to move faster, adapt more quickly, learn rapidly, and embrace dynamic career demands.
Careers and learning—real time, all the time	The new rules of competition call for organizations that deliver learning that is always on and always available over a range of mobile platforms.
Talent acquisition—enter the cognitive recruiter	Recruiting is becoming a digital experience as candidates come to expect convenience and mobile contact. Savvy recruiters will embrace talent acquisition technologies to forge emotional connections with candidates and constantly work to strengthen the employment brand.
The employee experience—culture, engagement, and beyond	Rather than focus only on employee engagement and culture, organizations are developing a focus on the entire employee experience. A new marketplace of tools, wellness and fitness apps, and integrated employee self-service tools is helping this transformation.
Performance management—play a winning hand	Companies are reevaluating every aspect of their performance management programs, from goal setting and evaluation to incentives and rewards. Changes are being aligned with business strategy and the ongoing transformation of work.
Leadership disrupted—pushing the boundaries	Organizations do not just need more strong leaders, they need a completely different kind of leader—younger, more agile, and *digital-ready*.
Digital HR—platforms, people, and work	As digital management practices and agile organizational designs become central to business thinking, HR must focus on people, work, and technology platforms.
People analytics—recalculating the route	Talent analytics is becoming a business function focused on using data to understand every part of a business operation, and embedding analytics into real-time apps and the way individuals work.
Diversity and inclusion—the reality gap	Fairness, equity, and inclusion efforts have not met expectations. The era of diversity as a *check-the-box* initiative owned by HR is over. CEOs must drive accountability among leaders at all levels to close the gap between what is said and the actual impact.
The future of work—the augmented workforce	Automation, cognitive computing, and crowds are paradigm-shifting forces reshaping the workforce. Organizations must experiment and implement cognitive tools, focus on retraining people to use these tools, and rethink the role of people as work becomes automated.

Adapted from Deloitte University Press, https://www2.deloitte.com/us/en/pages/human-capital/articles/introduction-human-capital-trends.html.

available over a range of mobile platforms. The half-life of skills is rapidly falling—a reality that is forcing companies to rethink the way they manage careers and deliver on-demand learning and development opportunities. Leading companies are moving to overhaul their career models and learning and development infrastructure for the digital age—though most organizations are still in the early stages of this transformation.[20]

Organizational Culture, Engagement, and Beyond Will Define the Employee Experience

Organizations are developing an integrated focus on the entire employee experience rather than a more narrow focus on employee engagement and culture. A new marketplace of pulse feedback tools, wellness and fitness apps, and integrated employee self-service tools is helping. Nearly 80 percent of respondents in Deloitte's research rate an employee's experience with his or her work environment as important or very important, yet only 22 percent say their companies are excellent at building a differentiated employee experience.

Talent Acquisition—Enter the Cognitive Recruiter

More than 8 in 10 executives say talent acquisition is important or very important. Talent recruiting is rapidly becoming a digital experience as candidates expect convenience and mobile contact. Smart recruiters will embrace new technologies to forge psychological and emotional connections with candidates. In today's transparent digital world, a company's employment brand must be highly visible and attractive because candidates often find the employer, not the reverse. Companies must manage their employment brand electronically, which can pull candidates toward them.

People Analytics—Recalculating the Route

Analytics is no longer just about finding interesting information and forwarding it to managers. Driven by the widespread adoption of cloud HR systems, companies are investing heavily in programs to use data for all aspects of workforce planning, talent management, and operational improvement. Talent analytics, or people analytics as it is called by Deloitte, is becoming a business function that stresses using data to understand every part of a business operation and embedding analytics into real-time apps that affect the way we work. This topic was discussed earlier in this chapter.

CONCLUDING THOUGHTS

A Delphi futures study predicted that the ability to integrate and manage strategic suppliers into a buyer's business will be considered a core competency that will not be outsourced. Gaining advantages from this integration requires human talent that has the ability to understand how to develop and manage critical relationships. Anything of significance that happens within the supply management domain requires the right people supported by the right IT, the right measurement systems, and the right organizational structure. Never diminish the importance of the four enablers of strategic supply management.

Experience reveals that there is a straightforward link between executive awareness of the value of strategic supply management and executive management's willingness to invest in supply management capabilities. Few would argue that one of these primary capabilities involves human talent. The journey toward success requires a commitment to all facets of talent management. This starts with an awareness of the current state of your company's supply management practices compared against best practices; identifying what defines a world-class organization; assessing the gap between the current and a desired future state; and creating a roadmap for acquiring the human talent that will transform your organization into a supply leader. It all starts with the right people.

REFERENCES

1. A. Bartolini, *CPO Rising 2017: Tools of the Trade*, a white paper by Ardent Partners, 2017.
2. R. E. Lewis and R. J. Heckman, "Talent Management: A Critical Review," *Human Resources Management Review*, 16, (2006): 139–154.
3. J. C. Hughes and E. Rog, "Talent Management: A Strategy for Improving Employee Recruitment, Retention and Engagement within Hospitality Organizations," *International Journal of Contemporary Hospitality Management*, 20, no. 7, 2008: 743–757, citing Lewis and Heckman, "Talent Management: A Critical Review," 139–154.
4. P. Cappelli, "Balance Your Talent Requirements," *Inside Supply Management*, 21, no. 10 (October/November 2010): 28.
5. R. J. Trent and R. M. Monczka, "Achieving Excellence in Global Sourcing," *Sloan Management Review*, (Fall 2005), from http://sloanreview.mit.edu/article/achieving-excellence-in-global-sourcing/.
6. S. Minter, "Identifying Your Future Leaders," *Industry Week*, 259, no. 9, (September 2010): 24.

7. J. Green, "Chowing Down on Boomers' Brains," *Business Week*, (January 25, 2016): 20.

8. D. Leonard and W. Swap, *Deep Smarts* (Cambridge, MA: Harvard Business School Publishing, 2005).

9. M. Vipal, "More Companies Freezing Corporate Pension Plans," *The Wall Street Journal*, March 3, 2016, from http://blogs.wsj.com/cfo/2016/03/03/more-companies-freezing-corporate-pension-plans/.

10. From http://www.gallup.com.

11. M. Nink and M. J. Robinson, "The Damage Inflicted by Poor Management," *Business Journal* (Gallup), December 20, 2016, from http://www.gallup.com/businessjournal/200108/damage-inflicted-poor-managers.aspx?g_source=engagement&g_medium=search&g_campaign=tiles.

12. J. Hughes and E. Rog, p. 749, citing Hewitt Associates, "What Makes a Best Employer?" *Insights and Findings from Hewitt's Global Best Employer's Study*, Hewitt Associates: 1–38.

13. J. Hughes and E. Rog, p. 750, citing Towers Perrin, "The 2003 Towers Perrin Talent Report: Working Today: Understanding What Drives Employee Engagement," Research Report, Towers Perrin, Stamford, CT, 2003.

14. Adapted from A. Mann and J. Harter, "The Worldwide Employee Engagement Crisis," *Business Journal* (Gallup), January 7, 2016, from http://www.gallup.com/businessjournal/188033/worldwide-employee-engagement-crisis.aspx?g_source=engagement&g_medium=search&g_campaign=tiles.

15. L. Weber, "Nowhere to Hide for Dead Wood Workers," *The Wall Street Journal*, (August 22, 2016): A1.

16. T. H. Davenport, J. Harris, and J. Shapiro, "Competing on Talent Analytics," *Harvard Business Review*, (October 2010): 52–58.

17. R. A. Rudzki and R. J. Trent, *Next Level Supply Management Excellence* (Fort Lauderdale, FL: J. Ross Publishing, 2011): 105–106.

18. 2017 Deloitte Global Human Capital Trends, from https://www2.deloitte.com/us/en/pages/human-capital/articles/introduction-human-capital-trends.html.

19. J. Bersin, T. McDowell, A. Rahnema, and Y. Van Daurrme, "The Organization of the Future: Arriving Now," Deloitte University Press, February 28, 2017, from https://dupress.deloitte.com/dup-us-en/focus/human-capital-trends/2017/organization-of-the-future.html?id=us:2el:3dc:dup3817:awa:cons:hct17.

20. B. Pester, D. Johnson, J. Stempel, and B. der Vyer, "Careers and Learning: Real Time, All the Time," Deloitte University Press, February 28, 2017, https://dupress.deloitte.com/dup-us-en/focus/human-capital-trends/2017/learning-in-the-digital-age.html?id=us:2el:3dc:dup3818:awa:cons:hct17.

4

EVOLVING ORGANIZATIONAL DESIGNS

When thinking about how companies achieve advantages from their supply management efforts, we often hear about some exciting initiatives. Hardly mentioned, however, is how organizational design promotes or hinders performance. This is something that is starting to change. In its worldwide study of challenges in business, Deloitte identified some interesting findings. For the over 7,000 companies in over 130 countries that responded to Deloitte's survey, the top-rated challenge facing leaders is *how to redesign our organizational structure* to meet the demands of the workforce and business climate today.[1]

Without question, how a company is organized affects its ability to achieve its objectives. Organizational design can act as a major enabler, or it can be a major inhibitor. Creating a set of objectives and then designing an organization that supports the attainment of those objectives is a major part of the supply management process. An effective design, supported by other supply management enablers, gives an organization the confidence to take on a set of challenges.

This chapter explores the often-overlooked topic of creating the right supply organization. The first section presents some important conclusions about this important topic. Next, a set of progressive design features in supply management appears. Third, a discussion of the use of teams will help us better understand this popular approach to work. The chapter concludes with some thoughts about the future of organizational design.

UNDERSTANDING ORGANIZATIONAL DESIGN

Organizational design refers to the process of assessing and selecting the structure and formal system of communication, division of labor, coordination, control, authority, and responsibility required to achieve organizational goals.[2] This includes the specific features put in place to support that design and is much more than what an organizational chart can ever depict. Its early placement in this book reflects the importance of organizational design as a critical supply management enabler.

A number of important conclusions relate to designing an effective supply organization. Organizational designs must continuously evolve as firms continue their transition from traditional purchasing to strategic supply management.

1. *A higher-level procurement office and executive is essential to the development of supply strategies and the effectiveness of strategic supply management.* While this conclusion seems intuitive, the importance of a higher-level chief procurement officer (CPO) who has access to the highest executive levels (although not necessarily the CEO) is essential when pursuing strategic supply management. Furthermore, regular presentations by the CPO to the CEO and Board of Directors also characterize an effective design.

It is not the formal executive position that makes this feature important. Rather, the visibility and resources that come with having a position that is on par with other functional executives is critical. Supply management initiatives flounder without an executive champion who has the authority to put in place a supportive organizational design. Companies that expect advantages from their organizational design must consider the importance of a higher-level supply officer as well as the reporting level of that position.

Another part of executive commitment through the organizational design relates to something called an executive steering committee, which a later section explores more fully. These committees are essential for setting the strategic supply direction of a company.

2. *Organizational size affects the type and intensity of the design features put in place.* Smaller, medium, and larger firms view the need for organizational design features differently. While some design features are common regardless of firm size, organizations also emphasize features that support their unique requirements. For medium and larger firms, this means relying on features that support coordination and integration across the supply chain. An important point is that larger firms rely on many parts of their organizational design to manage large, complex organizations. Some features that larger firms emphasize simply are not applicable to smaller firms.

3. *A continuing shift toward centrally coordinated or centrally led supply management reflects the need to leverage supply management volumes and capabilities.* Research evidence reveals an emphasis on centrally led or centralized governance, coordination, and decision making within supply management. We are witnessing a shift toward greater central control or coordination—something that is not likely to reverse. What is driving this shift are the competitive pressures brought about by new market entrants and global competition.

An inability to raise prices (largely due to this competition) demands the co-ordination of worldwide supply activities and the consolidation of purchase volumes in an effort to minimize total costs. The following highlights the emphasis placed on center-led or centralized authority and governance as identified during a study that included organizational design as a topic of interest:[3]

- Almost 75% of firms say their most important purchases are coordinated from a center-led or headquarters group
- Over 70% say their decision-making authority within supply management is centralized or highly centralized
- Over 50% say their business unit's strategy decisions are made from a worldwide perspective while 33% take a regional perspective
- Almost 60% say their overall business unit is structured and governed centrally, 39% say their business unit is decentralized with some coordination, and only 2% indicate their business unit is decentralized

Firms should consider putting in place features that support an expected movement toward centrally led or centrally coordinated purchasing. This includes the use of centrally coordinated commodity teams, formal positions that separate strategic and tactical supply responsibilities, lead buyers to manage non-centrally coordinated items, strategy review and coordination sessions between functional groups and locations, and a higher-level CPO. These features will enable organizations to capture the benefits of a centrally led organization while avoiding the poor perception that internal users or sites often associate with central control.

4. *The use of teams will remain a popular and even growing design option.* The use of teams over the last 30 years has proven to be a resilient part of organizational designs. The design features that supply organizations rely on continue to stress the use of cross-functional and cross-locational teams. However, few studies unequivocally establish a clear connection between teaming and better performance. The importance of this topic deserves a more thorough treatment later in this chapter.

5. *Certain design features may be the ideal solution if coordination and integration across the supply chain remains a challenge.* We often think of information systems as the enabler that promotes coordination across supply chains; and to a large degree this is true. If supply managers expect to achieve increased coordination and integration across the supply chain, they should take a closer look at design features that promote coordination and integration. Organizational design supports three kinds of integration—cross-functional, cross-locational, and cross-organizational.

Coordination across functions and organizations is becoming an increasingly important supply objective (a later chapter will define an objective as an aspiration to work toward). The focus in purchasing and supply management will shift from functional coordination to managing the interfaces that purchasing and supply management has with other functional units, thus leading to management of the white space that is present on the organizational chart.[4]

6. *Collocation of procurement personnel with internal customers is an increasingly important way to promote trust.* Physically collocating supply personnel with their internal customers, a feature that directly promotes trust-based relationships (along with a host of other benefits), is an attractive organizational design feature. Supply managers will increasingly rely on organizational design features to help manage the strategic connections with other functional groups as well as across enterprise boundaries. A later section highlights the collocation model.

7. *Supply organizations are shifting gradually from a vertical to a horizontal perspective.* A horizontal perspective features an organization designed around supply processes, such as supplier evaluation and selection, supplier development, and new product development. The extensive use of cross-functional teams, particularly teams that feature full-time members is one indication of a shift toward a process orientation. When organizing around processes, cross-functional participants work concurrently in an environment featuring the horizontal (i.e., cross-functional) flow of information across the supply chain.

The process rather than the functional group becomes the focus of the organizational design when shifting from a functional to a process orientation. It is unlikely, however, that firms will ever move totally away from functional groups. The placement of functional personnel into full-time teams would dilute the core expertise and knowledge required to operate a business. The need to maintain a critical mass of functional knowledge ensures that some functional structure, albeit a diminished one, will remain. Furthermore, the changes surrounding a shift from a functional to a process perspective (i.e., a shift from a vertical to a horizontal design) ensure any changes will be gradual. Chapter 14 addresses becoming a process-centric organization.

8. *Separating strategic and operational activities and authority supports the attainment of supply objectives.* Strategic and operational thinking involve different skill sets and time frames. It is a challenge, if not impossible, for an individual or department to engage in both types of thinking simultaneously. Given this challenge, we should see a continued separation between strategic and operational responsibilities. An emphasis on strategic tasks and objectives is a clear indication of the growing importance of supply management. A later section addresses this topic further.

PROGRESSIVE DESIGN FEATURES
IN SUPPLY MANAGEMENT

An abundance of design features is available to corporate planners. But, with so many features and options, the task of creating an effective design can be daunting. Table 4.1 identifies the wide variety of design features available to supply organizations.

Table 4.1   Possible supply management organizational design features

• Executive buyer-supplier council that coordinates activities and initiatives with key suppliers
• Formal strategy coordination and review sessions between supply management and other functional groups
• Centrally coordinated commodity teams that develop company-wide supply strategies
• Higher level executive officer with a supply-related title
• Lead buyers or site-based experts assigned to manage non-centrally coordinated items
• Regular presentations by the CPO to the CEO and/or Board of Directors
• Formal group or team responsible for demand and supply chain planning
• Executive position responsible for coordinating end-to-end supply chain activities
• Shared services model that provides support to business units or locations
• Cross-functional teams that manage some part of the supply management process
• Physical collocation between procurement and various internal customer groups
• Corporate level steering committee that oversees supply management initiatives
• International procurement offices (IPOs) to support worldwide sourcing
• On-site suppliers to perform activities such as replenishment and inventory control
• Customer advisory board that includes key customers and key suppliers
• Formal separation of strategic and tactical procurement and supply responsibilities, personnel, positions, and structure
• Specific individuals assigned responsibility for managing supplier relationships
• Formal supply strategy coordination and review sessions between business units or divisions
• A matrix reporting structure that features supply professionals reporting to more than one group, location, business, region, or manager
• Organization designed around supply processes rather than functions
• Value analysis or value engineering groups with supply involvement
• New product development teams that include supply professionals and/or suppliers
• Project teams that work on procurement and supply tasks
• Membership in a purchase consortium
• Virtual organizational design linked by information technology systems

Given the importance of organizational design as a strategic enabler, what are some features that supply managers should understand? The following presents four such features—executive steering committees, collocation models for promoting integration and coordination with internal participants, separating strategic and tactical responsibilities, and virtual designs.

Executive Steering Committee

Two design features tend to reveal the importance of supply management within the organizational hierarchy—a higher-level CPO and an executive steering committee or advisory board that provides strategic guidance. These boards or councils are usually comprised of executives from various functional and operating groups and are accountable for some serious work. The following highlights the responsibilities of a supply leadership council for a major global company:

- Ensure that consistent supply policies, procedures, and processes are followed worldwide
- Establish the strategic direction for purchase commodities
- Identify commodity candidates for company-wide leveraging and coordination
- Search creatively for new sourcing and supply methods
- Coordinate strategy development with other groups
- Verify compliance to corporate agreements
- Form, staff, and provide resources for strategy development teams
- Establish company-wide performance improvement targets

Just as leading supply organizations have a higher-level supply executive, progressive supply organizations also feature an active steering committee or council.

Promoting Integration and Coordination through Collocation Models

A design feature that supports integration and coordination between supply management and internal groups is the collocation model. Collocation involves physically placing supply personnel directly into the physical space of the internal customers they support. Do not forget that supply management is a support function, meaning that it serves internal customers. An effective organizational design can support the service that supply management provides.

In some ways collocation models represent a matrix organizational structure where the supply professional maintains a direct reporting line to the supply management group while supporting a dotted line or informal reporting line to the collocated group. Collocation can be a full- or part-time responsibility on the part of the supply professional who is assigned to an internal group.

Collocation models support frequent, face-to-face interaction between individuals from different functional groups or departments, something that we know directly promotes greater trust. Figure 4.1 provides some examples where supply management professionals interact directly with key internal customers. A special kind of collocation model occurs when suppliers place support personnel directly at the buyer's location.

What do we hope to gain from collocation? Supply personnel should gain first-hand insight into supplier performance; internal customer requirements; and capacity, material, and service needs when collocated with operating personnel. When collocated with engineering, we expect to gain insight into material specifications and new product, process, and technology requirements. When collocated with marketing, we should gain insight into demand requirements, new product ideas, and promotions and other planned shifts in demand. Collocation is not about simply working in the physical presence of other groups. Rather, it is about embedding the purchasing professional into the planning and operating systems of the collocated group.

Supply managers must consider a number of issues when considering a collocation model. One involves the amount of time to commit to collocation. Will supply professionals be collocated with other functional groups on a full- or part-time basis? Another issue is determining the reporting relationship that best supports collocation. In a typical collocation model, the collocated

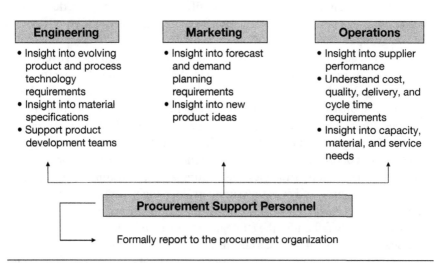

Figure 4.1   Examples of procurement collocation

employee maintains a dotted-line relationship to the collocation group with a solid-line relationship to the supply management group.

Some desirable outcomes can result when collocation models work as intended:

- Increased interaction with other functional groups
- Enhanced role clarity and understanding
- Development of positive internal relationships and trust
- Faster decision making and problem solving
- Enhanced creative thinking from working together physically
- Early insight into internal customer needs and requirements

Separating Strategic and Tactical Responsibilities

A model that features the physical and organizational separation of strategic and tactical responsibilities often accompanies a shift toward center-led supply management. Few people can pursue both strategic and tactical thinking simultaneously. Furthermore, operational or tactical activities almost always take precedence over planning, leaving less time for longer term planning and strategy development.

As mentioned, few individuals can manage strategic and tactical or operational duties simultaneously. After this reality becomes apparent (which it almost always does), separating responsibilities becomes a logical design option. Separation literally means maintaining separate groups to manage different kinds of work, something that makes sense since strategic supply management and tactical supply management feature different processes, procedures, time frames, and skill sets. Furthermore, performance measures differently across the two groups.

While a majority of supply organizations are centralized in their governance, not all tasks or responsibilities are managed at a central level. A separation between centrally led or centralization and decentralized decision making helps maintain responsiveness to internal requirements. Research reveals that certain activities are largely coordinated or managed at a centrally led or centralized level for the most important purchases while other activities remain the responsibility of sites or operating units. Activities such as developing category or commodity purchase family strategies, negotiating and establishing company-wide contracts, evaluating and selecting suppliers, locating potential supply sources, managing critical supplier relationships, and managing supplier development activities typically fall under the strategic activities umbrella.

Research also reveals that certain responsibilities typically remain part of a decentralized governance structure. Examples include executing schedules and inventory plans, expediting goods and services, issuing releases or purchase

- Develop and manage strategic relationships and suppliers
- Develop company-wide e-systems
- Pursue global opportunities
- Negotiate company-wide contracts
- Manage critical commodities

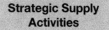

Strategic Supply Activities

- Manage transactions with suppliers
- Use e-systems to obtain standard or indirect items through catalogs
- Source items that are unique to the operating unit
- Generate and forward material releases
- Manage accounts payable and material control

Operational Activities

Figure 4.2   Separating strategic and tactical responsibilities

orders, planning inventory levels, developing requirements schedules, and routine communication and follow up with suppliers. Other activities such as resolving supplier performance problems and providing supplier performance feedback are somewhat more evenly distributed between centralized and decentralized responsibilities. Figure 4.2 illustrates how one company in the high-tech industry approaches this topic.

Virtual Designs

A defining characteristic of a virtual design is participants who are not necessarily located in close proximity, which makes face-to-face interaction a special occurrence. Supply leaders view virtual teams as a way to coordinate different supply locations and personnel across the world. Virtual communication has become a way of life at many organizations, particularly those with widely dispersed buying, engineering, and manufacturing centers.

Virtual organizations and teams do bring with them performance risks. Various research projects have concluded that even small physical dispersion between employees can affect efficiency and effectiveness negatively. And, performance often declines quickly as the geographic dispersion moves across countries and continents.[5] Building trust among virtual participants can also be a challenge.

How can the potential pitfalls of virtual organizations be mitigated or even overcome? The following set of practices characterizes successful virtual teams. Some of these practices are especially relevant when supply management personnel are located across the world:[6]

- Provide state-of-the-art communication tools
- Provide an online resource where members get to know one another

- Strive for 15% of the members of virtual teams to be individuals who are capable of crossing team, functional, and even organizational boundaries
- Select at least some members who have a previous working relationship
- Assign challenging tasks since team members demonstrate higher commitment and effort when given a challenging assignment
- Require participants to establish objectives and goals with ownership, accountability for results, and regular performance updates
- Divide work into modules that can be transferred between members, allowing participants to take advantages of time zone differences

Leading organizations will have gained a comfort level in the use of virtual designs. Interestingly, the last several years has witnessed a shift away from virtual work and teams. Boeing and IBM have joined a growing list of companies that have suspended working remotely away from the office. IBM stated that a remote model did not promote the collaboration among employees that the company was seeking.

This discussion provided only a glimpse of the design features available to supply managers. The bottom line is that many creative ways exist to organize and coordinate work today, which Table 4.1 highlighted. Take a good look at your organizational design. Is it promoting or hindering the attainment of your professional and organizational goals?

USING TEAMS TO ACHIEVE SUPPLY OBJECTIVES

Most companies have become enamored with teams, often for good reason, and the use of teams to support supply management is widespread. The ways that companies use teams to support supply and supply chain objectives are extensive. Figure 4.3 provides a sample of where we see groups and teams used within supply management and supply chain management. As this shows, there is no shortage of tasks assigned to groups and teams.

One might think that after years of research and experience, organizations would be confident in their ability to use teams. While over the last 50 years an abundance of information on work teams has emerged (far more than what could ever be presented here), this information has not always transferred to subsequent generations of managers, team leaders, and members. An understanding regarding how to use teams is still not an embedded part of many organizational cultures, and new generations of participants are not necessarily exposed to this understanding through academic or workplace training. And, never forget that teams invariably involve humans, something that introduces complexity and inconsistency to any process.

Group or Team	Description
Customer Advisory Boards	An executive level group that brings suppliers, customers, and the OEM/producer together to share information such as end customer requirements and expectations
Buyer-Supplier Councils	An executive level group that brings together the OEM/producer and a rotating group of suppliers to share information such as product forecasts and product development plans
Executive Steering Committees	A cross-functional, executive level group that has responsibility for overseeing centrally led supply initiatives and objectives
Commodity Management Teams	Cross-functional teams that develop commodity strategies with responsibility for supplier selection decisions and relationship management
Buyer-Seller Improvement Teams	Cross-organizational teams that focus on improvement opportunities and projects between the buyer and seller
Value Analysis/ Value Engineering Teams	Cross-functional teams that have responsibility for systematically analyzing the relationship between product/service function and cost
New Product Teams with Purchasing and Supplier Involvement	Cross-functional teams that have responsibility for developing new products and services with purchasing and supplier support
Supplier Development Teams	Cross-functional teams that have responsibility for managing supplier performance improvement opportunities

Figure 4.3   Examples of groups and teams

Anyone who says the use of teams guarantees better results does not really understand the complexities associated with using teams. High-performing teams, in theory, should deliver benefits that outweigh their cost. Conversely, poorly designed and managed teams can waste the time and energy of members, enforce lower rather than higher performance norms, engage in destructive conflict, and make notoriously bad decisions. Teams can also exploit, stress, and frustrate members—sometimes all at the same time.[7] Supply management teams are not immune from team dysfunctions.

The bottom line is that firms often face serious barriers when using teams, and it's important for supply managers to understand these barriers. Organizations can create barriers to teaming simply by how they structure their use—something that is addressed shortly. While a few organizations have created supply teams that are staffed by full-time members, teams with part-time members are still a prevalent way to work in teams. Members who provide a part-time commitment typically maintain their existing functional responsibilities while taking on additional team-related duties. Conflicting roles for individuals is often the result.

A second hurdle is a failure to recognize and reward the effort that team members put forth toward their assignments. Outdated reward structures that focus on traditional activities while ignoring the time a member commits to a team continues to be a common reason why teams fail. The results of various surveys reveal that too many companies have yet to revamp their compensation programs to increase the emphasis given to team participation and performance. Members often express frustration at their organization's inability to evaluate and reward individual and team performance.

A third hurdle relates to national culture. By nature, some countries—particularly the United States—are not group-oriented, especially when compared with countries such as Japan. While some cultures place group needs above individual needs, this is generally not the case within the U.S. Team members may perceive assignments to be a drain on their time or feel that working on a team stifles their individual creativity and personal recognition. Some team members find a shift away from individualism to be uncomfortable and threatening.

The use of teams has become so widespread that supply managers must have some understanding surrounding their use. While the issues related to using teams are not unique to supply management, their extensive use to support supply objectives demands thoughtful answers to some important questions. The time to think about what is going to impact team success is during the planning phase of team formation. Figure 4.4 summarizes the more important planning topics that supply managers should consider when using teams. Effective planning correlates directly with effective teaming.

The formation of work teams should not occur unless careful consideration is given to the kinds of issues and topics that affect their success. Without question, effective planning is essential to successful teaming. Second, post hoc analysis should occur at a team's conclusion or at various intervals for teams that operate continuously. Lessons learned and corrective actions identified during these post hoc analyses should be summarized and shared with other teams throughout the organization. This supports the continuous improvement of the teaming process.

Factors Affecting the Success of Organizational Work Teams

The reasons for the success or failure of teams are varied and not necessarily consistent from team to team, making generalizability an inexact science. The truth is many factors have the ability to affect team performance. This makes working with teams a challenge.

	Yes	No
Identify Appropriate Team Assignments		
Do assignments justify the use of teams?	☐	☐
Has the proper team model been identified?	☐	☐
Does executive and functional management support the use of a team for the assignment?	☐	☐
Form Work Team and Select Qualified Members and Leader		
Have core versus as-needed members been identified?	☐	☐
Do selected members have the proper skills, time, and commitment to support the work team?	☐	☐
Have team sponsors identified and selected a qualified team leader?	☐	☐
Are customers or suppliers part of the team if required?	☐	☐
Do members understand their formal team roles?	☐	☐
Determine Member Training Requirements		
Have team member training requirements been assessed?	☐	☐
Is required training available on a timely basis?	☐	☐
Identify Resource Requirements		
Are resources provided or available to support the team's task?	☐	☐
Determine Team Authority Levels		
Have team authority levels for the team been determined?	☐	☐
Have team authority levels been communicated across the organization?	☐	☐
Establish Team Performance Goals		
Has the team established objective performance goals that align with organizational expectations?	☐	☐
Determine How to Measure and Reward Participation and Performance		
Are approaches and systems in place that objectively assess team performance and member contribution?	☐	☐
Do reporting linkages exist to team or executive sponsors?	☐	☐
Is team performance effectively linked to performance reward systems?	☐	☐
Develop Team Charters		
Has a formal charter been developed that details team mission, tasks, broad objectives, etc.?	☐	☐
Has the charter been communicated across the organization?	☐	☐

Figure 4.4   Four quadrant team design model

The following addresses several important team-related topics, including effective feedback, team leadership, team design, and team size. By no means are these the only factors that can have a meaningful impact on team performance.

Providing Effective Feedback

Feedback is the process of providing information to staff, employees, or team members about their performance pertaining to job expectations. Numerous studies have found a strong link between effective feedback and performance. We know that goal directed effort is greater in teams that receive feedback regarding their progress. Furthermore, a team's performance increases as the feedback becomes more complete. Effective feedback also affords an opportunity to correct a problem that, if left unattended, will likely become more severe.

And, effective feedback usually involves some agreement or plan for moving forward. If delivered properly, feedback also offers an opportunity to strengthen relationships and performance. Do not discount the effect that feedback has on individual and group performance.

Importance of Team Leadership

Over 50 years ago Likert concluded that team leaders exert a disproportionate effect on group effort, cohesion, goal selection, performance norms, and goal attainment. While many variables affect team success, the influence of the leader is unusually important.

The formal role assumed by a team leader places this individual in a unique position to promote group interaction, guide teams toward consensus, establish high performance norms, promote member effort, and see to it that team tasks are important, challenging, recognized, and rewarding. Only a formal leader can perform many of the responsibilities associated with team leadership. Unfortunately, organizations usually underestimate the time and skills required to take on a formal team leadership position, thereby exposing teams to greater risk.

While different sources will have their own perspective regarding what defines an effective leader, most will agree that a team leader must fulfill a variety of roles well. Examples of team leader responsibilities include:

- Securing member involvement
- Managing conflict within and external to the team
- Maintaining team focus and direction
- Securing required resources
- Preventing team domination by a member(s) or functional group(s)
- Dealing with obstacles that confront the team
- Coordinating multiple tasks and managing the status of team assignments
- Helping the team establish goals
- Clarifying and/or defining each member's role
- Providing performance feedback to the team and/or individual members
- Guiding the team toward consensus decisions
- Acting as the liaison between the team and with other teams and executive management

As this reveals, the roles and responsibilities of a team leader are not trivial.

Proper Team Design Structure

Figure 4.5 presents a four-quadrant model that segments work teams according to their duration and member time commitment. Matching the right model to the team's task is an important consideration during team planning. While some organizations create teams staffed with full-time members, teams staffed with

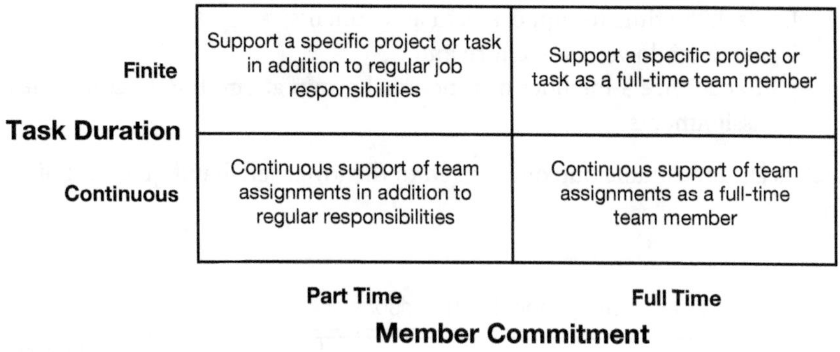
Finite
Task Duration
Continuous
Support a specific project or task in addition to regular job responsibilities
Support a specific project or task as a full-time team member
Continuous support of team assignments in addition to regular responsibilities
Continuous support of team assignments as a full-time team member
Part Time
Full Time
Member Commitment

Figure 4.5 Work team planning guide

part-time members remains a popular yet challenging design option. Organizations that rely on part-time teams typically maintain their existing functional structure with team-related duties as additional responsibilities. A part-time structure creates a *de facto* matrix organization where team members report to multiple entities—the team and their functional group. This has the potential to create stress and conflicting time demands.

Expected duration is also an important consideration. A major challenge when using continuous rather than finite teams (i.e., teams with a defined end point, such as project teams) involves maintaining member intensity and performance. The early positive effects of team formation often taper off and even diminish when members work over an extended period. Selecting the proper team model is no accident. It is the result of a well-thought-out decision that matches the right model with the team's task.

Table 4.2 presents data that reveal differences across the four quadrants in Figure 4.5. The first figure in the table represents the percentage of respondents that are in some level of agreement with a particular statement. The figure below each percentage is the average value for all respondents in that category where 1 = strongly disagree, 2 = disagree, 3 = slightly disagree, 4 = slightly agree, 5 = agree, and 6 = strongly agree with a statement. Lower values are more desirable than higher values given the wording of the statements.

Table 4.2 reveals that the design model employed likely affects a team's ability to succeed. Teams operating in a part-time/continuous environment are more likely to perform at a lower level compared with the other three quadrants. They are also more likely to have team members who:

1. Are confused about their role on the team;
2. Are part of a team that fails to become a collective unit;
3. Are more likely not to support the team;

4. Lack the time to support team assignments;
5. Put forth lower team effort; and
6. Experience a member or functional group attempting to control team assignments.

Each is an undesirable outcome linked to the lower left-hand quadrant of Figure 4.5.

Table 4.2   Team operating model comparisons

Item	PT/ Continuous	PT/ Finite	FT/ Continuous	FT/ Finite
Team members are confused about their role on this team	32%* 2.79**	32% 2.68	20% 2.31	17% 2.08
This team is a collection of individual members working on separate tasks— we have yet to become a collective unit	53% 3.32	25% 2.64	24% 2.59	33% 2.50
This team has a member who does not support this team's goals	42% 2.84	36% 2.79	22% 2.39	8% 2.42
Some team members fail to commit the effort required to support the team's task requirements	47% 3.42	46% 3.29	27% 2.63	17% 2.42
This team has a member or functional group that dominates the team's agenda	47% 3.47	46% 3.29	27% 2.63	17% 2.42
Our performance evaluation and reward system does not recognize the time and effort required by members to support this team's objectives	63% 3.58	57% 3.86	43% 3.32	42% 2.75
At least some of this team's members lack the time to support team assignments	68% 3.95	49% 3.70	40% 2.98	42% 3.25
Average across 23 items	38% 2.96	32% 2.79	31% 2.70	26% 2.47
Average rating	4.39	4.62	5.19	5.21
Average team size	6.0	6.3	6.6	6.3
	N = 23	N = 30	N = 58	N = 25

PT = part time, FT = full time commitment on the part of the team member

* Percent of respondents that slightly agree, agree, or strongly agree with the statement

** Figure below the percentage represents an average value for that group along a six-point scale where 1 = strongly disagree, 2 = disagree, 3 = slightly disagree, 4 = slightly agree, 5 = agree, and 6 = strongly agree

Understanding the Importance of Team Size

Both smaller and larger teams often face issues that affect team success. Members of larger teams often report less satisfaction from participation, less opportunity to influence decisions, and complain of poor coordination of activities and assignments. And, as size increases, individual members also have less opportunity to participate or lead with fewer members initiating leadership acts. We also know the pressure to conform to a team's majority position increases as team size increases, a condition that can lead to groupthink.

Large teams are often affected by two phenomena—social loafing and group process loss. Social loafing, first studied in 1913 and at multiple times thereafter, describes the tendency of individuals to put forth less effort as group size progressively increases.[8] A second condition associated with larger groups is process loss. Process loss results from difficulties associated with coordinating member activities, motivational problems, and inefficiencies that result when members work together on teams.[9] And, process loss grows at an increasing rate as a team adds members. Size becomes an issue when the number of team members increases beyond a point that allows effective communication and coordination.

Table 4.3 highlights the issues associated with larger teams. As team size increases the probability also increases that: members will say they are confused about their role on the team; the team becomes a collection of individual members working on separate tasks rather than a collective unit; the team has a member(s) who does not support the team's goals; some team members fail to commit the effort required to support the team's task requirements; and the performance evaluation and reward system does not recognize the time and effort required by members to support the team's objectives. The potential drawbacks associated with larger teams should cause team planners to think carefully before using them. If larger teams are used, careful thought is required about how to manage the risks that naturally come with larger teams.

Some Guidance when Using Teams

As mentioned, many factors can affect team success. And, a precise understanding of what affects success or failure often varies from team to team. The challenge becomes one of taking the insights gained from many years of work and developing a set of recommendations that enhance the probability of a successful outcome.

The Teaming Process Starts with Planning and Leadership

Many outcomes flow from the presence of effective planning and leadership at the team and executive level. Selecting a team leader requires careful

Table 4.3   Team size comparisons

Item	Smaller	Medium	Larger
Team members are confused about their role on this team	18%* 2.36**	23% 2.30	32% 2.71
Communication barriers exist among team members	46% 3.18	55% 3.45	66% 3.78
Distrust exists between team members	5% 1.82	25% 2.66	36% 3.02
This team has a member who does not support this team's goals	9% 1.82	30% 2.57	34% 2.93
Some team members fail to commit the effort required to support the team's task requirements	18% 2.95	25% 2.62	53% 3.60
Team members lack the tools to support effective communication and interaction	5% 2.05	19% 2.38	28% 2.80
Our performance evaluation and reward system does not recognize the time and effort required by members to support this team's objectives	41% 3.09	43% 3.19	64% 4.00
Destructive conflict occurs between team members	14% 2.05	17% 2.34	28% 2.54
At least some of this team's members lack the time to support team assignments	33% 2.71	60% 3.49	45% 3.50
Average across all 23 items	25% 2.54	30% 2.66	37% 2.98
Average team performance rating	4.92	5.09	4.65
	N = 24	N = 47	N = 60

* Percent of respondents that slightly agree, agree, or strongly agree with the statement

** Figure below the percentage represents an average value for that group along a six-point scale where 1 = strongly disagree, 2 = disagree, 3 = slightly disagree, 4 = slightly agree, 5 = agree, and 6 = strongly agree

In this research, teams with four or fewer members were classified as smaller teams; five to seven members were classified as medium teams; and teams with eight or more members were considered larger teams.

consideration early on during the team planning process (almost all supply management teams have a formally designated team leader). Never assume that an individual has the qualifications or experience to assume demanding team leadership responsibilities. Even if a team has no formally selected team leader, the probability that a leader will emerge increases as team size increases. The question becomes whether the emergent leader will lead the team effectively. Team designers must also consider a range of other important, but often subtle planning topics, which Figure 4.4 identified. This figure should be used whenever an organization is establishing a team.

Teams Must Understand the Change Process

Unless a team is responsible for generating ideas, making a recommendation, or solving a problem with a single correct answer, the chances are good that at some point the team must manage the change process, something that will invariably involve others outside the team. This is especially true for teams that structure their work as projects. An inability to manage change can easily undermine success, particularly when performance measurement systems conflict with team goals and objectives.

Do Not Discount the Importance of Team Size

Only after determining that a team is an appropriate organizational response should managers identify the skills, knowledge, and abilities required to support a task. This, in turn, affects team size. As mentioned, team size becomes an issue when the number of members increases beyond a point that allows the effective coordination of activities—although, teams that are too small present their own challenges. While there is no accepted standard of what defines a large team, most observers would agree that teams exceeding eight members begin to invite coordination and commitment issues.

Think About Team Authority Earlier Rather than Later

A potential area of conflict, and one that requires early attention, relates to the authority granted to a team. Whether explicitly stated or not, teams have varying degrees of authority to perform their tasks or make decisions. Teams may not understand the limits to their authority because managers have ignored this issue, something that often leads to conflict. A recommended action is to create a formal charter that, at a minimum, conveys a team's responsibilities, defines the team's authority, and identifies core and as-needed members. Charters legitimize teams, particularly when a team must make decisions that affect others external to the team. Refer back to Chapter 2 for a discussion of team authority.

The Right Structure or Model Can Affect Team Success

An earlier section addressed this important topic in detail. We know that teams staffed by part-time members, particularly those that operate in a continuous rather than finite environment, usually present challenges. Not only do members experience conflicting demands on their time, continuous teams usually progress through a life cycle that, much like products, features a decline phase.

Identifying the best model given a specific task is an essential part of the planning process.

Organizations must continuously enhance what they know about how to design and use teams. Ignoring the abundance of issues that can affect team success increases the risk that supply leaders will wonder why the reality of using teams does not match the expectations surrounding their use. We should not assume that team members necessarily understand or appreciate how to work as a collective unit. And, even if an organization and its members have a higher intelligence quotient regarding teams, the need to improve is never ending.

WHERE NEXT FOR ORGANIZATIONAL DESIGN?

Looking toward the future, we expect supply organizations to continue to transform themselves into something that looks dramatically different than earlier designs.[10] Less involvement with day-to-day transactions should mean a smaller staff that, if not located at a central location, will likely report to a central location. Centrally led and centrally coordinated supply management will be the norm. A clear delineation between the placement of planning and execution authority will also occur.

At least some of the activities that supply organizations manage will be described as strategic. This includes an even greater emphasis on developing strategies that support important corporate initiatives. At times this will mean supporting regional rather than global strategies as companies increasingly build where they sell, a trend we are witnessing across a variety of industries. For various reasons we are also witnessing a shift toward insourcing in some industries, a shift that supply managers must support.

The supply groups that are responsible for managing nontraditional items and services will increasingly coordinate their efforts, often in a virtual setting. These sourcing groups will move beyond the purchase of direct items and manage anything that involves significant expenditures, particularly items that can be organized into commodity groups. Acquiring or developing the expertise required for managing a large portfolio of goods and services worldwide will continue to be a challenge from a human talent perspective, something that Chapter 3 addressed.

Supply organizations will also be responsible for managing a set of critical internal and external relationships, which later chapters address. Accomplishing this will require supply managers to be boundary spanners, particularly across external boundaries. Specific design features will be established that support these boundary spanning requirements.

We also expect to see tighter linkages between supply management and finance, a linkage that certain design features will promote. In fact, it is reasonable to conclude that supply managers must expand their skill set to become risk and financial managers.

The use of matrix organizational designs should continue as supply management increasingly assumes a regional and even global perspective. As mentioned, movement toward a center-led model should continue as supply organizations work to coordinate their processes and activities across a company. One thing is clear: organizational design is dynamic and ever changing.

Networks of Teams

A staggering 92% of the companies surveyed by Deloitte during its research cited *redesigning the way we work* as a key challenge. Clearly, organizational design is a key component related to this challenge. Today's digital world has dramatically altered the foundation of organizational structures; shifting from a traditional functional hierarchy to one Deloitte calls a *network of teams*. This network features authority provided to highly trained and empowered teams with a real-time information and operations group to centralize information and provide teams with real-time and accurate data. This new work model is forcing organizations to change job roles and job descriptions, rethink careers and internal mobility, emphasize skills and learning as keys to performance, redesign how to set goals and reward people, and change the role of leaders.[11]

According to Deloitte, the challenge that organizations face is how to coordinate and align a wide variety of teams in terms of tasks and locations, how to get them to share information and work together, and how to move and reward people in an environment where upward mobility is no longer so prevalent. Work will increasingly be structured as projects where people bring their skills and abilities to projects and programs, build and deliver a solution, and then move on to the next assignment or project. This new mode of organization—a network of teams with a high degree of empowerment, strong communication, and rapid information flow—is going to transform businesses and governments around the world. A network of teams organization is built on various principles:[12]

- Empower teams to set their own goals and make their own decisions within the context of an overarching strategy or business plan—reversing the traditional structure of goal and performance management
- Replace functional silos with an information and operations center to share integrated information and identify connections between team activities and results
- Organize teams around mission, product, market, or integrated customer needs rather than business functions

- Teach and encourage people to work across teams, including the use of open office spaces that promote collaboration and job rotation to give teams a common understanding
- Enable people to move from team to team as needed and then ensure that people have a home to return to once a team-based project is completed
- Shift senior leaders into roles that are focused on planning, strategy, vision, culture, and cross-team communication

Two major factors are driving a shift toward networks of teams. First, pressure to get products to market quickly combined with greater empowerment among the workforce, is making small teams a more natural way to work. Smaller teams (recall the discussion of team size earlier in the chapter) should deliver faster results, engage better, and stay closer to their mission. Second, digital technology helps teams stay aligned. Teams can use web or mobile apps to communicate extensively and build a common culture. Rather than sending messages up and down a corporate hierarchy, employees can access information immediately. Roles such as liaison officers will provide valuable linkages between teams, so that teams are current about what other teams are doing.

CONCLUDING THOUGHTS

A number of years ago the *Corporate Executive Board* issued a report concluding that supply management executives must think about how their organizational structure can enable improvements in performance and operational excellence. There is no reason to believe this conclusion is any less relevant today. While other topics generate more excitement than organizational design, we should not overlook the linkage between effective designs and enhanced supply management performance. In the hyper-competitive environment that characterizes global business, overlooking any supply management enabler is a serious mistake.

Over time, a debate has occurred regarding several important questions. Does a company pursue activities because it has the organizational capabilities to do so (strategy follows structure) or does a company identify what it must accomplish and then create the organization that it needs (structure follows strategy)? In terms of supply management, it is probably best for structure to follow strategy, simply because most supply organizations have been limited in their capabilities. When a supply organization resembles something barely beyond a traditional purchasing department, any ideas about contributing at the corporate level are going to be constrained. The desire to be world-class will remain unfulfilled without an organizational design that supports supply management excellence.

REFERENCES

1. From http://joshbersin.com/2016/03/the-new-organization-different-by
   -design/.
2. G. Hamel and C. K. Pralahad, *Competing for the Future*. Harvard Business School Press, Cambridge, MA, 1994, as referenced in D. Hellriegel,
   J. W. Slocum, and R. W. Woodman, *Organizational Behavior* (Cincinnati:
   South-Western College Publishing, 2001): 474.
3. R. M. Monczka, R. J. Trent, and K. J. Petersen, *Effective Global Sourcing
   and Supply for Superior Results*, (Tempe, Arizona: Center for Advanced
   Purchasing Studies, 2006).
4. J. R. Carter and R. Narasimhan, "Purchasing and Supply Management:
   Future Directions and Trends," *International Journal of Purchasing and
   Materials Management*, 32, no. 4 (Fall 1996): 2–12.
5. F. Siebdrat, M. Hoegl, and H. Ernst, "How to Manage Virtual Teams,"
   MIT Sloan Management Review, 50, no. 4 (Summer 2009): 66.
6. L. Gratton, "Working Together ... When Apart," *Wall Street Journal*, June
   16–17, 2007, R4.
7. J. R. Hackman, "The Design of Work Teams," in *Handbook of Organizational Behavior* (Englewood Cliffs, NJ: Prentice Hall, 1987), 315–342.
8. B. K. Latane, K. Williams, and S. Harkin, "Many Hands Make Light the
   Work. *Journal of Personality and Social Psychology*, 37 (1979): 822–832.
9. J. E. McGrath, *Groups: Interaction and Performance* (Englewood Cliffs,
   New Jersey: Prentice-Hall, 1984).
10. Updated from R. A. Rudzki and R. J. Trent, *Next Level Supply Manage-
    ment Excellence* (Fort Lauderdale, FL: J. Ross Publishing, 2011): 83.
11. J. Bersin, from http://joshbersin.com/2016/03/the-new-organization
    -different-by-design/, March 5, 2016.
12. T. McDowell, D. Agarwal, D. Miller, T. Okamoto, and T. Page, "Orga-
    nizational Design: the Rise of Teams," from https://dupress.deloitte
    .com/dup-us-en/focus/human-capital-trends/2016/organizational-models
    -network-of-teams.html, Deloitte University Press, February 29, 2016.

5

NEW DIRECTIONS IN SUPPLY MEASUREMENT

It should come as no surprise that measurement is a critical enabler supporting supply management excellence. The right measurement system and measures can provide a wide range of benefits. Unfortunately, a strong argument can be made that measurement systems are not nearly as well developed within supply management as they are within other groups, particularly marketing and finance. For example, experience tells us that when supply professionals are asked in a group setting whether they are satisfied with how their organization measures supplier performance, few hands are ever raised. For many firms, the development of supply measurement systems is still on their to-do list. Effective supply organizations have in place a well-defined set of performance measures backed by supportive information technology systems.

Since measurement is one of the four key enablers of strategic supply management, it is worth exploring in some depth. This chapter presents an overview of supply management measurement, including the reasons for measuring performance and the characteristics of an effective measurement system. The chapter next discusses four primary areas of supply measurement and the important role that benchmarking plays within the measurement process. The chapter concludes with a set of lessons learned from a seemingly state-of-the-art but deceptively complex supplier scorecard system.

THE CONTINUING NEED FOR SUPPLY MEASUREMENT

For some good reasons the need to measure supplier and supply management performance is as great as it has ever been. What are those reasons? Without question performance measurement motivates people to act in certain ways. It's therefore important to act in ways that support organizational goals rather than in a narrow and sometimes conflicting manner. Develop the right set of measures and the chances are good that the right kind of behaviors will result. Measurement also helps identify areas that are most in need of improvement. It helps identify internal areas that might benefit from benchmarking against best-in-class companies, a topic that is addressed later in this chapter.

Another reason to measure performance is to identify rates of change. Measurement provides a picture of performance over time that supply managers can use to project into the future. These trends can relate to supplier performance or internal indicators such as budget compliance. Performance measurement also conveys what is important within an organization. This includes the set of performance targets that suppliers must achieve.

Performance measurement also supports some important principles of quality management. Supply measurement, particularly the measures used to evaluate supplier performance, is an ideal way to convey a buying organization's (i.e., customer) requirements and expectations. Measurement also helps supply managers base decisions on objective rather than subjective analysis, another important quality principle. The measurement process is also an ideal way to promote continuous improvement. Once a performance target is achieved, it is safe to assume that a new, more challenging target will be established.

A final reason for measuring supply management performance is somewhat self-serving. Supply leaders can use the right set of measures, particularly those that are financially oriented, to convey the value of strategic supply management. Without measures that show the impact that supply initiatives have on corporate indicators, including top and bottom line performance, the supply management story often remains untold. This need is specifically addressed in a later chapter.

A set of criteria exist that helps us identify whether a measurement system is effective or not. Disagreeing with one or more of the following criteria likely indicates a problem with the measurement system:

- Measures use data from sources that are visible throughout the supply organization
- Performance objectives are reviewed regularly and adjusted as required
- Measurement targets are based on world-class performance, ideally through performance benchmarking
- Performance measures link to and support corporate strategies and objectives
- Performance measures link to and support the performance strategies and objectives of other functional groups
- Individuals or groups are held accountable for achieving performance goals
- Supply measures do not encourage unintended consequences or behavior

- Supply measures promote teamwork, continuous improvement, and cross-functional cooperation
- Key supply performance results are reported throughout the organization to executive leaders
- Performance measures focus primarily on accomplishments rather than activities
- Performance measures include well-defined action plans regarding how to achieve each measure

Effective supply measures contain four parts. The first part pertains to what the measure addresses. What is being evaluated should be unambiguous. The second part includes the performance target for the measure. Preferably, these targets are established through external analysis rather than simply internal performance. The third part is the actual performance. The fourth component is often absent. This includes the action plans (also called tactics) that will be put in place to achieve the performance target. Along with these plans is a clear identification of the individual or group that has accountability for the success or failure of the measure.

WHERE DO WE SEE MEASUREMENT IN SUPPLY MANAGEMENT?

Our discussion about measurement up to this point has been somewhat broad. What exactly do we mean by supply management measurement? Perhaps the best way to address this question is by identifying the areas where supply measurement primarily occurs.

Supply management measurement occurs primarily, but not exclusively, in four distinct areas—during supplier evaluation and selection; during the ongoing assessment of supplier performance; when evaluating the performance of the supply management organization; and when evaluating suppliers' perception of the buying company as a customer. An additional area could include the measurement that takes place when certifying supplier quality performance (such as during ISO 9000 certification). The following addresses these four areas.

Supplier Evaluation and Selection

Supplier evaluation and selection decisions are complex and important. Given the performance demands placed on suppliers, and the extremely high cost of switching suppliers after selection, the use of site visits to evaluate supplier capabilities is an important part of the selection process. Visits to more than one supplier may also occur since these visits usually determine which suppliers are invited to final negotiations. And, if considering a global supplier, buyers must likely visit multiple sites around the world. While the cost of making worldwide site visits is high, the cost of making a poor selection decision is even higher.

A buying firm should evaluate suppliers as if it were buying the supplier. Leading supply organizations have developed tools and templates that support the formal assessment of supplier capabilities. The supplier evaluation and selection process offers ample opportunity to engage in various kinds of measurement.

Not all selection decisions are created equally, nor do they warrant comparable effort. Firms that excel at supply management understand the need to approach the selection decision based on the attributes of a purchase requirement. The way that buying firms subsequently manage their suppliers will also differ from requirement to requirement. Segmenting supply requirements using the portfolio matrix approach presented in Chapter 7 begins to define the intensity of the search, the contracting approaches and performance measures to employ, and the kind of relationship to pursue with a selected supplier.

Continuous Supplier Performance

Supplier performance measurement includes the methods and systems to collect and provide information to measure, rate, or rank suppliers on a continuous basis.[1] Many companies use the term *scorecards* to describe the report or system that conveys supplier performance data. A later section addresses how to create an ideal supplier scorecard.

Supplier Assessment of the Buying Company (Reverse Scorecards)

Most buying companies still do not measure how their suppliers feel about doing business with them. Some firms will say they don't ask their suppliers what they think because the buyer is the customer, and the customer is the big dog. Others will say these assessments are too much work. Still others will (grudgingly) admit they might not like what their suppliers have to say.

Companies that are serious about strategic supply management regularly assess how their suppliers feel about doing business with them. Formal surveys, usually conducted on an annual or every other year basis, are forwarded by a third party to suppliers that the buying company feels are critical to the performance of the supply chain. A later section discusses this important topic in depth.

Supply Management Performance

An important set of measures are those that formally report on supply management performance. Developing measures that encourage the desired behavior and then collecting data and information that accurately reports actual performance is not easy. Too often, measures result in unintended consequences that have longer term detrimental effects. The need for continuous cost reductions, for example, will always be a major supply management focus. However, there are instances where suppliers have been so pressured for price reductions that they eventually stopped selling to a buyer, or at the extreme, went out of business. Sometimes, buyers choose to do business with suboptimal suppliers because those suppliers offer a lower unit price. Never forget that unit price never equals total cost.

A general observation is that lower level performance measures should be tactically focused while higher level measures should be strategic in scope. Another way to look at supply management measurement is that lower level supply groups tend to emphasize efficiency indicators while higher level supply groups tend to emphasize effectiveness. A simple way to differentiate between efficiency and effectiveness is that efficiency is doing things right while effectiveness is doing the right things. This is an important point as a transition occurs from traditional purchasing to strategic supply management.

A relevant set of performance metrics must focus on accomplishments that reflect the objectives of a strategic supply organization. This does not mean that some of the new metrics will not be activity focused. The percent of total dollars under longer term agreement, for example, reflects activity more than accomplishment. Recall, however, that measures should promote desired behaviors. An organization that wants to pursue longer term agreements as part of its supply model might want to have a measure that promotes the development of longer term agreements. The downside is that this measure does not tell us whether the agreements are providing the return that is expected of them. Presumably, a set of accomplishment measures will reflect the value that results from these agreements.

With any performance measure, the challenging part is capturing the data that accurately reflect performance or compliance. The involvement of the finance department will be critical for validating measures that are financially oriented.

CREATING THE IDEAL SUPPLIER SCORECARD SYSTEM

As the opening to this chapter noted, a revealing exercise when working with supply professionals is to ask them to raise their hand if their organization measures supplier performance. Those with their hands raised (usually a high percentage) are then asked to keep them raised if they are satisfied with their company's supplier measurement system. While we can view the number of hands that drop as a less than positive endorsement of these systems, the rush of falling hands does provide a refreshing breeze across the room.

The development of effective supply measurement systems is still on the *to-do* list for many organizations, particularly smaller companies. Even supply organizations with mature systems should recognize that continuous improvement is an ongoing challenge and that most supplier measurement systems have shortcomings.

If anyone is asked why their company should measure supplier performance, a logical response might be: "Why would it not?" Taken as a whole, few could argue convincingly against the virtues of measuring supplier performance, especially since suppliers are becoming more rather than less critical to a buyer's success. Since measuring supplier performance is such a key part of strategic supply management, let's at least do it well.

A Primer on Scorecards

Supplier performance measurement includes the methods and systems to collect and provide information to measure, rate, or rank suppliers on a continuous basis.[2] Many companies use the term *scorecard* to describe the report that conveys performance results to suppliers.

The types of scorecards a supply organization uses typically fall into one of three categories—categorical, weighted point, or cost-based. *Categorical* measurement systems require simple check offs to items that describe a supplier's performance across different categories. For relatively unimportant items this may be an effective way to evaluate performance. As it relates to supplier scorecards, most supply organizations use a *weighted point* system that includes a variety of performance categories, provides weights for each category, and defines the scales used for scoring each category. The third type, *cost-based* systems, is the least used when measuring supplier performance. This approach attempts to quantify the total cost of doing business with a supplier over time. Some companies use a hybrid approach that covers one of more of these approaches. Figure 5.1 summarizes the advantages and disadvantages of each type of measurement system.

No standard measurement approach exists across industries, although supply organizations should strive internally for some consistency, particularly as it relates to the technical aspects of the system. It does not make sense for every business unit or internal location to re-invent how they measure performance. The challenge is to develop a scorecard system that offers some flexibility to internal locations while maintaining company-wide consistency.

Categorical Model	Weighted-Point Model	Cost-Based
Advantages	**Advantages**	**Advantages**
• Easy to implement • Requires minimal data • Requires minimal resources to develop or operate • Low cost to maintain • Good for less critical requirements	• Allows flexibility in assigning weights to categories • Allows ranking of suppliers • Moderate cost to implement • Does not require extensive support to develop or maintain	• Provides a total cost perspective • Identifies specific areas of supplier non-performance • Allows objective assessment of cost elements • Offers greatest potential for long-range improvement
Disadvantages	**Disadvantages**	**Disadvantages**
• Less reliable • Relies on broad, subjective assessments • Usually manual, although some use spreadsheets	• Often focuses on standard performance categories • Ratings may be subjective and inconsistent between raters • Usually requires manual data collection and input	• Usually requires a cost accounting system • High development costs • Cross-functional support required to provide data • Sometimes relies on cost averages rather than actual costs

Figure 5.1   Advantages and disadvantages of measurement models

Supplier Measurement Shortcomings

It would be great to say that most supply organizations are fully mature as it relates to measuring supplier performance. Unfortunately, that simply is not the case. Some supplier scorecards are so ill-conceived that at times it might be better if they were not even used. Far too often measurement is an activity that fails to lead to improved results. Consider the following examples.

Several years ago a consumer products company with $100 million in annual sales developed a scorecard to evaluate its suppliers, most of whom were substantially larger than the buyer. The system as presented to suppliers can only be described as a failure that deterred this company from moving forward with its measurement objectives. Besides creating a scorecard that was not pilot tested and was slightly less than professional in appearance, many larger suppliers challenged the accuracy of the scores, particularly when these scores were lower than what they received from more sophisticated customers.[3] A supply organization must take a hard look at its measurement process when suppliers challenge the legitimacy of scores. An executive at a major supplier described the scorecard process with one of his customers as: *they present and we refute.*

A second example highlights the shortfalls that confront too many measurement systems. Almost every supply organization has at least thought about developing a supplier scorecard system. And the ones that are serious about measuring supplier performance likely committed some serious time, budget, and resources toward system development. One such company is a major logistics company located in the U.S. On the surface, this company's system is one that most can only dream about. Do you want a ranking of supplier performance by commodity group? Do you want a listing of the company's best and worst performing suppliers? This, and much more, is available with a few keystrokes.

While many supply managers may look at this system with envy, sometimes the grass really is not greener on the other side. During a training session with this company, an instructor asked a buyer to name one of his best-performing suppliers, or what this company called an elite supplier. Without hesitation the buyer provided a supplier's name. Across the room another participant responded by saying this was one of the worst suppliers his operations group worked with on a day-to-day basis. How can one person say this is a supplier worthy of a preferred status while another would like to see this supplier go away? And, what are the dangers of a system that awards high scores to poorly performing suppliers?

These differences of opinion led to some conclusions that most in attendance could agree upon. The group agreed that although the scorecard system was supported by a server and a database that allowed all kinds of analyses, the data to support that system were still collected and input manually. Second, most buyers had responsibility for inputting data quarterly for about 25 suppliers, a heavy burden that was in addition to their normal workload. Many in attendance also agreed that the data for the scorecards were input just before, and sometimes after, the quarterly cutoff. Third, attendees acknowledged that supplier scores were used as an indicator of a buyer's job performance, potentially creating a conflict of interest. Finally, many scorecard items required subjective judgments.

The group also agreed that all material suppliers were held to the same criteria and weights, even though all suppliers were not equally important. Participants further agreed that internal customers or stakeholders had no way to be part of the measurement process. There was also some confusion about what qualifies as a supplier since some suppliers provide material from more than one location. Finally, and perhaps most troubling, no clear agreement emerged that the measurement process was contributing to better supply chain performance.

What are some lessons here? Clearly, an effective scorecard system requires much more than a sophisticated database that can present data in many ways. While that capability is important, technical capabilities do not guarantee success. And, scorecards should not ignore the voice of internal customers. When was the last time a truck unloaded material into a supply manager's office or cubicle? On a day-to-day basis, operating sites are well positioned to evaluate supplier performance, at least in some important performance categories.

Another lesson is that scorecards often place a heavy work burden on the individuals who are responsible for maintaining them. This burden often results in scorecards that are late or completed at the last minute, raising a concern about data integrity. Is a reliance on subjective and last-minute evaluations affecting the integrity of the scores?

A further learning is that scorecard systems can result in excessive averaging of data for suppliers that provide goods from more than one location. One supplier to this company provides goods from a dozen locations around the world. Should this be one scorecard or 12? If this supplier pursued ISO 9000 certification, the certification would apply to individual sites, not the entire company. So, why does the scorecard apply to the entire company? The number of suppliers and the number of shipping points are often different figures.

A final lesson is to be careful that scorecard systems do not drive the wrong behavior. Here a buyer's performance evaluation is based partly on the performance of the buyer's suppliers. That performance is determined by scorecards that these same buyers are responsible for completing. This presents a possible conflict of interest that could work to the detriment of the entire organization.

No one at this company believes that measuring supplier performance is not worthwhile. What this company is starting to realize is that measurement involves more than creating a database that turns out some impressive looking reports. Supplier measurement, like forecasting, is a process that requires more than a technical solution.

Characteristics of an Ideal Scorecard System

We are at the point of this discussion where we should think about the characteristics that define an ideal scorecard system. Research and work with hundreds of supply organizations has provided a unique opportunity to define what an ideal supplier measurement system should look like.

The Measurement System Allows Scoring Flexibility

Perhaps the most obvious shortcoming of most scorecards is that they treat suppliers the same in terms of how they are measured. If segmentation occurs, it might simply be between material and service suppliers. If all suppliers are not created equally in terms of importance, and it is unlikely we can argue convincingly that suppliers are equally important, then why apply equivalent scorecard measures? Better systems will allow adjustments to the performance categories and their weights to reflect the realities of different supply requirements. One measurement scheme does not fit all suppliers, although it is surprising how prevalent the one-size-fits-all approach is applied at well-recognized supply organizations.

An automotive original equipment manufacturer (OEM) has changed the way it evaluates suppliers by involving more employees in the process and giving them the power to adjust the weights used to evaluate suppliers.[4] The company now relies on internal boards, with at least four employees on each board, to determine the weights of the performance categories that suppliers are evaluated against. Each board consists of specialists in cost, technology, quality, and logistics who are responsible for posting supplier data monthly to a global supplier portal. Suppliers are even able to see the names and performance evaluations of their competitors, although the product boards have the authority to withhold names within their product groups if they so choose.

Internal Customers Evaluate Supplier Performance

Internal customers should have the ability to submit comments and ratings about a supplier's performance directly into the scorecard system. Internal customers are often in an ideal position to evaluate a supplier's operational performance on a day-to-day basis. Ignoring the voice of the customer is usually not a good practice.

The buyer should consider allowing suppliers to enter a web-based portal to view any free-form comments or scores that internal customers submit. This supports the open exchange of information—something that helps build trust and is widely practiced with other supply chain applications (such as demand forecasts).

Scorecards Are Distributed Electronically and Widely to Suppliers

It should go without saying that any supply organization that still relies on paper-based scorecards is behind the technological curve. Besides being more efficient, electronic distribution allows widespread distribution to key internal and external personnel.

Scorecards Are Reviewed by Executive Managers at the Supplier

Related to the previous characteristic, a set of key executives at each supplier should receive scorecards electronically. Perhaps most important, the party sending the scorecard should track acknowledgments that the scorecards were received and reviewed, including any responses to specific queries.

Forwarding scorecards directly to executive managers supports two important purposes. First, these executives will have access to information that their own personnel may not willingly share. More than one executive has been caught off guard because he or she was unaware of issues that affected customers. Second, information will likely reach those individuals that can affect meaningful changes—if changes are required.

The distribution list should include more than one executive. For smaller suppliers the buying company should consider placing the CEO on the distribution list. Providing vital information to those who are ultimately accountable for performance results makes a great deal of sense.

Suppliers with More than One Location Receive Multiple Scorecards

When looking at the size of a supply base, the tendency is to count a supplier as a single entity. As the earlier example pointed out, some suppliers provide material from multiple locations. To aggregate these different locations into a single scorecard can be misleading. This also limits our ability to assign scores to specific locations.

A possible solution is to evaluate each supplier's shipping locations across a basic set of operational metrics (such as cost, quality, and delivery), while the supplier as a corporate entity is evaluated by some higher-level metrics. Examples of higher-level metrics include assessments of supplier innovation, responsiveness, and willingness to invest in the buyer-seller relationship.

One OEM has addressed the issue of multiple supplier locations by assigning a separate code to each of its suppliers. Each shipping location for that supplier receives a suffix to identify it as a unique location that will receive a scorecard. A supplier with three shipping locations, for example, will have a corporate supplier code (say, 23455). The three shipping locations are then designated as 23455A, 23455B, and 23455C. This approach keeps the shipping locations grouped within the supplier's corporate code, which is helpful when conducting any analyses.

Scorecards Include Cost-Based Measures Wherever Possible

Most scorecards include price as a performance category simply because price is perhaps the easiest indicator to measure. Unfortunately, price never reflects the total cost of doing business with a supplier. To compensate for any disconnect between price and total cost, progressive supply organizations calculate metrics that reflect more than unit price.

An example of a total cost metric is the supplier performance index (SPI). The SPI assumes that any quality or performance infraction committed by a supplier increases the total cost of doing business with that supplier. If a supply manager can track these infractions and assign a cost to them, the index can be used in a scorecard to supplement a price metric. The SPI or even the adjusted price can be included in the scorecard rather than simply the price paid. The adjusted price is the unit price multiplied by the SPI value. Supply managers are urged to learn more about total cost measures and their many valuable uses.

Scorecards Are Updated in Real Time

Too many scorecards still resemble a batch system that features periodic input of data submitted manually on a periodic basis. In a perfect world, anyone who is granted access to a scorecard system should be able to view supplier performance levels in real time. Whenever a transaction occurs, whether it involves the results of a quality audit or an accounts payable transaction, data records should flow into the scorecard database with real-time updating of supplier performance. Of all the attributes presented here, this is likely the furthest from implementation.

In order for real-time updating to work, the scorecard system must be linked to other supply chain groups—including accounts payable, quality control, and transportation. Theoretically, any system that stresses objective assessment rather than subjective assessment, particularly in a real-time environment, should receive serious consideration. It is safe to conclude that most supply chain systems are moving toward real-time data visibility. Some buying companies are relying on suppliers to self-report and submit their performance to the scorecard system on a frequent basis. A few leading companies are even beginning to solicit performance data from or about second-tier suppliers.

The Scorecard System Separates the Critical Few from the Marginal Many

In an era when fewer suppliers are providing a greater share of total purchases, the need to separate the critical few from the marginal many has never been greater. At a major consumer products company, for example, 400 suppliers (out of 90,000 worldwide) receive 25% of the company's $50 billion in annual purchases.

If a supply organization is adamant about measuring most of its suppliers, then the less critical suppliers should receive a basic scorecard, perhaps one that is categorical. At some point, depending on the level of effort required to obtain scorecard data, the cost to measure a supplier could outweigh the value of measuring the supplier. When this is the case, a logical response is to not measure a supplier, measure a supplier less frequently, or simplify the type of scorecard used.

The Measurement Database Allows User Flexibility in Retrieving and Displaying Data

A value of databases is their ability to support the easy retrieval and analysis of data, including the generation of supply base reports. Besides the scorecard generated by the system, an effective system will allow for the presentation of data in a variety of reporting formats. Various on-demand reports can include suppliers that improved or deteriorated in performance over a certain period, performance changes by category, and side-by-side supplier rankings. A database that takes raw data and turns it into information by adding value is an essential requirement of a scorecard system.

The System Has Predictive Capabilities

Most measurement systems are reactive in the sense they report what has happened, not what is likely to happen. An ideal measurement system would have the capability to look ahead to spot troublesome trends and nonrandom performance changes before performance becomes out of control. An ideal system would notify supply managers of potential problems before the impact of those problems are even realized. The system would have predictive capabilities— something the next chapter discusses.

Consider the possibility of generating early warnings when using advance shipping notices (ASNs). Anytime an ASN reveals a possible late supplier delivery after comparing expected transit times against a due date, a material planner would receive a warning of a potential shipping delay. Or, real time GPS tracking systems might reveal that supply chain delays are occurring with a notification sent to the appropriate parties. In this case being proactive is a better way to go through life.

Suppliers Have the Ability to View and Compare Their Performance Online

For many years, almost every supply organization concealed the scores and names of competing suppliers within a category or commodity group. Then, some supply organizations became more willing to show relative comparisons against competing suppliers identified by letters (but not names). The time has come to accept that scorecards present a healthy way to create supply-base competition. That means providing suppliers with the ability to access their scores online with comparisons to other suppliers in the same or similar commodity groups.

Scorecard transparency is an idea whose time has come. This transparency does not violate any buyer-seller ethics, laws, or standards of confidentiality. An analogy involves looking at the standings of any sports league. Doesn't every team know precisely where it stands in relation to competing teams? At the academic level, colleges and universities are routinely rated and ranked against one another. Somehow these institutions survive the ordeal. Suppliers will be no different.

The Measurement System Is Benchmarked
Against Best-Practice Companies

As mentioned in Chapter 2, performance benchmarking involves comparing products, practices, processes, or strategies against key competitors or companies considered best-in-class. Benchmarking methodologies can involve working directly with other companies to compare scorecard practices, searching databases and the Internet to find information on performance measurement, and working with professional contacts to obtain scorecard information. Some supply organizations belong to research consortiums that share best-practice information. In an era where almost too much information is available, there is no excuse for not remaining current regarding the trends and technologies related to performance measurement.

The challenge for supply organizations is to step back and take an unbiased view of their performance measurement systems. The objective should be to take a poor system and make it better while transforming a good system into an excellent one. While measuring supplier performance is a worthy pursuit, the reality is that measurement is simply an activity. It is natural to feel good when pursuing activities that prevailing wisdom says are good. Activity means nothing, however, unless it leads to tangible accomplishments.

THE NEED FOR REVERSE SCORECARDS

The one constant that corporate leaders will always face is a relentless pressure to improve performance. Enlightened leaders are increasingly recognizing that the link between positive relationships with suppliers and improved corporate performance is a strengthening rather than weakening one. And, these leaders understand that by satisfying the diverse needs of their suppliers, they stand a better chance of receiving preferential treatment from suppliers compared with firms with less satisfied suppliers. They understand they can become the customer of choice.[5]

Gaining objective insight into how to become the customer of choice is one of the primary objectives for using a comprehensive measurement instrument called the *Supplier Satisfaction Survey*.[6] This survey is a reverse scorecard in which suppliers evaluate and score a specific customer rather than the customer evaluating and scoring a supplier, which is traditionally the case in buyer-seller relationships. The survey is divided into sections that explore a supplier's perception of a specific customer's performance. Table 5.1 identifies these sections.

As part of this comprehensive survey, suppliers evaluate their customer against 25 performance areas that were identified as being important to supplier-buyer relationships. Suppliers compare their customer against an ideal

Table 5.1 Supplier assessment of buyers

Suppliers evaluate a buyer's performance or ability within the *supplier satisfaction survey* for the following areas:

- Performance within 25 areas compared to an ideal customer
- Importance to the supplier of 25 performance areas
- Ability to define quality and performance expectations
- Quotation, negotiation, and contracting practices
- Ability to provide supplier performance feedback
- Procurement knowledge and skills
- E-procurement and transaction systems
- Responsiveness to supplier concerns or questions
- Business opportunities and payment terms
- Managing the supplier-buyer relationship
- Ethics and business conduct
- Cross-organizational communication and information sharing
- Supply chain planning and execution systems

customer on a scale where 0 = much worse than the ideal, 3 = somewhat less than the ideal, and 6 = equal to the ideal. The total points across the 25 items are summed and divided by 150 (the highest possible points) to arrive at a percentage score out of 100. Suppliers evaluate a customer's ability to:

- Share relevant supply chain information
- Provide a fair financial return on the supplier's investment
- Provide adequate lead times for planning
- Provide accurate forecasts
- Share cost savings from supplier-provided improvement ideas
- Provide correct and clear material specifications
- Provide smoothly timed order releases
- Protect proprietary information and technology
- Exhibit ethical and respectful behavior
- Provide objective performance feedback
- Provide payment in a reasonable amount of time
- Minimize last minute product and order changes
- Pursue efficient negotiating and contracting practices
- Offer longer term business opportunities
- Provide opportunities for early involvement during new product development
- Design parts to match the supplier's process capabilities
- Respond to inquiries in a timely manner
- Provide clear channels of communication
- Use electronic systems to facilitate transactions
- Be receptive to improvement ideas

- Be knowledgeable about the supplier's business and industry
- Be committed to continuous improvement
- Develop effective buyer-seller relationships
- Provide tangible support if problems arise
- Be clear regarding the customer's performance expectations

Next, suppliers evaluate the importance of each of the 25 items. A comparison is made between a supplier's assessment of the customer for a particular item and the importance the supplier attaches to that item. Addressing the items with the largest gaps should provide the best opportunity for a customer (i.e., buyer) to satisfy the needs of its suppliers, which in turn will increase the probability of being viewed by the supplier as a customer of choice.

The following presents actual gap analysis data for a producer of transportation equipment. From this data we can calculate the size of the gap between how important an item is to suppliers, on average, compared against the customer's (i.e., the buyer's) performance score. Items with the largest negative gaps represent the most significant opportunities to engage in discussions about how to improve as a customer. The following items provide a clear opportunity for this company to focus its improvement efforts with suppliers:

- Providing a fair financial return on the supplier's investment (gap between importance and performance = −2.81)
- Payment in a reasonable time (−2.50)
- Opportunities for early involvement during new product development (−2.28)
- Adequate lead times for planning (−2.22)
- Opportunities for a longer term business relationship (−2.10)
- Efficient negotiating and contracting practices (−1.94)
- Providing accurate forecasts (−1.89)
- Smoothly timed order releases (−1.81)
- Effective buyer-seller relationships (−1.78)
- Minimum last-minute product and order changes (−1.75)
- Sharing of costs savings from improvement ideas (−1.74)

Financial considerations, concerns surrounding that buyer's negotiating practices, adequate supply chain planning and execution practices, and the supplier's desire to engage early in product development with longer term business relationships are consistent themes throughout the supplier satisfaction survey with this customer. Objective data helps this buyer focus its improvement efforts where they should have the largest payback with suppliers. How to become the customer of choice is explored in depth in Chapter 10.

CONCLUDING THOUGHTS

Never forget that a performance measurement system can be your best friend or your worst enemy. A well-designed system can focus supply management attention on what truly provides value to an organization. Conversely, a poor system can cause employees to exhibit the wrong behavior; provide data that are not timely, relevant, or even accurate; stress activity over accomplishment; create conflict between groups and with suppliers; or measure the wrong things. It is not that hard to imagine something we call an enabler easily becoming an inhibitor if not managed well.

REFERENCES

1. R. M. Monczka, R. J. Trent, and R. B. Handfield, *Purchasing and Supply Chain Management* (Mason, Ohio: Thomson South-Western, 2005): 269.
2. This part of the chapter is adapted from R.J. Trent, "Creating an Ideal Supplier Scorecard," *Supply Chain Management Review*, 14, no. 2 (March/April 2010): 24–29.
3. This is not to say the scores were wrong. It is possible the suppliers did not give the same level of service to smaller customers.
4. This example is adapted from J. Armstrong, "Chrysler Changes Scorecard," *Automotive News*, 79, no. 1610 (November 8, 2004): 16.
5. Some sources use the term *customer of choice* to describe preferred customers. The terms *customer of choice* and *preferred customer* are viewed interchangeably here.
6. The *Supplier Satisfaction Survey* is a survey instrument developed by Robert J. Trent. A PDF copy of the survey is provided as a WAV resource on the J. Ross Publishing website.

6

THE INFORMATION-ENABLED
SUPPLY ORGANIZATION

Without question, industries of all kinds are witnessing an era of rapid disruption featuring unprecedented rates of change. This disruption is facilitated largely by the widespread adoption of new and creative kinds of information technology (IT) hardware and software. Hardly a day goes by without hearing about a new application, a creative use of big data and predictive analytics, or some new technology product that promises more efficient supply chain operations. It almost goes without saying that successful supply chains must be information enabled.

This chapter focuses on a supply management enabler that is evolving at a dramatic rate—the use of IT to support an organization's supply objectives. This chapter presents a set of conventional IT applications that most supply managers will find useful. Next, a set of exciting IT developments that have supply chain and supply management implications are discussed. The chapter concludes with a set of predicted trends that reveal the rapidly changing nature of the IT world.

NO SHORTAGE OF TOOLS AND APPLICATIONS

Hardly anyone would argue against the notion that IT has made our lives easier. Whether we use laptops, PC's, tablets, or smartphones to conduct transactions of all kinds or to retrieve information using powerful search engines, the uses of IT grow daily. Using IT to support our supply chain needs also seems to grow daily. Whether we want to manage transactions or to gain visibility to expenditures across an entire company, someone is offering software that will support that task.

Dozens of applications and hundreds of software suppliers make a discussion of IT a bit of a challenge. *Inbound Logistics* magazine, for example, regularly features its listing of the 100 top supply chain and logistics IT companies, which is narrowed from a much larger list. The supply chain domain features many areas where IT solutions are offered, and each of these areas will have their own set of subapplications. Figure 6.1 identifies some areas where IT applications and solutions are available to support the broad domain of supply chain management.

Within the procurement and supply management arena, the number of IT providers and applications is also large. A suite of tools and applications that are available from one software provider includes electronic applications such as e-RFX, e-auction, e-contract management, and e-procurement along with spend analysis, vendor management, project management, catalog management, print procurement, and supplier performance management. It would take an entire book to address all the IT tools and applications that are available to support supply management. We will focus instead on a selected set that is probably the most relevant to supply managers. One research group argues that four pillars serve as the foundation for any strategic sourcing program—spend analysis, sourcing, contract management, and supplier management.[1] And guess what? It is not a surprise that IT tools and approaches are available to support each of these pillars.

Although many companies use supply management technologies successfully, their use is not yet as routine or widespread as we might believe. An Ardent Partner research report concluded that while a majority of chief procurement officers (CPOs) state that among the different competencies that their procurement organization possesses, *leveraging technology to drive business value* is one of the least-developed and lowest rated.[2] Only 15% of CPOs in Ardent's research rated their procurement group's technical proficiency as advanced or very advanced. Almost 60% rated their proficiency as adequate or below. Ardent also reports that the drive to improve the use of technology by investing in new

Supply Chain IT Applications

- Cross-enterprise collaboration
- Customer relationship management
- Demand management
- Distribution requirements planning
- Enterprise resource planning
- Freight payment
- Freight auditing
- Inventory control
- Logistics
- Load planning
- Materials requirements planning
- Network modeling
- Optimization
- Procurement
- Reverse logistics
- Routing and scheduling
- Security
- Supplier relationship management
- Trade compliance
- Transportation management system
- Vendor management
- Warehouse management system
- Yard management systems

Figure 6.1 IT software applications in supply chain management

systems and/or improving current systems is the top strategy that CPOs expect to pursue over the next several years. Recent changes to U.S. corporate tax laws may accelerate this investment. The following are some of the key IT systems that support supply management.

e-Procurement Through the Internet

E-procurement is a broad term that relates to the application of Internet technology to the buying and selling of goods and services. It is also a widely adopted procurement technology. An e-procurement network provides a secure marketplace, sales platform, and transaction tracking system to buyers and sellers.[3] An e-procurement system generally consists of four components—content management, requisition management, transaction management, and connectivity management.[4] A variety of applications reside within the e-procurement domain, including auctions, trading exchanges, e-RFX, and online catalogs.

Internet Auctions

This application consists of auctions and reverse Internet auctions. Reverse auctions differ from regular auctions in two ways. First, the buyer initiates the auction rather than the seller. And second, the objective of a reverse auction is to drive a price lower rather than higher. For many supply managers the use of IT tools to conduct reverse auctions became a quick and easy way to reduce prices across a wide range of purchase categories. There is no denying that reverse auctions became fashionable among supply organizations.

The misapplication of reverse auctions can harm any semblance of a supplier-buyer relationship. It is important to know when and where to use these auctions. They are best suited for standardized items that are clearly specified, have known volume requirements, and feature lower supplier switching costs. When using reverse auctions most suppliers will say that the only thing a buyer is interested in is a lower price, even if it harms the supplier's profitability or adversely affects the supplier-buyer relationship. An obsession with price during reverse auctions increases the risk of overlooking other important variables such as quality, capacity, delivery, and financial stability. Just because a supplier participates in a reverse auction and quotes a marvelously low price does not necessarily mean it is a qualified performer.

We do not hear quite as much about reverse auctions today as when they were first introduced. This may be due partly to the novelty of this approach wearing off. It may also be due to a realization that not all purchase requirements are candidates for reverse auctions. We also hear about reverse auctions less when a supply market tightens. These auctions work best when an industry has excess capacity. During a seller's market where capacity is tight, suppliers are not going to be quite as anxious to participate in an auction. Few suppliers want to reduce their price if they can readily sell their output at a preferred price.

Any concerns about this approach do not mean reverse auctions should not be an IT approach to consider. When conditions are right, reverse auctions can be an efficient way to create a competitive marketplace that results in attractive price reductions. Even incumbent suppliers that have been complacent about lowering prices are often able to come up with price reductions when participating in an auction. Just make sure the suppliers that are invited to a reverse auction are capable of meeting your requirements in areas besides price.

Trading Exchanges

Another major part of e-procurement involves trading exchanges, or what some call e-marketplaces. These exchanges or marketplaces provide an electronic forum where buyers and sellers meet online to exchange information and bids—greatly expanding sales opportunities for sellers and often reduced prices for buyers.[5] While precise figures are hard to determine, the number of trading exchanges in operation today is likely in the hundreds.

A major consulting firm has developed a classification of exchanges to provide some order to this discussion:[6]

- Independent trading exchanges—these exchanges, which are usually targeted to a specific industry, are owned by third parties rather than industry buyers or sellers
- Vendor-managed trading exchanges—these exchanges, which are a subgroup of independent exchanges, are created by software vendors that include trading exchange operations in their product offering
- Consortia trading exchanges—these exchanges are formed by a group of industry buyers and sellers coming together to create an exchange for themselves or an entire industry
- Private trading exchanges—these exchanges are established by one large buyer or seller exclusively for its own set of customers or suppliers

This firm recommended using independent trading exchanges for commodity-like, nonstrategic direct and indirect manufacturing goods and services; using private trading exchanges for noncommodity, low-volume strategic direct materials and services; and using private exchanges supplemented by traditional electronic data interchange (EDI) for strategic, high-volume direct materials and services.

e-RFX

This application is designed to streamline the paper, transactions, time, analysis, and decisions that are associated with managing requests for information, quotes, and proposals. One supply chain software provider describes its e-RFX application as a way to simplify and automate the process of creating bid documents by multiple team members, forward requests to suppliers, collect responses, and score responses. The primary benefits of e-RFX are that this removes time and costs from the request process.

Electronic Catalogs

E-catalogs are electronic representations of information on the products and services a company offers, and they are a means for buyers to view and interact with a supplier's information.[7] E-catalogs are usually more current and less cumbersome than manual catalogs, quicker to reference, and, with the help of third-party software, offer the opportunity to compare supplier prices for similar items.

There are typically three kinds of e-catalogs—supplier-managed catalogs, buyer-managed catalogs, and third-party managed catalogs.[8] With supplier-managed catalogs, the suppliers host the content and its presentation. With the buyer-managed model, data must be applied, or massaged, into the exact format required to load correctly into the buyer's target application. Third-party catalogs consist of aggregated catalogs containing data from multiple suppliers. The data are then made available on a commercial basis, often by the same people who manage trading exchanges. With the buyer and third-party managed models, purchasing companies and e-marketplaces or exchanges play the role of catalog aggregators. Suppliers and distributors play the role of catalog providers in the supplier-managed model.

While e-procurement through the Internet was revolutionary a decade or more ago, the suite of capabilities supported by the Internet (and now the cloud) are largely taken for granted. Because e-procurement has entered a more mature phase compared with other emerging IT applications (such as artificial intelligence) it is still a critical part of a company's IT architecture.

Electronic Data Interchange

A well-established approach for sharing information between supply chain parties involves EDI. EDI is a communications standard that supports the electronic exchange of common business documents and information across businesses. EDI systems and protocol are typically comprised of at least three parts:[9]

1. A set of EDI standards and forms—this includes the rules for formatting and syntax agreed to by the users in the EDI network. The American National Standards Institute ACS X12 EDI standards is a common format.

2. Translation software—this translates the company-specific database information into EDI standard format for transmission and receipt.
3. Third-party network provider—this party is responsible for transmitting documents through a value-added network, or VAN. This network, which is operated by a third-party provider on a subscription basis, serves as an intermediary between the EDI parties.

The promise of EDI during the 1990s never matched the hype surrounding its use.[10] Many small suppliers balked at the costs associated with a full-blown EDI system. Early cost estimates to establish an EDI system were grossly underestimated. And, many suppliers had difficulty adopting the different EDI systems that their trading partners were using. We have also come to realize that forwarding documents electronically, while essential for driving out waste and transactions costs, is not leading-edge. EDI does not offer an opportunity to interact and reach decisions through two-way communication. With EDI, a decision is reached unilaterally and then that decision is forwarded in the form of an electronic document to another supply chain member. EDI is best suited for managing documents and transactions.

The technology underlying EDI systems has changed dramatically since the early days, making it easier for firms to adopt EDI. The new version of EDI is called EDI XML, which is a standardized framework in which EDI-based business documents and messages are described using XML (extensible markup language) syntax. This form of EDI relies on virtual private networks (VPNs) supported by the Internet. This format replaced the use of third-party VANs because it is was less expensive and presented fewer standards issues. As an example, VANs add document transmission fees that range from 10 cents to 50 cents per kilocharacter, while a basic Internet-based private exchange service may charge five cents to seven cents per kilocharacter.

While EDI is not considered leading-edge today, it's hard to imagine a progressive supply organization not endorsing some sort of technology to reduce the transactions costs of moving information across the supply chain.

Supplier Relationship Management Applications

Given the importance of supplier relationships, we knew it would not be long before software companies bundled a set of software applications and named that bundle *supplier relationship management* (SRM). After all, the downstream side of the business has *customer relationship management* (CRM) software. It only seems fair that the supply side should have its own important sounding acronym.

SRM software encompasses a broad suite of capabilities that facilitate collaboration, sourcing, transaction execution, and performance monitoring between an organization and its trading partners.[11] Some of the more interesting capabilities housed within an SRM package include:

- Automated requests for information, quotes, and proposals from suppliers
- Weighted attributes and scoring that apply complex algorithms for quantitative scoring of supplier responses with side-by-side comparisons
- Event scoreboards that provide side-by-side comparisons of supplier responses to promote faster, better-informed decisions based on total costs
- Real-time bid graphs that visually graph bids from all suppliers in a dynamic, real-time display, including during auctions
- Supplier scorecards that allow the configurable development of supplier report cards based on user-defined parameters
- Capabilities for online information sharing, collaboration, and negotiation with suppliers
- Online Internet auctions, including English auctions, Dutch auctions, sealed bids, and dynamic ascending and descending events
- Alert notifications of upcoming events
- Search filters and capabilities that allow buyers and suppliers to find events, items, and partners that meet their objectives
- Document support, such as allowing end users to create their own requisitions 24/7 using established contracts with appropriate controls
- Contract repositories that serves to store company-wide contracts electronically for easy retrieval and analysis

Sourcing Data Warehouses and Databases

A data warehouse is a collection of integrated, subject-oriented databases designed to support a specific function. A database is a large collection of data that is organized especially for rapid search and retrieval. In a data warehouse each unit of data is relevant to some moment in time and contains atomic data and lightly summarized data. Atomic data represent the lowest level of process analysis data stored in a data warehouse.[12] While databases have been in existence for decades, they are still an essential part of IT systems.

Assume you are assigned the task of developing a company-wide supply contract for a specific commodity. Several types of information would be valuable to your task—including a listing of existing contracts and suppliers, supplier performance by individual sites, supplier capability, projected worldwide volumes by commodity or category, information about new suppliers, internal customer requirements, part numbers that are part of the commodity, and volume requirements across buying units. Databases and data warehouses are designed to overcome the inherent problems associated with trying to collect data from diverse sources. The productivity improvements that are provided by easy access to data, especially when developing supply strategies, can be staggering.

Data warehouses are an important part of spend management systems. Spend management is about gaining visibility of expenditures so they can be grouped and managed more effectively. The objective of a spend management system is to cleanse and feed data that have been correctly classified according to some scheme, such as the United Nations Standard Products and Services Code, into a data warehouse. Classifying the data is critical—this is what supports future retrieval and analysis. There are dozens of companies that offer spend management software solutions.

Procurement Cards

Many companies have issued corporate credit cards (i.e., procurement cards) to their personnel. Procurement cards may not be the first thing that comes to mind when we think of IT or electronic tools and applications, since their use has become so ubiquitous. Procurement cards are an effective way for obtaining low dollar goods and services that are not part of corporate contracts. Some companies even use their cards as a releasing mechanism for items that are covered by contracts. These companies say they like the control and reporting features that their card provider offers. The use of procurement cards, while important and well established, is not particularly glamorous or innovative.

Most organizations provide procurement cards to internal users so that supply personnel can focus on tasks that are more important than chasing around low dollar purchase requirements. What is sometimes overlooked is that card programs require many administrative duties. Procurement groups are often responsible for administering a card program. Responsibilities include selecting a card provider, controlling access and distribution of the cards, training new cardholders, compiling usage and spending reports, performing card audits, developing guidelines and a user manual, establishing spending limits, and working with the card provider to continuously improve the program. Administering a card program is not a trivial matter.

Most firms that have put a card program in place have successfully captured the benefits they wanted from their use. The most common benefits of a card program include faster response to user needs, reduced transactions costs, reduced total transaction time, improved accounts payable process, and streamlined payments made on a monthly consolidated statement. A procurement card system may also support decentralized purchasing and improved user perception of purchasing's responsiveness.

Widespread use of procurement cards has led to some observations regarding this technology:

- While it is tempting to restrict suppliers, most organizations eventually realize that the program benefits from opening up the number of suppliers that can participate.
- Card administrators caution against setting transaction limits too low since this restricts card usage.
- While it is tempting, do not track too much data. Excessive data begins to undermine the objectives of the card program.
- When establishing a pilot program, cardholders should be placed throughout the organization rather than in a single location.
- It often becomes necessary to eliminate other low dollar procurement systems to force card usage.
- Do not discount the important role that accounts payable and finance play in a card program.

EMERGING IT SYSTEMS AND APPLICATIONS

A discussion of IT, particularly as it relates to trends and developments within the IT space, can become complicated very quickly, which does not serve our purposes. This section presents a somewhat scaled-back set of emerging IT technologies that supply managers should at least be aware of.

Predictive Analytics Comes of Age

Rarely a day passes without hearing about a new application involving large quantities of data to make predictions, or something called *predictive analytics*. When a practitioner hears the term predictive analytics, he or she can assume that a model has been developed that uses algorithms to arrive at a predicted outcome.

Predictive analytics includes the branch of advanced analytics that uses data to make predictions about unknown future events. It uses techniques from data mining, statistics, modeling, machine learning, and artificial intelligence to analyze current data to make predictions about the future.[13] Other descriptors for predictive analytics include big data, business intelligence, data analytics, and business analytics. Without question, predictive analytics is today's hot topic at the corporate and academic level.

Predictive models and techniques have been around for decades, although practitioners and academics did not historically use the term predictive analytics.

Some commonly used predictive approaches include statistical process control, failure mode and effects analysis (FMEA), supplier and customer bankruptcy predictors, process capability studies, deterministic forecasting techniques, pro forma financial statements, multiple regression modeling, scheduling algorithms that predict order delays, equipment sensors that monitor process variation, what-if scenario planning, and facility and network simulations.

So, what is different today? Its relevance in industry has increased, together with the amount of data being captured from people (e.g., from online transactions and social networks) and sensors (e.g., from GPS mobile devices) as well as the availability of cost-effective processing power, be it cloud- or Hadoop-based. Some might recognize the term Internet of Things (IoT) as part of this discussion. The IoT is "a system of interrelated computing devices, mechanical and digital machines, objects, animals, or people that are provided with unique identifiers and the ability to transfer data over a network without requiring human-to-human or human-to-computer interaction."[14]

Without question, analytics tools are more rigorous today, particularly in their ability to glean insights from unstructured data, such as videos. Traditional predictive tools and techniques rely largely on structured data sets.

Predictive analytics is part of a hierarchy of analytics that address some important questions. The hierarchy consists of three distinct levels:[15]

- *Descriptive analytics* use data aggregation and data mining to provide insight into the past and answer the question: "What has happened?" Descriptive analysis (i.e., statistics) summarizes raw data and makes it something that can be understood by humans. They are analytics that describe the past.
- *Predictive analytics* use statistical models and forecasting techniques to understand the future and answer the question: "What could happen?" These analytics are about understanding the future. Predictive analytics provide companies with actionable insights based on data.
- *Prescriptive analytics* use optimization and simulation algorithms to provide guidance on possible outcomes and answer the question: "What should we do?" These analytics go beyond descriptive and predictive analytics by recommending one or more possible courses of action. Prescriptive analytics are relatively complex to administer, and most companies are not yet using them in their daily course of business.

While predictive analytics will be applied across all business disciplines, supply chains will benefit greatly from this technology. The following examples comprise a small set that illustrates where areas that are related to the supply chain are capitalizing on big data:

- *Telematics* involve the branch of IT that deals with the long-distance transmission of computerized information. Using sensor technology, truck fleet owners can monitor the real-time performance of transportation vehicles, including location, engine performance, fuel consumption, driver habits, and predicted mechanical issues. Telematic service providers are designing systems to provide benefits within three main areas—safety, compliance (such as hours of service monitoring), and efficiency. Remote telemetry is also being used to gather real-time data, such as predicting remotely the need to replenish inventory, such as gases and raw materials, at customer locations.
- *Wearable technology* involves technology that is worn by a human to monitor vital signs. One application in the supply chain space is to monitor brain waves to identify if vehicle drivers are falling asleep.
- *Delivery tracking* involves real-time monitoring of freight shipments and deliveries to predict early, on-time, or late supply chain deliveries. Tracking supports a sought-after supply chain objective called transparency.
- *Smart sensors,* as part of the IoT, will collect and communicate data on a wide range of conditions. Equipment will no longer be maintained or repaired on a maintenance schedule; instead, maintenance will be based on a predicted need. In the rail industry, trains will arrive in yards for maintenance with prepositioned yard crews already having an understanding of engine and rail car maintenance requirements.[16] Data from supplier processes can also be visible on a real-time basis.
- *Weather analytics* helps predict supply disruptions, forecast effects on future demand, analyze the effect on fuel prices, and sense transportation hub congestion to dynamically reroute to less congested locations.[17]

Most companies are asking themselves, "We have all this data, why don't we do something with it?" Predictive analytics represent their attempts to do something with it. The uses of big data only seem to be limited by our imagination.

The Rise of the Cloud

Cloud computing is a relatively new form of Internet-based computing that provides shared computer processing resources and data to computers and other devices on demand. It is a model for enabling ubiquitous, on-demand access to a shared pool of configurable computing resources such as computer networks, servers, storage, applications, and services.[18] The rise of cloud computing has created major structural changes within the IT world. Gartner provides a good explanation of cloud services when they say:

> *"Cloud computing differs from other historical IT models in that it fo-*
> *cuses primarily on services, rather than technology. As a result, the deliv-*
> *ery of cloud computing services is analogous to a traditional supply chain*
> *in which services are offered to users in terms that they understand, and*
> *the underlying technical details are abstracted away from them. Consum-*
> *ers of the service can place service requests via self-service and are billed*
> *for what they use."[19]*

The rise of the cloud has certainly changed the power structure within the high-tech industry. Instead of a company buying a limited number of servers, for example, to support its internal IT requirements, these companies may now rely on services from providers such as IBM, Apple, Google, Microsoft, and Amazon. These companies purchase servers (and other equipment and hardware) by the thousands to operate their server farms. This has changed the hardware market, as these large buyers gain leverage over hardware and software suppliers.

Why would a company use cloud computing services? Besides the obvious reasons that using the cloud simplifies the management of the information network and could provide a lower total cost of IT ownership, other reasons help explain why a cloud approach is attractive:[20]

- *Infrastructure as a service*: Using an existing infrastructure on a pay-per-use basis makes sense for companies looking to save on the cost of acquiring, managing, and maintaining an IT infrastructure (such as servers). Some fixed costs may become variable costs.
- *Access to a private or hybrid cloud*: There are times when organizations want to evaluate some applications they intend to deploy through the use of a public cloud. Adopting a cloud approach allows for testing application workloads without the investment that might be wasted should the testing fail. A hybrid cloud offers the ability to expand capacity during periods of limited peak usage, which may be preferable to hosting a large infrastructure that is seldom used. An organization can access additional capacity on a pay-as-you-go basis.
- *Testing and development*: Testing and development offers one of the best scenarios for using cloud services. In a traditional IT setting, testing and development entails securing a budget, setting up physical assets, and installing and configuring an internal platform. Cloud computing can offer readily available environments that are tailored to specific needs.
- *Big data analytics*: An attractive feature of cloud computing is the ability to tap into vast quantities of structured and unstructured data that is available on the cloud, enabling the use of predictive analytics.

- *File storage*: The cloud offers the possibility of storing files and retrieving them from any web-enabled interface using simple interfaces. Organizations only pay for the amount of storage they consume without having to take on the task of overseeing the daily maintenance of the storage infrastructure.
- *Disaster recovery*: Cloud-based disaster recovery solutions may provide for faster recovery of data compared with traditional disaster recovery sites that have fixed assets, rigid procedures, and higher costs.
- *Backup*: Backing up data is a complex and time-consuming operation involving maintaining a set of tapes or drives, manually collecting them, and dispatching them to a backup facility. Cloud-based backup transfers this responsibility to the cloud provider.

While this list is not exhaustive, it highlights why the cloud is increasingly attractive to IT managers.

Supply managers need to understand what the cloud is about. Instead of negotiating directly with individual hardware and software providers, supply managers will increasingly find themselves negotiating with cloud computing service providers. Hardware and software as a service is a very different world than supporting hardware and software in a traditional IT environment.

Software Applications in New Product Development

The pressure to reduce product development times is ongoing. One of the primary ways that firms have achieved dramatic reductions in development times is through the use of IT-enabled tools and applications. Software tools are available that support product and process development through the design of experiments, quality function deployment (i.e., translating customer wants and requirements into design specifications), and the methodical assessment of design for manufacturability or assembly, something that is essential when taking a concurrent product and process development approach. And, the importance of CAD (computer-aided design), CAM (computer-aided manufacturing), and rapid prototyping applications have supported impressive development improvements in quality, cycle time, and cost. Keeping within the software theme, FMEA tools support the assessment of potential failures in a design or process while TRIZ software supports a disciplined approach to complex problems that are encountered during development. 3-D printing is also making a major impact on the product development process. Product development leaders are familiar with some or even all of these software applications.

IT TRENDS—THE WOW FACTOR

The rate of change surrounding IT is a bit overwhelming. Gartner has been at the forefront of analyzing and predicting IT trends for a number of years. Based on their work, Gartner concludes that today's IT trends cluster into three primary categories or themes called intelligent, digital, and mesh. Gardner concludes that these technologies are beginning to break out and have the potential to be serious disruptors. Whether or not these trends will affect supply management directly is anyone's guess. But, it is in every supply manager's best interests to appreciate what is going on within the IT world. So, what are these trends within the categories of intelligent, digital, and mesh?[21]

Intelligent

Creating intelligent systems that have the ability to learn, adapt, and act autonomously rather than simply execute predefined instructions is a primary battleground for technology suppliers and researchers.

Artificial Intelligence and Advanced Machine Learning

Artificial intelligence (AI) and advanced machine learning (AML) includes technologies such as deep learning, neural networks, and natural-language processing. AI and AML can also encompass more advanced systems that understand, predict, adapt, learn, and potentially operate autonomously. The combination of parallel processing power, advanced algorithms, and massive data sets that feed computational algorithms is enabling this trend.

Intelligent Apps

Intelligent apps include technologies like virtual personal assistants that transform the workplace by making everyday tasks easier and its users more effective. Intelligent apps are not limited, however, to new digital assistants. Existing software categories from security tooling to enterprise applications will include AI-enabled capabilities. Using AI, technology providers will focus on advanced analytics, AI-powered and increasingly autonomous business processes, and AI-powered immersive, conversational and continuous interfaces. Gartner expects most of the world's largest companies to exploit intelligent apps and benefit from the full array of big data and analytics tools to improve the customer experience.

Intelligent Things

Intelligent things generally include robots, drones, and autonomous vehicles. As intelligent things evolve they will shift from a stand-alone model to a collaborative model featuring intelligent things communicating with one another and acting in concert to accomplish tasks.

Digital

The lines between the digital and physical world should continue to blur, thereby creating new opportunities for digital businesses. The digital world will increasingly become a detailed reflection of the physical world and the digital world will appear as part of the physical world. This creates opportunities for new business models and digitally enabled ecosystems.

Virtual and Augmented Reality

Virtual reality (VR) and augmented reality (AR) are transforming the way in which individuals interact with each other and with software systems. VR, for example, can be used for training scenarios and simulating different experiences. AR enables a blending of the real and virtual worlds, which allows a business to overlay graphics onto real-world objects, such as hidden wires on the image of a wall. Over time VR and AR will expand beyond the visual sense to include all human senses.

Digital Twin

Using data on how the components of something operates and responds to the environment as well as data provided by physical world sensors, a digital twin can analyze and simulate real-world conditions, respond to changes, and improve operations. Digital twins function as substitutes for skilled individuals (such as technicians) and traditional monitoring devices and controls (such as pressure gauges). Those who understand the maintenance of real-world things will collaborate with data scientists and IT professionals to create digital twins. Digital twins will enable an increasingly detailed digital representation of the real world for simulation, analysis, and control.

Blockchain

Blockchain is a distributed ledger in which value exchange transactions are sequentially grouped into blocks. Currently it is used widely to support crypto-currency transactions, such as Bitcoin. An analogy will help us better conceptualize blockchain technology—blockchain is to Bitcoin as the internet is to e-mail. It is a large electronic system that supports different applications. Bitcoin currency is just one of those applications.[22]

Blockchain is an open, distributed ledger that can record transactions between two parties efficiently and in a verifiable and permanent way.[23] Each time a digital transaction occurs it is grouped together in a protected block with other transactions that have occurred in the last 10 minutes. Members in the network with high levels of computing power compete to validate the transactions by solving complex coded problems. The validated block of transactions is time-stamped and added to a chain (i.e., the ledger) in a linear, chronological order. New blocks of validated transactions are linked to older blocks, making a chain of secure blocks that show every transaction made in the history of that blockchain. The entire chain is continually updated so that every ledger in the network is the same, giving each member the ability to prove who owns what at any given time.

Blockchain users expect this technology to add trust and provide transparent access to the information in the chain. Most blockchain initiatives and applications are still in an early phase of development.

Mesh

Mesh refers to the dynamic connection of people, processes, things, and services to support intelligent digital ecosystems. As the mesh evolves, the user experience and the supporting technology, security architectures, and platforms must evolve as well.

Conversational Systems

Conversational systems can range from simple, informal, bidirectional text or voice conversations to complex interactions such as collecting oral testimony from crime witnesses to generate a sketch of a suspect. Conversational systems shift from a model where people adapt to computers to one where the computer hears and adapts to a desired outcome. These systems do not use text or voice as the exclusive interface but enable people and machines to use multiple modalities such as sight or sound to communicate across the digital device mesh, such as sensors, appliances, or the IoT systems.

Mesh App and Service Architecture (MASA)

MASA is a multi-channel solution architecture that leverages cloud and serverless computing, containers, and microservices to deliver modular, flexible, and dynamic solutions. Solutions ultimately support users in various roles using multiple devices and communicating over multiple networks. MASA is a long-term architectural shift that requires significant changes to development tooling and best practices.

Digital Technology Platforms

Digital technology platforms are the building blocks for a digital business. Every organization will have some mix of various digital technology platforms: information systems, customer experience, analytics and intelligence, the IoT, and business ecosystems. Companies should identify how industry platforms will evolve and plan ways for their platforms to meet the challenges of digital business.

Adaptive Security Architecture

The evolution of the intelligent digital mesh and digital technology platforms and application architectures means that security must become fluid and adaptive. Security in the IoT environment, for example, is especially challenging. Security teams will need to work with application, solution, and enterprise architects to consider security objectives early in the design of applications or IoT solutions.

It is unclear how these trends will affect supply and supply chain managers. However, this discussion illustrates that the next generation of IT systems and applications are evolving at a rapid pace.

CONCLUDING THOUGHTS

Even though this chapter focused on a wide variety of IT tools and applications, the primary message should not be ignored. That message is that IT is a critical enabler of strategic supply management. Managing even the most mundane supply activities is a cumbersome process without a supporting set of IT tools and applications. A supply organization that spends an inordinate amount of time chasing insignificant purchase items and managing transactions, paperwork, data collection, and reporting and compliance requirements will not have the time to pursue the supply management activities that make a difference at the corporate level.

REFERENCES

1. A. Bartolini, *CPO Rising 2017: Tools of the Trade*, a white paper by Ardent Partners.
2. ibid.
3. M. P. Papazoglou and P. Ribbers, *e-Business: Organizational and Technical Foundations* (West Sussex, England: John Wiley & Sons, 2006), 227.
4. Papazoglou and Ribbers, 241.
5. D. Neef, *e-Procurement*, (Upper Saddle River, New Jersey: Prentice Hall, 2001): 9.
6. T. Stevens, "Exchange for the Better?" *Industry Week*, 249, no. 8 (August 21, 2000): 39.
7. Papazoglou and Ribbers, 243.

8. The information presented on e-catalogs is adapted from Papazoglou and Ribbers: 242–245.
9. R. M. Monczka, R. J. Trent, and R. B. Handfield, *Purchasing and Supply Chain Management* (Mason, Ohio: Thomson South-Western, 2005): 603.
10. R. M. Monczka, and R. J. Trent, "Purchasing and Supply Management: Key Trends and Changes throughout the 1990s," *International Journal of Purchasing and Materials Management*, volume 34, issue 4, (Fall 1998): 2–11.
11. From an industry white paper titled *Accenture Builds High Performance in Supplier Relationship Management with mySAP SRM Solutions*, www.accenture.com.
12. W. H. Inmon, J. D. Welch, and K. L. Glassey, *Managing the Data Warehouse* (New York: John Wiley & Sons, 1997): 365–366.
13. From http://www.predictiveanalyticstoday.com/what-is-predictive-analytics/.
14. From http://internetofthingsagenda.techtarget.com/definition/Internet-of-Things-IoT.
15. From https://halobi.com/2016/07/descriptive-predictive-and-prescriptive-analytics-explained/.
16. From http://data-informed.com/five-supply-chain-opportunities-in-big-data-and-predictive-analytics/.
17. E. Rusch, "Using Analytics to Differentiate Your Customer Service, *Inbound Logistics*, (September 2015): 34.
18. From www.wikipedia.com.
19. "Cloud Computing Deployments Should Begin With Service Definitions," retrieved from https://www.gartner.com/doc/reprints?id=1-3G2H8FE&ct=160826&st=sb.
20. M. Ferkoun, "The 7 Most Common Uses of Cloud Computing," https://www.ibm.com/blogs/cloud-computing/2014/02/top-7-most-common-uses-of-cloud-computing/, February 6, 2014.
21. These trends are adapted from *Gartner's Top 10 Strategic Technology Trends in 2017*, http://www.gartner.com/smarterwithgartner/gartners-top-10-technology-trends-2017/.
22. This section is adapted from C. Thompson, "How Does the Blockchain Work (for Dummies) Explained Simply," October 2, 2016, https://medium.com/the-intrepid-review/how-does-the-blockchain-work-for-dummies-explained-simply-9f94d386e093.
23. M. Iansiti and K. R. Lakhani, "The Truth About Blockchain," *Harvard Business Review*, 95, no. 1, (January–February, 2017): 120.

Part III

Contemporary Topics in Supply Management

7

STRATEGY IS STILL KING
(OR QUEEN)

Without question, strategy development is one of the most important parts of strategic supply management. It is hard to imagine a company that has gained a competitive advantage from its supply efforts without putting in place a set of formal supply strategies. As was pointed out in Chapter 1, the presence of well-thought-out strategies is one of the defining features of an effective supply management organization. Just about anything that represents a meaningful endeavor should have a strategy underlying it.

This chapter addresses the topic of supply strategies by first presenting a primer to position our thinking about strategy as a concept. We next summarize the strategy development process at a company that is recognized for its ability to develop worldwide supply strategies. We conclude with a discussion of the portfolio matrix, a tool that should be a part of every supply manager's tool kit, and present examples showing how to apply the portfolio matrix to real-life scenarios.

WHAT IS A STRATEGY?

Strategy is a word that we all have heard used many times over our lifetime. Recall from Chapter 2 that a concept closely related to strategy—strategic—is one of the most overused and misused terms in business today. An important point is that strategy development is not unique to supply management. In fact, supply management has often lagged in its strategy development efforts compared with more established groups such as finance and marketing.

Historically, combining purchasing and strategy in the same sentence has not been taken all that seriously. At many companies the purchasing department simply reacted to requests from internal customers. The development of strategies that could affect corporate success was something that challenged our grasp of reality. A clear indication today that supply management is evolving in terms of maturity is the presence of sophisticated strategies, many of which are formalized through supply contracts.

When asked to define the term, more often than not the respondent will say that a strategy is a plan. While partially true, that perspective fails to fully capture the essence of the concept. Richard Vancil of Harvard University provides what is still one of the better definitions of this concept.[1] He writes that the strategy of an organization, or of a subunit of a larger organization, is a conceptualization, expressed or implied by the organization's leaders, of (1) the long-term objectives or purposes of the organization, (2) the broad constraints and policies that restrict the scope of the organization's activities, and (3) the set of plans and near-term goals that have been adopted in the expectation of contributing to the achievement of the organization's objectives. The plans that allow us to carry out a strategy are also called tactics. One of the virtues of this perspective is that it is easy to summarize—effective strategies consist of objectives, constraints, plans, and goals.

The development of any strategy requires a realistic assessment of the constraints that create boundaries around what we can realistically accomplish. Although something that constrains us is usually viewed negatively, the reality is that constraints should have a neutral connotation. They interject a sense of realism.

It is hard to conceive of a time when a strategy does not have constraints that limit the boundaries of that strategy. A company may have contract language that restricts outsourcing, supplier development initiatives may lack budgetary support, human talent may not be available to manage collaborative supplier relationships, or a company may want to expand its buying efforts to Asia but lacks the logistical and in-country support that is required to do so. All constraints can be classified into one of two categories—internal or external. Table 7.1 describes a set of internal and external constraints that can affect a company's supply strategies. Every proposed strategy must include a realistic assessment of the constraints that can affect success.

Something that is also essential when thinking about supply strategies is to appreciate the differences between objectives and goals. One of the challenges here is that these terms are often used interchangeably. A popular dictionary defines an objective as something that one's efforts or actions are intended to attain or accomplish; a purpose; a goal; a target. The definition of a goal is that it is the result or achievement toward which effort is directed; an aim—an end. The clear overlap of these two terms will not satisfy our needs.

If you remember nothing else from this chapter, remember the following. An objective is an aspiration while a goal is an accomplishment. The presence of objectives is like a compass: they point us in a certain direction. That direction

Table 7.1 Supply strategy constraints

Internal Strategy Development Constraints
Corporate Policies and Objectives: Supply strategies are often influenced by and must support higher-level organizational objectives. An emphasis on doing business with large suppliers, for example, may conflict with a corporate policy that supports doing business with small and disadvantaged suppliers.
Strategy Development Within Other Functional Groups: Many supply strategies are intended to support strategies that were developed by other functional groups. The purchasing group is a support function with an extensive array of internal stakeholders, each of whom has requirements that purchasing may be called upon to support.
Financial Resources: Most strategies require some level of financial resources. A commodity management team that performs site visits to suppliers, for example, will require budget support. Operating an International Purchasing Office (IPO), something that is often part of a company's organizational structure, will not be inexpensive.
Human Resource Capabilities: A shortage of qualified participants continues to be one of the most serious internal constraints facing supply organizations.
Labor Contracts: Labor contracts may prohibit certain actions, such as the outsourcing of work or prohibiting suppliers from working onsite.
Internal Customer Demands: A support function such as purchasing must always be ready to satisfy the demands of its internal customers. Satisfying these demands, many of which are not known until they are made, often take priority.
External Strategy Development Constraints
Competitor Actions: Supply strategies are sometimes developed as a response to actions by competitors. The purchase of a tier-one supplier by a competitor, for example, can force the development of new supply strategies that reflect a changing supply market.
Economic and Market Risk Conditions: Economics and risk affect supply strategies because of the increasingly global nature of supply activities as well as the effect these conditions have on supply markets. Currency changes, interest rates, supply and demand changes, and worldwide growth affect supply strategies.
Laws and Regulations: Domestic and foreign laws and regulations can affect the strategy development of any organizational unit. Strategy development involving international procurement, for example, will require an evaluation of which country's laws apply within a purchase agreement.
Customer Demands: Many suppliers have grown because of the demands placed on them by their industrial customers. Customer demands at all levels of the value chain influence supply strategies. Your customers influence your strategies, and your strategies influence your suppliers' strategies, and so on down the line.

may involve cost reduction, quality improvement, cycle time reduction, better supplier relationships, or dozens of other worthwhile aspirations.

Goals align with aspirations (i.e., the objectives) and provide guidance regarding specific accomplishments to achieve by some future date. Ideally, goals align clearly with the objectives of the organization as articulated by its leaders.

And, the presence of goals makes objectives actionable. Effective strategies include both objectives and goals, making an understanding of the differences between these terms important. Beyond differentiating between objectives and goals in terms of aspirations and accomplishments, other meaningful differences exist between the two terms. Table 7.2 presents four areas where goals and objectives may differ.[2]

Table 7.2   Differences between objectives and goals

Time Frame: Objectives are timeless or open-ended while goals are time-phased and intended to be superseded by subsequent goals. Improving supplier quality is an ongoing objective, while lowering the average supplier's defect level from 4,000 ppm to 2,000 ppm within two years is a goal.
Specificity: Objectives are stated in broad, general terms while goals are much more specific—stated in terms of a particular result that will be accomplished by a certain date. A desire to reduce purchase costs of plastic parts is a broad objective, while reducing the purchase price of plastic parts by 10% within a six-month period is a specific goal.
Focus: Objectives are often stated in some relevant environment external to the organization while goals are internally focused and imply how resources shall be used. Being regarded (externally) as an environmentally friendly company is an objective, while committing 3% of pretax profits (internally focused) to sustainability efforts is a goal.
Measurement: Quantified objectives are stated in relative terms, while a quantified goal is stated in absolute terms. Seeking to have the largest market share compared to competitors is a relative objective. Increasing sales by $5 million annually is a goal stated in absolute terms.

THE SUPPLY STRATEGY DEVELOPMENT PROCESS

If strategies are such an important part of strategic supply management, then it makes sense that a process for developing strategies should be in place. The primary objective of any strategy development process should be to craft a set of supply strategies that differentiate your company from your competitors. While no agreed-upon or standardized development process exists, it is important to have a process that builds in best practices and provides guidance when developing strategies.

Not all strategy efforts include the development of supply contracts, although strategy development and contract development are often embedded as part of the same process. Much of the strategy attention in supply management involves developing commodity or category strategies, almost all of which are formalized through written contracts. Conversely, a firm could develop strategies for increasing supplier involvement in product development, something that may or may not involve formal contracts. Or, strategies may be put in place that stress cost reduction across the supply chain.

Table 7.3 summarizes the development process that a Fortune 500 company follows when developing its worldwide supply strategies. This process contains some best practices that are not immediately obvious. First, an executive steering committee oversees this process and takes an active role in identifying a set

Table 7.3   Supply management strategy development process

Step 1: Identify sourcing and supply opportunities An executive steering committee identifies supply strategy development opportunities offering the best return.
Step 2: Establish strategy development teams Executive steering committee forms strategy development teams with members from worldwide locations participating. The committee provides resources as required.
Step 3: Evaluate sourcing opportunities and propose strategies Teams validate project assumptions; verify current volumes and expected savings; identify potential suppliers; evaluate specifications between design centers; consider supply chain risks; and propose preliminary supply strategies. The executive committee reviews the recommendations developed by the strategy development teams.
Step 4: Identify requirements for supplier proposals Strategy development teams prequalify suppliers and develop the request for proposal that suppliers receive.
Step 5: Forward proposals to prequalified suppliers Teams forward proposal requests, on average, to six suppliers with responses expected within six weeks.
Step 6: Evaluate the technical and commercial viability of proposals The team performs a commercial and technical evaluation of supplier proposals and conducts supplier site visits as required.
Step 7: Negotiate with most qualified suppliers A smaller team negotiates with suppliers at the buying company's U.S. headquarters. Negotiations, which last up to three days, lengthen if the buying company does not achieve its previously established improvement goals.
Step 8: Award final contract(s) to winning supplier(s) Information concerning the awarded contract is communicated throughout the company. The steering committee reports expected savings to executive management and finance.
Step 9: Manage transition to new contracts and/or new suppliers Agreements are loaded into the appropriate corporate and contract management systems. The sourcing team manages the transition if the supplier and/or part numbers change from previous agreements or designs.
Step 10: Monitor supplier performance and review expiring contracts Performance measurement systems assess supplier performance and validate savings. The contract repository system notifies supply managers of expiring agreements six months prior to expiration.

of sourcing opportunities. Second, executive managers make budget support available for any travel and living expenses that may be incurred by team members during the development process. Third, executive managers require strategy development teams to meet stringent milestones before they move from one step to another. Teams have to present their progress to the steering committee regularly with progress posted on the company's intranet. Finally, lessons learned sessions are conducted after the completion of each strategy development project to identify the good, the bad, and the ugly that resulted.

Most strategy development efforts, especially those that involve formally negotiated supply agreements, will benefit from analyzing some important topics. It is important to evaluate a wide range of issues when developing a formal supply strategy:

- Broad objectives of the strategy
- Functional groups to involve during strategy development
- Current expenditures by commodity and supplier
- Future volumes for this commodity
- Performance of current supplier(s)
- Other suppliers in the marketplace and their capabilities
- Internal customer requirements the strategy must support
- Type of supplier relationship to pursue
- Responsibility for managing the supplier relationship
- Specific clauses to include in a supply contract
- Domestic, regional, or worldwide contract
- Reliance on single or multiple suppliers, and if multiple suppliers are used, how to divide purchase volumes
- Other issues besides price to consider
- Services, such as inventory management or design support, sought from the supplier
- Power relationships in the market
- Other buyers competing for supply
- Expected negotiating strategy
- How best to measure supplier performance
- Short-term or longer term contract
- Pricing targets
- How to promote continuous improvement
- Contract performance risks and how to manage them

Clearly, the strategy development process will benefit from up front planning.

USING THE PORTFOLIO MATRIX TO SEGMENT SUPPLY STRATEGIES

It almost goes without saying, but it will be said anyway, that strategy development is not an easy process. Fortunately, a prescriptive tool is available that provides valuable guidance when crafting supply strategies. This tool, called the *portfolio matrix*, is one that every supply manager should understand and routinely apply when developing strategies. Figure 7.1 presents the portfolio matrix.

Presented in a classic 2×2 format, this matrix recognizes that an effective supply organization applies a variety, or portfolio, of strategies and approaches that reflect the realities of the supply market as well as a supply manager's desire regarding where to position a requirement. The 2×2 supply matrix, although not this specific version, was first articulated by Kraljic in his 1983 *Harvard Business Review* article titled *Purchasing Must Become Supply Management*.

Users of this matrix segment their purchase requirements across two dimensions—the number of active suppliers in the marketplace and the value of the good or service to the buying organization. Both of these dimensions are purposely vague. For some requirements an active supply market might consist of three or four suppliers. For other items there may be dozens, even hundreds, of qualified suppliers. The concept of value also does not have a specific definition. Value can be a function of total dollars spent on an item, or it could be a relatively inexpensive item that has a disproportionate effect on product or service performance.

Figure 7.1 The portfolio matrix

The most important reason for using a tool such as the portfolio matrix is its prescriptive nature. Once a supply manager or commodity team quantifies the total spend for each commodity or category, the good or service can be positioned within the most appropriate quadrant. This positioning helps identify (1) the type of supplier relationship to pursue, (2) whether to engage in a win-lose or win-win negotiation, (3) whether to take a price or cost analytic approach when managing the commodity or item, (4) the types of supply strategies and approaches that should work best within a specific quadrant, (5) how to measure suppliers, and (6) how best to create value across different purchase requirements.

Items that reside in the lower half of Figure 7.1 will benefit most from price analytic techniques. Price analysis refers to the process of comparing one price against another price or against other available information without in-depth knowledge about underlying costs. At times an item may have such a low value or be part of such a highly competitive market that any analysis beyond competitive price comparisons is not worth the effort. At other times, supply managers must apply innovative cost management techniques to manage costs and cost drivers for items that are more important or higher in value. Cost analytic techniques focus on the cost drivers and elements that combine to create a purchase price, which applies more to the top half of the matrix.

The portfolio matrix also suggests the type of relationship to pursue with suppliers. A solid understanding of supply relationships is essential for effective supply management. This does not mean that all relationships are equally important. Knowing when, where, and how to apply an appropriate relationship is an area where supply professionals bring value to their organization.

Recall that Chapter 2 presented a framework that characterizes relationships along a continuum. That framework recognized that different approaches to supplier management apply to different settings. A *one-size-fits-all* approach does not apply to buyer-supplier relationships. As a review, the four kinds of buyer-supplier relationships include:

- *Counterproductive relationships*: Also called antagonistic or lose-lose relationships, this relationship features the parties in a relationship working actively against each other's interests. While this type of relationship is not recommended, they do occur—particularly when one party in a contract takes legal action against the other party.
- *Competitive relationships*: Also referred to as distributive, win-lose, or adversarial relationships, this relationship features supply chain members acting primarily in their own self-interests as they compete over a fixed amount of value. Beyond the transaction or arm's-length activities taking place, few benefits result from a closer supplier-buyer relationship.

While competitive relationships will likely form the majority of a buying firm's relationships, they usually do not comprise a majority of total purchase dollars.

- *Cooperative relationships*: Also referred to as integrative relationships, cooperative relationships, which are by definition win-win, recognize the value of closer interaction and open sharing of information. Cooperative relationships are often formalized through longer term contracts that lead to discussions about how to improve cost, quality, delivery, packaging, inventory management, product innovation, and service—all factors that can affect performance.
- *Collaborative relationships*: Collaborative relationships, which represent the pinnacle of win-win relationships, involve a limited number of suppliers that provide items or services that are essential or unique to a firm's success. These relationships represent the most intensive relationship that is possible between a buyer and seller—and often involve the sharing of risk, resources, and rewards. The parties ideally share a co-destiny and recognize that the value they receive would be far less than if collaboration did not exist. Collaborative relationships are dealt with in detail in Chapter 9.

Understanding the Four Quadrants

Part of the value that supply managers bring is an understanding of their organization's purchase requirements, and then knowing how to pursue an appropriate supply strategy. The strategy response is a primary way that supply managers enhance the value they bring to their organization. It is also important to understand how to shift items across quadrants to derive even greater value. An understanding of the four quadrants is essential when using the portfolio matrix.

Transaction Quadrant

The goods and services in the transaction quadrant have a lower total value with a limited supply market. Miscellaneous office supplies, one-time purchases, magazine subscriptions to trade journals, and emergency tools needed at remote locations usually qualify as transaction items. Reducing the transactions cost of a purchase is the primary way for supply professionals to create value here, usually through electronic systems or procurement cards. Even when a requirement has many possible suppliers, the cost of comparing these options outweighs the value of a supplier search. Any price analysis that occurs is cursory due to the low value of the good or service.

Relationships and the number of suppliers that reside in this quadrant are not concerns to supply managers. Negotiation rarely occurs for these items since supply managers should not involve themselves in their direct acquisition. And, these items are often one-time or infrequent purchases. Supply managers will likely be involved in negotiating with the vendors that provide low-dollar purchase systems, such as the provider of a procurement card. Procurement is often responsible for managing any low-dollar systems.

Market Quadrant

The market quadrant includes standard items or services that have an active supply market, lower-to-medium total value, many suppliers that can provide substitutable products and services, well-defined specifications, and lower supplier switching costs. Commodity chemicals, fasteners, packaging, and other basic raw materials that do not have an unusually high dollar value are logically part of this quadrant. Any negotiation with suppliers is lower level and focuses primarily on price and delivery.

The way that supply managers create value within this quadrant is to let market forces determine the most efficient producer. Competitive bidding or price comparisons, spot buys, shorter term contracting, reverse Internet auctions, and blanket purchase orders are often-used techniques when obtaining market items. Relationships with the providers of market items are typically competitive (i.e., win-lose) and price focused. Supply managers should use the power of the marketplace to have suppliers actively compete for the buyer's business.

Leverage Quadrant

The upper-right quadrant of the portfolio matrix, the leverage quadrant, includes those items where consolidating purchase volumes and reducing the size of the supply base should provide a host of benefits. Examples of leverage items include any grouping or family of items whose volumes can be combined for economic advantage, such as plastic injected molded parts, transportation services, electric wiring harnesses, and facility maintenance services. Market quadrant items that are grouped into commodity families can be treated as leverage quadrant items.

Since leverage items are typically candidates for longer term agreements, supply managers should negotiate a range of issues with suppliers beyond price. The development of longer term contracts is the primary way that supply managers create value within this quadrant. Contract development should lead to discussions about cost, quality, delivery, packaging, logistics, and inventory management, all factors that affect supply chain performance. Supply managers leverage their requirements to gain advantages in price and other non-price areas. Depending on the leveraged item, a cost rather than a price focus should take place in this quadrant.

The management of leverage items will benefit from cooperative relationships that feature an extensive sharing of information between parties. While this quadrant will not have the most suppliers in terms of numbers, the dollar value of the leverage items should be high.

Critical Quadrant

The critical quadrant includes goods and services that consume large sums of money, are essential to a service or product's function, and/or the end customer values the differentiation offered by the good or service. This quadrant also features fewer suppliers that can satisfy a purchaser's requirements, which often involves customization rather than standardization. This quadrant often features the seller having a power advantage over the buyer. It is not easy, if at all, for the buyer to reposition items away from this quadrant. The marketplace is such that an item often gets locked into this quadrant. The buyer cannot magically cause an item to have a lower value, and the marketplace will not suddenly spawn a slew of new suppliers.

Although critical items usually represent a small portion of total transactions and part numbers, they often have a disproportionate impact on cost or performance. Supply managers create value when managing critical items by pursuing collaborative and alliance-type relationships with suppliers.

SUPPLY STRATEGY EXAMPLES

At times the marketplace determines the position of an item within the portfolio matrix, which may limit your flexibility to reposition an item to your advantage. At other times a buying company, through its strategy development process, consciously positions an item in a desired quadrant. While a good or service may be treated historically as belonging within a certain quadrant, this does not mean it must always remain a permanent resident of that quadrant.

The following examples illustrate the development of supply strategies that can be explained through the use of the portfolio matrix. The matrix provides insights into how each company manages a supply requirement, how it should manage the requirement, or how it plans to manage the requirement.

Chrysler Leverages Its Packaging Volumes

The packaging facility of Chrysler's aftermarket division (MOPAR) relies extensively on corrugated boxes to package replacement parts for distribution to its vast dealer network. At first glance, corrugated boxes are a classic market item—no individual box is particularly high in value, switching costs from one supplier to another are relatively low, the technology to make a box is well established, and many producers are usually available within a geographic region. A logical supply approach has been to treat boxes as a market item and rely on market forces to identify the most efficient producers.

In one part of the MOPAR packaging facility, the company relied on six suppliers to provide 50 separate box sizes. Unfortunately, spreading purchase requirements across 50 box sizes and six suppliers resulted in Chrysler forgoing any opportunity to leverage its purchasing power. A decision was made to purchase high-speed packaging equipment and to shift thousands of part numbers from slower equipment and manual pack areas to the high-speed equipment. Because the new equipment had high set-up charges each time a carton change occurred, another decision was made to reduce the number of box sizes for the new equipment from 50 to 12. A third decision was to rely on a longer term relationship with a single supplier for all 12 box sizes. This represented a shift within the portfolio matrix from managing individual box sizes as market items to treating the combined corrugated requirement as a leverage opportunity supported by a longer term agreement.

Almost overnight Chrysler went from having minimal influence with any one supplier to being a single supplier's most important customer. Besides the lower prices that resulted from larger volumes, the supplier agreed to deliver boxes twice a week instead of the more traditional weekly deliveries, thereby allowing the facility to reduce its average inventory levels. Order lead times were also reduced, which reduced forecast uncertainty. The buyer also received preferential scheduling in the supplier's production queue as well as design support for new corrugated applications. The supplier also began to send higher level managers and technical people to visit the packaging facility rather than salespeople.

This example highlights the benefits of shifting purchase requirements from the market quadrant to the leverage quadrant. A review of the benefits from this shift reveals that most have nothing to do with the physical product. Combining similar market items into leveraged contracts is probably the most beneficial shift that occurs within the portfolio matrix. Sometimes it really pays to think outside the box.

General Motors Bets Big on Bethlehem Steel

A number of years ago General Motors entered into a longer term supply agreement with Bethlehem Steel.[3] The two companies agreed on a four-year contract with a 3-to-5% decrease in prices with fixed pricing covering 18 million metric tons of cold-rolled steel annually. Historically, steel contracts covering one year in duration with an annual price increase were the accepted industry practice. GM's contract was part of the company's overall strategy for managing $13 billion of annual steel purchases.

GM correctly viewed steel as a leverage item during strategy development. The company consumes massive amounts of steel, making it a high-value item. The steel market also features many producers. GM does business with dozens of steel producers on a worldwide basis. Steel is also not a rapidly changing item from a technological or growth perspective. In fact, automakers are searching for ways to remove steel from their vehicles to reduce weight. GM's steel contract with Bethlehem Steel is a textbook example of using a longer term agreement for a leverage item. The agreement also changed the way a supply market typically operates by shifting from one-year agreements featuring price increases, which more closely resembles how companies manage market items, to multi-year agreements, which are characteristic of leverage items.

At this point, astute readers will note that Bethlehem Steel is no longer a viable company. This brings us to the second part of the story. GM entered into a longer term agreement with a financially distressed company. During the GM contract, Bethlehem Steel entered into bankruptcy and its assets were purchased by Integrated Steel Group (ISG). ISG was then purchased by a foreign firm (Mittal) whose goal was to control a disproportionate share of the worldwide steel market.

What is the lesson learned here? A detailed assessment of Bethlehem Steel's financial health would have indicated that the company was in distress. (An approach for analyzing a supplier's financial condition from a risk management perspective will be discussed in Chapter 8.) A buyer should evaluate longer term suppliers as if the buying company were buying the supplier, not just buying the supplier's output. How many supply managers want to do business with suppliers that are in bankruptcy?

The strategy development process must take into account supply risk and how to manage it. One way to accomplish this is to require fully-developed risk assessments that become a required part of any proposed strategy. The following provides guidance regarding the format and content of a risk assessment plan that should be part of any major commodity or purchase strategy. Risk assessments can also be developed independently of strategies:

- *Section 1—External Analysis*: This section includes an external intelligence report that describes in detail the supply market for the commodity/material. Who are the major suppliers and where are they located? Who are the major customers? What are the supply trends? Are there specific supply and demand price drivers? What is the overall competitive environment of the market for this commodity?
- *Section 2—Risk Identification*: This section identifies and categorizes risk(s), including a detailed description of each risk (i.e., not a generalization such as *potential supply disruption* or *bad weather*).

- *Section 3—Risk Mapping*: This section requires the development of a risk scenario map with each risk plotted on the map. The dimensions of the map can include the probability of a risk occurring and its expected impact if it were to occur.
- *Section 4—Risk Management*: This section contains a comprehensive risk management plan that identifies risk management actions that describe how to manage the risks identified in Section 2. This section should also include a timeline that shows how and when to carry out risk management actions.
- *Section 5—Risk References*: This section includes a listing of objective references and information sources about the demand and supply market for that item and its supplier(s). It should identify why each information source is valuable. Particular emphasis should be given to sources that are updated on a regular basis.

The topic of supply chain risk is addressed in Chapter 11.

General Motors Sees the Future and the Future Is Not Steel

Aluminum versus steel is not likely a matchup or battle that overly excites the typical individual. As it relates to supply markets, however, aluminum and steel are radically different. First, aluminum, like steel, is a high-value item in the context of the portfolio matrix. Second, and this is where a major distinction takes place, aluminum only has a handful of major producers in North America. Recall from the GM/Bethlehem example just presented that the steel industry features many suppliers worldwide. Within the matrix, aluminum is a critical item while steel more closely resembles a leverage item. Third, a trend in the automotive industry is to replace steel with lighter weight aluminum, plastic, and composite parts to better manage fuel efficiency. Aluminum is becoming increasingly critical to automotive companies.

To promote a shift toward aluminum, GM signed a multibillion-dollar agreement to buy substantial amounts of aluminum from Alcan, a Canadian-based producer of aluminum. A closer examination reveals four reasons why the agreement and relationship that GM is pursuing with Alcan is truly collaborative and that GM is managing aluminum correctly as a critical item. First, the CEO of GM personally signed the purchase agreement with Alcan, something that is highly unusual. Second, the agreement was initially for 10 years, something that again is highly unusual in supply agreements. Third, the agreement contains a formula for keeping aluminum prices stable that involves the sharing of risk and a guarantee that Alcan will receive a certain return on its investment.

Historically, the volatility of aluminum prices has been a major deterrent to its expanded use in the auto industry. Finally, the agreement called for GM and Alcan to set up a joint research program at GM's technical center in Warren, Michigan, staffed with 15 to 40 engineers drawn from the two companies. The research center is charged with inventing new ways to use aluminum in vehicles and to make aluminum parts as recyclable as soda cans.

While the average consumer likely cares less about the supply markets for aluminum and steel, supply managers understand the differences well. Aluminum is a critical item within the portfolio matrix, and GM is managing it correctly by pursuing a collaborative relationship with one of the few capable suppliers in the aluminum industry.

Lockheed Martin Goes 3-D

Without question, we are witnessing an era of profound disruption which Chapter 1 touched upon. One technology that will be a market disruptor is 3-D printing, or additive manufacturing as it is formally called. A company that is endorsing this technology is Lockheed Martin, a global aerospace company. The company expects to 3-D print over half of the parts required for its A2100 satellite bus. Some new system designs for the satellite cannot even be machined with existing technology. They can, however, be printed. The change brought about by additive manufacturing will lead to drastically reduced hardware development costs, decreased parts counts, fewer suppliers, and production cycle times that are shortened by 50%.[4]

What does 3-D printing have to do with our discussion of supply strategy development and the portfolio matrix? Without question, many of the items on a complex satellite system such as the A2100 are available from a limited supply base. And, almost all are critical-to-quality, higher-value items. A failure of even one part can cause a devastating system failure.

Recall that items that reside in the critical quadrant of the portfolio matrix often present significant sourcing challenges, often because suppliers have a certain degree of power over the buyer. One way to manage critical items is to remove them as critical items, something that is easier said than done. What 3-D printing offers companies is the opportunity to become more vertically integrated by printing parts and subsystems that were previously sourced from external suppliers. Instead of relying on suppliers for a variety of often critical items, companies such as Lockheed Martin become their own supplier. The company can now develop less complex sourcing strategies for the raw materials required in order to print their parts, as compared with buying finished items from suppliers. Many critical items and applications are now brought in-house, offering a degree of control over design, cost, cycle time, performance, and quality. Other aerospace companies that are adopting 3-D technology are Boeing, SpaceX, Pratt & Whitney, and Aerojet Rocketdyne, to name a few. 3-D printing technology is what we call a game changer.

Supply Risk Becomes Corporate Risk at Ford

One of the more public supply contracting missteps over the last 20 years occurred at Ford Motor Company.[5] Just how big was this misstep? In the end Ford had to write off $1 billion of its precious metal inventory and was sued by shareholders who alleged the company misled them about the risks associated with the company's handling of precious metals. How could this happen?

Let's step back and talk about a relatively unknown element called palladium. For many years, auto companies used platinum in catalytic converters for emission control. However, in anticipation of tougher government emission rules, auto companies designed palladium into their pollution control equipment, suddenly consuming over half the world's palladium demand. Besides being more effective at cleaning vehicle exhaust, it was (at least at the time) also less expensive than platinum.[6] The end of the Cold War left a large stockpile of inexpensive palladium in Russia, one of two primary palladium producing regions.

As engineers created designs that replaced platinum with palladium, the worldwide price of palladium became very volatile. As demand skyrocketed during the latter 1990s, palladium peaked at almost $1,000 an ounce (and each vehicle required about an ounce of palladium). At this point, macroeconomics should kick in as high commodity prices encourage suppliers to provide more output, helping to bring supply and demand closer to equilibrium. Unfortunately, several factors helped to ensure that a move toward equilibrium would not be smooth. First, the two primary supply sources of palladium are Russia and Africa, two areas not known for their supply stability. In Russia, the size of the palladium stockpile is a state secret. The Russian government also showed a willingness to delay releases from its stockpile, thereby creating major supply and price disruptions. Second, palladium occurs in nature with other elements. It is mined with platinum in Russia and with nickel in Africa, and the amount of palladium present is less proportionally than platinum or nickel. A producer would have to increase the production of platinum and nickel to increase the output of palladium. That would drive down the price of nickel and platinum as the new supply flooded the market with no change in demand.

Now, let's get back to Ford. Assurance of supply and a fixed price were clearly the procurement group's primary objectives as it developed its precious metals strategy. Ford entered into a longer term palladium contract with a fixed price at near record levels. As Ford's buyers stocked up on expensive precious metals, Ford's engineers, as well as engineers at other companies, figured out how to reduce by half the amount of palladium that was required in each vehicle. The net effect of these engineering changes was to quickly lower total palladium demand, and lower demand resulted in a lower per ounce cost. The value of the inventory that Ford locked into and stockpiled was now worth much less. The eventual $1 billion write off for precious metals clearly upset some shareholders.

Palladium's value and limited supply base clearly placed this item in the critical quadrant of the portfolio matrix. So, what was Ford's mistake? Ford's procurement managers treated palladium as a leverage item, similar to steel and copper, rather than the critical item that it truly resembled. Treating palladium as a critical item would likely have resulted in some strategy changes. Procurement did not consider, for example, the input of finance, a group who likely would not have recommended a high fixed-price contract, or engineering, who might have mentioned something about the ongoing effort to reduce the palladium required in each vehicle. Ford's chief financial officer later said publicly that the purchasing staff did not take the sort of precautions that sophisticated buyers routinely take to hedge risk in volatile markets.

Remember a critical point here—procurement is functional while supply management is organizational. There are good reasons why important supply initiatives, including longer term contracts, involve groups besides procurement. In this example procurement lacked the expertise to source this volatile element on its own. While it is easy for outsiders to stand back and determine what went wrong, there are still valuable lessons to take forward from this saga.

Shifting Between Quadrants at Lehigh University

Almost every buying organization has a procurement card program in place. At Lehigh University in Bethlehem, PA, academic departments and faculty rely on procurement cards to obtain transaction items and services that do not justify purchase contracts or purchase orders. Procurement cards are a popular way to obtain transaction items.

A major assumption is that the card is used for items that truly belong in the transaction quadrant. An analysis of the spending patterns by the purchasing group revealed that while no single department required an unusual amount of goods or services obtained with procurement cards, there was enough overlap between departments to justify a different buying approach. The procurement manager blocked some items from the procurement card that had commonality between departments and instead created blanket purchase orders to obtain those items. The manager made a conscious decision to shift some items from the transaction quadrant to the market quadrant within the portfolio matrix and manage them accordingly. Competitive bidding and blanket purchase orders now became appropriate approaches for managing these newly shifted items.

The analysis also revealed that half of the university's 350 blanket purchase orders showed no activity during the previous year. The procurement manager found he was committing too much time reestablishing unnecessary contracts on an annual basis. The decision was made to cancel over half of the university's blanket purchase orders and use procurement cards in the event these items were required. Here, the procurement manager made a conscious decision to shift items from the market quadrant to the transaction quadrant. Positioning items in their appropriate quadrant provided clear guidance regarding how best to manage these items.

Ford Makes a Revolutionary Change

In its quest to lighten vehicle weights to better meet government-mandated mileage requirements, Ford made the strategic decision to design and build a large part of its trucks using aluminum instead of steel. Why was this strategic? The F-Series trucks, which Ford's former CEO refers to as the company's *crown jewels*, represent over $30 billion in annual revenue. Tinkering with a company's cash cow can be a risky proposition.

The move to an aluminum truck body represented a radical change in terms of technical and supply issues. As mentioned, aluminum, as compared with steel, clearly resides in the critical quadrant of the portfolio matrix. Besides featuring a limited number of capable suppliers, the use of aluminum presents other challenges. Aluminum cannot be welded like steel, making Ford's welding robots a thing of the past and forcing a major retrofitting of Ford's assembly plants. Instead of being welded, aluminum must be riveted or bonded with adhesives. Consumer perceptions of the strength of aluminum versus steel are also a concern. When consumers think of aluminum they often think of a lightweight beverage can that anyone can crush with one hand. Next, new suppliers from a limited pool had to be located and qualified. And, these suppliers had to ramp up and produce at volumes never before seen. Finally, dealers and repair shops did not have the expertise or equipment to repair aluminum. Repair facilities had to make an investment in specialized aluminum repair equipment. The required supply chain changes and issues associated with switching from steel to aluminum were complex.

How did Ford address the technical and supply issues associated with this switch? The company established four working groups to address specific concerns. One group focused on the availability of aluminum in the marketplace. This group was responsible for developing Ford's single-source supply strategy. A second group addressed internal assembly issues. A third focused on serviceability (i.e., repair) issues. The last group addressed consumer perceptions of aluminum, or what Ford terms *likeability*. A multifaceted strategy was put in place to support the launch of the new F-Series trucks. This reflected the complexity of managing an item that resides squarely within the critical quadrant versus a more understood one that resides within the leverage quadrant.

These examples highlight how the use of the portfolio matrix not only provides guidance when crafting supply strategies, the matrix also helps us understand the rationale behind the strategy. The matrix even helps us spot the mistakes that are made when managing a supply requirement incorrectly.

CONCLUDING THOUGHTS

Crafting a set of supply strategies is no guarantee that these strategies will be successful. To that end, effective supply strategies share some important characteristics. They are the result of an iterative process involving different groups and personnel, they provide a proper match between opportunities and resources, and they support and align with original corporate objectives. They are also drafted (at least partially) by those who are responsible for their attainment, provide operational guidance to supply managers across an organization, and are dynamic and subject to review and change as conditions warrant. Perhaps most important, well-executed strategies can result in performance outcomes that lead to competitive market advantages at the corporate level. Supply strategies can be strategic in the true sense of the word.

REFERENCES

1. The strategy discussion in this section draws from R. F. Vancil, "Strategy Formulation in Complex Organizations," *Sloan Management Review*, 17, no. 2 (Winter 1976): 1–18.
2. ibid.
3. P. Galuszka, "An Ironclad Deal with GM," *Business Week*, 3619 (March 8, 1999): 36.
4. A. S. Farnborough, "Adding Up: Lockheed Martin Is Testing 3-D Printed Subsystems on A2100 Space Bus," *Aviation Week and Space Technology*, (August 4, 2014): 51.
5. G. L. White, "Precious Commodity: How Ford's Big Batch of Rare Metals Led to a $1 Billion Write-Off," *Wall Street Journal*, February 6, 2002, A1.
6. G. L. White, "Unruly Element: Russian Maneuvers Are Making Palladium More Precious than Ever," *Wall Street Journal*, March 6, 2000, A1.

8

LINKING SUPPLY MANAGEMENT AND CORPORATE SUCCESS

Everything that a supply professional does affects one or more components of his or her company's balance sheet, income statement, and/or cash flow statement. The time has come to understand, and articulate when necessary, the linkages between supply management and corporate financial success. One of the primary reasons for applying financial tools, techniques, and thinking to support supply chain decisions is to utilize a body of knowledge that is well regarded and well developed. Learning to speak a language called finance—which is spoken at the highest echelons of governments, nonprofit organizations, and corporations—and showing how supply and supply chain initiatives affect corporate performance will only enhance your professional stature.

This chapter provides an overview of five areas that have clear overlap between supply management, supply chain management, and corporate financial management. The following sections address the diverse and wide application of financial thinking that can be applied within the supply and supply chain management domain. Today's supply manager must think like a financial manager.

KNOWING MORE ABOUT YOUR SUPPLIERS THAN THEY KNOW ABOUT THEMSELVES

One of the most important processes undertaken today is the evaluation and selection of suppliers. Mistakes made during this process can have long and lasting consequences, particularly when a supplier is the beneficiary of a longer term purchase agreement. A key part of the selection process is understanding how to analyze supplier financial data and information to predict potential supplier bankruptcy and other financially related problems.

A supplier financial analysis is performed primarily to manage business risk and to eliminate marginal suppliers from the selection process. Many firms require suppliers to attain a certain level of financial stability before they receive further consideration, such as a site visit. Financial assessments should also occur for incumbent suppliers as a way to manage supply chain risk.

Suppliers that are under financial duress or have some red flags should be placed on a watch list that results in more frequent reviews. Few supply managers want to get caught off guard because of supplier financial difficulties. And, let's face it, troubled suppliers may not always tell you they are in financial trouble. A supplier that tells a potential buyer about its financial problems may accelerate its own demise, as buyers will likely avoid these suppliers. Exceptions to this do exist, of course. A supplier's financial issues may be temporary, or the supplier could be the only source that offers something the buyer needs, such as a new technology. And, a supplier, while still under some duress, may also be trending in the right direction.

Financial Ratio Analysis

A common approach when evaluating a company's financial situation involves ratio analysis. Ratios, also called financial performance metrics, simply represent one number divided by another to arrive at a value that is then compared to an industry benchmark, an internal target, a historical performance, or other companies. Since hundreds of financial ratios exist, the first step is to determine if a ratio tells us something of importance rather than simply being numbers thrown into a formula.

The reasons for evaluating financial ratios are compelling. We use supplier financial ratios to manage risk by providing insights that line-item data from financial statements cannot provide. Ratios take financial data and turn them into value-added information that is then interpreted. Furthermore, ratio analysis, when performed on a regular basis, can highlight trends. Ratios can also be used to determine the relative financial strength of a supplier compared with other suppliers in an industry. Perhaps most important, various tools use financial ratios to predict the potential of supplier bankruptcy (which will be discussed later).

Financial ratios should be calculated when evaluating potential suppliers, especially when a purchase requirement involves a significant amount of dollars or when buying items that are critical to your business or product. Very important, ratios analysis should occur when supplier switching costs are high and changing suppliers because of a poor selection decision is difficult. Finally, ratio analysis is warranted when conducting regular risk scans of your supply base.

A supplier may be rejected early during the selection process for reasons other than concerns about financial health. These include, but are not limited to, a history of poor performance; a lack of available capacity; pending litigation involving the supplier; the supplier is a direct competitor; the supplier has environmental or other workplace infractions; the supplier demonstrates relative indifference about doing business with the buyer; the supplier has questionable ethics; or unfamiliarity with the buyer's industry.

Not everyone agrees on the categories of financial ratios. A search of financial resources reveals that while some overlap exists regarding ratio categories, complete overlap is rare. Regardless of the categories used, each ratio category should answer a specific question or satisfy a specific objective that is unique to that category. The following presents six categories of ratios:

- *Liquidity ratios*: Liquidity ratios help identify if a firm (i.e., the supplier) is capable of meeting its short-term financial obligations.
- *Leverage ratios*: This category includes any ratio that is used to evaluate a company's methods of financing or to measure its ability to meet financial obligations.
- *Activity ratios*: Activity ratios indicate how effectively a firm is managing its assets.
- *Profitability ratios*: Ratios in this category indicate how well a firm is performing in terms of its ability to generate a profit.
- *Market ratios*: These ratios indicate how well a supplier is performing compared with market indicators such as price/earnings and shareholder return.
- *Growth ratios*: Growth ratios provide insight into the rate of growth that is occurring over time, such as sales or net income.

Using financial data and ratios is not without challenges. First of all, gaining access to reliable and timely data is not always easy or convenient. While public companies are obligated to make their financial information available in the form of financial statements, private suppliers are under no such obligation. Second, gaining the right level of data about public companies can be problematic. Large companies almost always have multiple operating units that are aggregated within financial statements. Finally, the quality of financial data might be questionable when using international suppliers. The *two sets of books* method, which is unthinkable (and illegal) in developed countries is not so far-fetched in some countries. In practice, companies should establish an information technology (IT) repository that houses financial information that has been collected from multiple sources.

Some words of caution are in order when performing ratio analysis. As mentioned, data access and reliability are often concerns, particularly for private and foreign companies. Furthermore, ratio analysis is simply a tool that should be part of a broader supplier evaluation and selection process. Care must also be taken when comparing suppliers from different industries. While the numerical values of some ratios are interpreted similarly across industries, the value of other ratios may not be comparable. Some industries have different perspectives, for example, about the assumption of debt versus equity (i.e., stock). Also, financial statements, which are the basis for most ratios, represent only a point in time for balance sheets or a relatively short period of time for income and cash flow statements. And, these statements are always backward looking. Finally, avoid relying on a single period or snapshot. Multiple time periods should be considered to identify possible trends. Table 8.1 provides examples of selected ratios.

Is the Supplier Going Bankrupt?

The financial crisis of 2008 put a huge spotlight on the need for supply managers to assess the financial health of suppliers, both during the selection process and during ongoing operations. Whether we realize it or not, bankruptcy predictors are an early use of predictive analytics. As mentioned in Chapter 6, predictive analytics is the practice of extracting information, usually from large data sets, to identify patterns to predict future outcomes and trends.

Perhaps the most well-known bankruptcy predictor is the Altman Z-Score. Edward Altman, an NYU Stern Finance Professor developed the Z-score formula

Table 8.1   Selected financial ratios

	Ratio	Preferred Direction
Liquidity	**Current ratio**: (current assets / current liabilities)	Higher
	Cash ratio: (cash / current liabilities)	Higher
	Quick ratio: ((current assets – inventories) / current liabilities)	Higher
Activity	**Asset turnover**: (sales / total assets)	Higher
	Current asset turnover: (sales / current assets)	Higher
	Inventory turnover: (sales / inventory)	Higher
Leverage	**Debt to equity**: (total liabilities / equity)	Lower
	Current debt to equity: (current liabilities / equity)	Lower
	Interest coverage: (earnings before interest and taxes / interest)	Higher
Profitability	**Net profit margin**: (net income / sales)	Higher
	Gross margin: ((sales – cost of goods sold) / sales)	Higher
	Operating margin: (operating income / sales)	Higher
	Return on assets: (net income / total assets)	Higher
	Return on equity: (net income / equity)	Higher

in 1967. As recently as 2012, he released an updated version called the Altman Z-score Plus for evaluating public and private companies as well as manufacturing and non-manufacturing companies of U.S. and non-U.S. origin.[1] The Z-Score combines a series of weighted ratios for public and private firms to predict the likelihood of financial bankruptcy. While sources sometimes differ on the predictive validity of the Z-Score, most users operate under the assumption that the Z-Score is around 90% accurate in predicting bankruptcy one year in advance and 75% accurate in predicting bankruptcy in two years.

Supply chain managers will find that the Z-score, as with other bankruptcy predictors, supports some worthwhile objectives. The Z-Score is ideal as a screening tool at the earliest stages of supplier evaluation and selection. This assessment helps provide a *go or no-go* concerning whether to continue viewing that supplier as a possible sourcing option. The Z-Score calculation is also valuable during routine risk scans of the supply chain. And, along with other supplier performance indicators, it provides guidance regarding which suppliers to keep or eliminate from the supply base. The following are the Z-Score formulas for private and public firms:

Private Company:

$$Z\text{-Score} = 6.56 \times \frac{\text{Working Capital}}{\text{Total Assets}} + 3.36 \times \frac{\text{Retained Earnings}}{\text{Total Assets}} +$$

$$6.72 \times \frac{\text{EBIT}}{\text{Total Assets}} + 1.05 \times \frac{\text{Net Worth}}{\text{Total Liabilities}}$$

Where:

Z-Score < 1.1   Red Zone—Supplier is financially at risk
Z-Score between 1.1 and 2.6   Yellow Zone—Some area of financial concern
Z-Score > 2.6   Green Zone—Supplier is financially sound

Public Company:

$$Z\text{-Score} = 1.2 \times \frac{\text{Working Capital}}{\text{Total Assets}} + 1.4 \times \frac{\text{Retained Earnings}}{\text{Total Assets}} +$$

$$3.3 \times \frac{\text{EBIT}}{\text{Total Assets}} + 0.6 \times \frac{\text{Net Worth}}{\text{Total Liabilities}} + 1.0 \times \frac{\text{Net Sales}}{\text{Total Assets}}$$

Where:

Z-Score < 1.8   Red Zone—Supplier is financially at risk and is
                                                 likely to enter bankruptcy

Z-Score between 1.8 and 3.0   Yellow Zone—Some area of financial concern
Z-Score > 3.0   Green Zone—Supplier is financially sound

The required data for calculating Z-Score ratios appears in the balance sheet and income statement. The following explains the financial location of each piece of data required for the Z-Score calculation.

- *Total assets*: Total assets appear in the first section of the balance sheet.
- *Working capital*: Working capital requires a calculation on the user's part. Working capital represents the difference between current assets and current liabilities, which is found on the balance sheet.
- *Retained earnings*: Retained earnings are the net earnings that are not paid as dividends. Retained earnings appear directly on the balance sheet within the stockholders' equity portion of the balance sheet.
- *Earnings before interest and taxes* (EBIT): This figure may require some calculation since EBIT is often not presented directly as a line item on the income statement. When this is the case, take the net income figure and add back *interest expenses* and *taxes*. Both of these figures will appear on the income statement.
- *Net worth*: The net worth figure is presented as shareholders' equity on the balance sheet.
- *Total liabilities*: This figure appears between total assets and total stockholders' equity on the balance sheet.
- *Net sales*: This is the top line of the income statement. It is likely that this will not appear as net sales but rather as sales or revenue.

Keep in mind that the Z-score is a financial risk indicator—it does not tell us if the supplier has adequate capacity or whether or not it can satisfy quality or delivery requirements. It would be a mistake to place undying faith in the Z-Score (or any bankruptcy predictor), just as it is a mistake to rely on a single indicator for almost anything. After the financial meltdown of 2008, any models that were backward looking (which includes most financial statements and forecasting models) became questionable in terms of their validity.

Because of its longevity, the Z-Score is ingrained as a bankruptcy predictor in the minds of most practitioners and academics. Relying on a single predictor of supplier health, however, is a risky strategy. You would not go to a doctor for a physical and then have only your temperature taken. And, if you had a serious illness you might not want to rely only on one opinion. Combining the Z-Score technique with other third-party bankruptcy indicators as well as a set of financial ratios should lead to more robust conclusions about the financial state of a supplier or customer.

Other Third-Party Supplier Bankruptcy Predictors

Not every company has the resources or expertise to evaluate hundreds or even thousands of suppliers from a financial risk perspective. It is also safe to assume that financial data about suppliers is not always easy to obtain. For these reasons, buyers often rely on third-party assessments to support their efforts. Rapid Ratings (www.rapidratings.com) provides a multi-part report that provides a detailed discussion of a company's financial health rating. The rating, which ranges from 0 to 100, includes multiple years of trend data for comparison purposes. Dun & Bradstreet (www.dnb.com) offers a suite of risk management products under a category called *supplier risk manager*. Two analytic tools are available that use predictive scores, including the Supplier Stability Indicator, a predictor of near-term (90–120 days) financial and operational stability, and the Supplier Evaluation Risk Rating, which predicts the likelihood that a company will obtain legal relief from creditors or cease operations without paying creditors in full over the next 12 months. These reports are especially useful when evaluating private suppliers.

EXPENSES ARE BAD, INVESTMENTS ARE GOOD

The world of finance deals extensively with investments while supply and supply chain management deals extensively with expenses. It is safe to conclude that most corporate executives generally think about supply management activities as expenses rather than investments that offer a clear and substantial payback. Unfortunately, a basic tenet of financial thinking is that expenses are bad, investments are good. Expenses are a necessary evil, and as such, this evil should be minimized whenever possible.

Certain investment techniques are used whenever a company evaluates capital projects, such as building a new facility, buying a piece of equipment, or installing a new IT system. It is not realistic to assume that every initiative in supply management involves a capital project. In fact, most supply initiatives will not involve capital projects. When the initiative is not part of a capital expenditure, it is usually treated as an expense. Never forget, the prevailing view among most managers is that investments are good and expenses are bad.

What if we could present certain initiatives, such as supplier development, as investments rather than expenses and apply financial techniques that are well recognized by executive management? The following summarizes the three financial investment techniques—simple payback, net present value (NPV), and internal rate of return (IRR)—that will help supply managers present their initiatives in terms of investments rather than expenses.

Simple Payback

Simple payback represents the length of time required to recover the cost of an investment without considering the time value of money. Payback may be best suited for less complex projects or applications where management wants a relatively quick snapshot of the payback period. This method does not consider the time value of money, so the calculations are relatively straightforward. The payback method is popular because it is relatively simple and provides a quick indication that shows how soon a company will recover invested funds.[2] If more than one alternative is being considered, the alternative with the quickest payback is considered the best choice. Payback analysis is all about how quickly a company recoups its investment.

Assume that a company decides to put forth a cash outlay of $150,000 to purchase equipment to support an upgrade at a supplier's work cell. Project planners have identified the savings that are a direct result of the upgrade to be $85,000 each year over a three-year expected life. A payback analysis reveals that the payback is one year and nine months, or 1.75 years.

How did we arrive at the payback of 1.75 years? During Year 1 $85,000 of the $150,000 in investment was realized as savings, leaving $65,000 of the investment outstanding. Given that the second year savings are also expected to be $85,000, the remaining $65,000 of the investment will be realized after just over nine months ($65,000 is approximately three-quarters of $85,000, and nine months is three-quarters of a year). The logic applied here is the same even if cash flows from the investment are not uniform each year—which Table 8.2 illustrates. A lower payback period is better than a higher payback period.

Table 8.2 Simple payback period illustrated

	Alternative A	Alternative B
Cash outflow Year 0	($500)	($475)
Cash inflow Year 1	$230	$200
Cash inflow Year 2	$200	$210
Cash inflow Year 3	$140	$220
Payback period	2.5 years	2.34 years

Figures are in thousands of dollars.

Alternative A: In Year 1, a $230 cash inflow leaves $270 of the $500 Year 0 investment remaining; in Year 2 a $200 cash inflow leaves $70 of the $270 investment amount remaining; in Year 3 a $140 cash inflow will cover the remaining $70 investment amount in six months, ($70 / $140 = .5 of a year).

Alternative B: In Year 1, a $200 cash inflow leaves $275 of the $475 Year 0 investment remaining; in Year 2 a $200 cash inflow leaves $75 of the $275 investment amount remaining; in Year 3 a $220 cash inflow will cover the remaining $75 investment amount in four months, ($75 / $220 = .34 of a year).

Net Present Value

A company may require a more complex financial assessment of a project. A well-established evaluation technique in the finance world is called NPV, which represents the present value (PV) of projected future cash flows or benefits discounted at an appropriate cost of capital or hurdle rate less the cost of the investment.

NPV, which is a more complex financial evaluation compared with the simple payback method, follows a multistep process:[3]

1. *Estimate the initial cash outlay*: This includes the primary capital expenditures as well as any other costs to pursue the project. Unless told otherwise, initial cash outlays occur at *Time 0*.

2. *Determine annual incremental operating cash flows*: This requires quantifying the net savings that result from the project. One way to identify these savings is to perform a cost-benefit analysis to arrive at annual benefits due to the project. Another way is to prepare an estimated income statement and cash flow with and without the project (what is called *pro forma* statements). The difference represents the incremental impact due to the project.

3. *Project the terminal cash flow or expected salvage value*: Add the salvage value of any assets at the final project year's operating cash flow.

4. *Determine the PV of the future cash flows*: This represents the value in today's dollars of the benefit stream over each year of the project. Future flows are discounted by some percentage provided by finance, such as a hurdle or discount rate.

5. *Determine the NPV of the project*: The project's NPV is the sum of the PVs of the discounted cash flows (benefits received each year) less the outflows (investment cost). A positive number means the current value of the discounted future benefits exceeds the project hurdle rate.

The challenge when using any financial investment technique is arriving at accurate investment costs and incremental savings due to the project. Most of us have sat through presentations where financial costs and savings are taken as absolutes without question. Oftentimes no one challenges the savings since they appear in a highly regarded financial format. These investment models always arrive at an output number. The question becomes whether the costs are modeled correctly.

The Hurdle or Discount Rate

An important financial topic is something called the hurdle rate. In capital project evaluation, the hurdle rate, which is presented as a percent, is the minimum rate that a company must earn before approving a project.[4] If a proposed investment or project is considered to have an unusually risky outcome, the hurdle rate could be adjusted to reflect higher risk. Most companies establish their hurdle rate as equivalent to the cost to obtain capital, or the cost of raising cash through equity and debt. Companies with no equity only use the cost of debt, while companies with equity and debt arrive at a weighted average of the two.[5] Calculating the hurdle rate is the responsibility of finance.

Technically, the rate at which we subject investments in an NPV analysis is called the discount rate. It does not have to be the company's hurdle rate. Companies have different ways of identifying the discount rate, including using the expected return of other investment choices with a similar level of risk.

An essential part of the NPV process is the formula that is used to discount future cash inflows at an appropriate rate into current values. While tables and calculators are available that provide values to discount future flows to the present, the following formula shows how to arrive at the present value of a future value:

$$(PV) = \text{Future Value (FV)} / (1 + r)^n$$

Where r = the discount or hurdle rate and n = the future value period. Table 8.3 illustrates the mechanics of the NPV calculation. Project A provides higher expected return.

Table 8.3   NPV illustrated

	Alternative A	Alternative B
Cash outlay Year 0	($750)	($675)
Cash inflow Year 1	$300	$310
Cash inflow Year 2	$425	$300
Cash inflow Year 3	$400	$350

Discount rate = 13%; figures are in thousands of dollars.

Project "A" NPV calculation:

Present value for Year 1 inflow: PV = $300 / (1 + .13)^1 = $265.48
Present value for Year 2 inflow: PV = $425 / (1 + .13)^2 = $332.03
Present value for Year 3 inflow: PV = $400 / (1 + .13)^3 = $277.78

Present value of inflows: $875.29
Less Year 0 outlay: $750.00

Project "A" NPV: **$125.29**

Project "B" NPV calculation:

Present value for Year 1 inflow: PV = $310 / (1 + .13)^1 = $274.34
Present value for Year 2 inflow: PV = $300 / (1 + .13)^2 = $234.37
Present value for Year 3 inflow: PV = $350 / (1 + .13)^3 = $243.05

Present value of inflows: $751.76
Less Year 0 outlay: $675.00

Project "B" NPV: **$ 76.76**

Internal Rate of Return

A similar concept to NPV is IRR, which represents the discount rate that makes the NPV of all future cash flows from a particular project equal to zero.[6] While NPV and IRR are conceptually similar, they have a major difference. The first three steps of the five steps for arriving at the NPV presented earlier are identical for the IRR. With NPV, the rate at which we discount the future cash flows (Step 4) is provided by finance at the onset of the analysis. The NPV analysis cannot happen without knowing that rate. With IRR, the output of the analysis is a rate of percentage return for the project that makes the PV of the discounted cash flows equal to the cost of the investment or project. A company's hurdle or discount rate has no direct bearing during the calculations. Obviously, we want to select projects that have the highest IRR and exceed the company's hurdle rate.

Table 8.4 illustrates the mechanics of arriving at an IRR. Our objective is to identify the IRR where the percentage return for the project makes the PV of the discounted cash flows equal to the cost of the investment or project. Here

Table 8.4 IRR illustrated

	Project
Cash outlay Year 0	($900)
Cash inflow Year 1	$300
Cash inflow Year 2	$325
Cash inflow Year 3	$425
Cash inflow Year 4	$350

Project IRR calculation at 22%:

PV for Year 1 inflow: PV = $300 / (1 + .22)^1 = $245.90
PV for Year 2 inflow: PV = $325 / (1 + .22)^2 = $218.12
PV for Year 3 inflow: PV = $425 / (1 + .22)^3 = $234.05
PV for Year 4 inflow: PV = $350 / (1 + .22)^4 = $158.06

PV of cash inflows: $856.13
Less cash outlay at Year 0 $900.00

Difference between inflows and outlay: **($43.87) (22%, too high)**

Project IRR calculation at 20%:

PV for Year 1 inflow: PV = $300 / (1 + .20)^1 = $250.00
PV for Year 2 inflow: PV = $325 / (1 + .20)^2 = $225.69
PV for Year 3 inflow: PV = $425 / (1 + .20)^3 = $245.95
PV for Year 4 inflow: PV = $350 / (1 + .20)^4 = $168.79

PV of cash inflows: $890.43
Less cash outlay at Year 0: $900.00

Difference between inflows and outlay: **($9.57) (IRR = appx. 20%)**

we use a trial-and-error method to identify the return rate where the discounted cash flows equal the initial cash outlay. Financial calculators are available that allow the user to input the data to calculate the IRR with the push of a button. In this example, a 22% IRR is too high, while 20% is the rate where the PV of the discounted cash flows equals the initial cost of the investment. Whether this IRR is good or not depends on a number of factors, including a comparison to a company's required hurdle or discount rate or comparisons to other possible projects. As with NPV, higher values are better.

One way to shift management's attitude toward expenses is to remove expenses as the primary focus. Applying financial investment techniques to supply initiatives, such as supplier development projects, represents a radical new way of thinking.

"R" YOU READY TO RUN WITH THE BIG DOGS?

Supply management and supply chain management professionals need to articulate the impact of their initiatives on corporate level indicators. Rest assured that a corporate performance indicator that starts with the word *return* is almost always a key indicator. They are the big dogs of the corporate world. We will highlight three indicators here—return on assets (ROA), return on investment (ROI), and return on invested capital (ROIC). Understanding how your supply efforts affect these indicators conveys a higher level of financial sophistication on your part.

Return on Assets

ROA, which is a ratio usually presented in the form of a percentage, reflects the return generated from invested capital (assets). ROA provides an idea of how efficiently assets are utilized to generate earnings.

The basic formula for ROA is net income divided by total assets. If a company earns $5 million and has assets of $50 million for a certain period, its ROA is 10%. The ROA formula appears in a variety of formats, which is true for most "R" level indicators. Some companies use average assets over a time period for the denominator, while others use the asset figure that appears on the balance sheet. Others rely on a return on net asset (RONA) calculation, which uses fixed assets plus net working capital rather than total assets in the denominator. Still others replace net income in the numerator with EBIT.

Supply and supply chain professionals affect ROA primarily in two ways. First, inventory is treated as a current asset on a company's balance sheet. Effective inventory management (which should be an obsession with supply chain professionals) should lead to less on-hand inventory to support a given level of business requirements. Lower inventory reduces the size of the ROA denominator (a good thing). More effective inventory management will also lead to lower inventory carrying costs, which lower expenses and raise net income. This benefits the numerator of the ROA calculation. Second, supply management professionals can take actions to reduce the unit cost of inventory, which results in two outcomes: (1) the total value of inventory becomes lower on the balance sheet, which benefits the denominator of ROA and (2) the unit cost of the inventory becomes lower, which lowers the cost of goods sold and increases gross profit and eventually net income. This benefits the numerator of the ROA formula.

At first glance, ROA appears to be just another corporate indicator. In fact, many finance professionals do not view this indicator as anything special. In the supply chain world, however, it should be thought of as a superordinate measure. A superordinate measure is one that cannot be achieved unless functional groups work together and coordinate their efforts. The presence of superordinate measures demands that different groups succeed or fail collectively. Supply and supply chain professionals from one end of the supply chain to the other have their fingerprints all over the ROA measure. This indicator is a big deal.

Return on Investment

ROI attempts to measure the profitability of an investment and, as such, there is no one right calculation.[7] ROI is often used to calculate the return from specific investments, and the term investment might be used too loosely. A marketing executive might be interested in the financial return from a marketing campaign (i.e., the investment) while an investor wants to know the return from a particular stock. When it is used in these contexts the ROI is a relatively straightforward calculation: ROI = (gain from investment − cost of investment) / (cost of investment).

Many sources interchange the definition of ROI and the basic definition just provided for ROA, particularly when looking at returns at the corporate level. This can be confusing. Keep in mind that the calculation for ROI and its definition can be modified to suit a particular situation. This flexibility has a downside, since ROI calculations can be easily manipulated to suit a particular purpose.[8]

Even though ROI is widely used, and most people would say ROI as their first choice if asked to name a measure that starts with the word *return*, supply professionals should probably rely on ROA when evaluating the impact of supply initiatives on corporate performance.

Return on Invested Capital

ROIC is one of the most important financial indicators in use today. ROIC is also referred to as *return on capital* or *return on total capital*. It is a calculation that assesses a company's efficiency (i.e., its return percentage) at allocating the capital under its control to profitable investments. The ROIC measure gives a sense of how well a company is using its money to generate returns.[9] ROIC is always calculated as a percentage and is usually expressed as an annualized or trailing twelve-month value. It should be compared to a company's cost of capital or hurdle rate to determine whether the company is creating value.[10]

An ROIC that is less than a company's cost of capital or hurdle rate means the company is losing value and liquidating itself, potentially to the point where the company becomes insolvent. Similar to the ROA indicator, a search of respected financial sources reveals different ways to calculate ROIC. Some of those ROIC formulas include:

- ROIC = (net income − dividends) / (debt + equity)
- ROIC = (net income − dividends) / (total capital)
- ROIC = (EBIT) / (employed capital)

Although agreement about the exact contents of this measure is hard to come by, many finance professionals will agree that ROIC is the granddaddy of corporate financial performance. Understanding how ROIC is derived and appreciating how your supply initiatives affect its components is something that most of your counterparts will not be able to do.

If you can articulate how your accomplishments affect these corporate indicators, you might just be ready to run with the big dogs. The importance of linking supply management outcomes to corporate-level indicators is growing. Since finance is the language of business, why not learn to speak that language? When an executive asks, "What have you done for me lately?" you will be able to show this individual in no uncertain terms the linkage between supply management initiatives and corporate results.

MANAGING WORKING CAPITAL THE RIGHT WAY

An area where finance falls short from a supply chain perspective relates to managing working capital. Finance and supply chain professionals view working capital and its management quite differently. Recall from the Z-Score discussion that the technical definition of working capital is the difference between current assets and current liabilities. Unfortunately, the way that finance experts manage working capital is often harming rather than helping supply chain relationships. Finance professionals stress the management of receivables and payables when managing working capital. Most finance professionals have no problem holding off payments to suppliers for as long as possible.

Supply chain managers have (or should have) a different perspective of working capital and its management. Besides defining working capital from an operational rather than a financial perspective, supply chain professionals generally focus on managing the inventory portion of the working capital equation. The inventory portion is not trivial at most companies. The following provides an operational definition of working capital:

Operational working capital = (raw materials + work in process + finished goods) + accounts receivable − accounts payable

As mentioned, the most common approach taken by finance professionals when managing working capital is to pay less attention to inventory and more attention to accelerating receivables and delaying payables. Unfortunately, delaying payables to suppliers often damages buyer-seller relationships. A number of research studies have concluded that getting paid in a reasonable time is one of the most important outcomes that suppliers seek from their relationship with a buyer (this will be discussed further in a later chapter). Far too many finance professionals disregard this important point as they unilaterally extend payment terms with suppliers.

In any economic downturn, or in the quest to show financial improvements quickly, companies often consider improving cash flow by extending their payment cycle to suppliers. Larger companies in particular will use this strategy since they are not worried about being cut off by suppliers.[11] Typically, this strategy involves stretching payments from net 30 days to 45, 60, or even 90 days and beyond. Suppliers usually see this as a coercive use of power.

Working cooperatively with functional groups, suppliers, and customers offers another way to improve working capital that does not involve an excessive reliance on extending payment terms. Better firms know that not all working capital management techniques are equal in their effectiveness or how they affect buyer-seller relationships. Why then does finance insist on emphasizing the one approach that we know angers suppliers?[12]

Managing inventory is the best way for supply and supply chain professionals to make a financial contribution through the effective management of working capital. Literally dozens of ways exist to manage the volume, velocity, and value of inventory across a supply chain. Some powerful approaches include:

- Pursuing perfect inventory record accuracy
- Developing well-established procedures for handling physical inventory and inventory records
- Relying on perpetual rather than periodic inventory systems
- Using IT-based supply chain planning and execution systems
- Improving the accuracy of demand estimates (forecasts are part of a demand estimate)
- Simplifying and reusing components during product development to lower component costs

- Financially modeling the impact of inventory initiatives on corporate indicators
- Modeling the supply chain to identify bottlenecks that affect the flow of material from suppliers to customers
- Relying on cross-functional improvement teams for better management of the volume, velocity, and value of inventory across the supply chain
- Pursuing lean supply chain initiatives, including pull systems, just-in-time delivery, and reduced machine set-up times
- Using quantitative techniques to better manage inventory, including economic order quantity models and min-max reorder point systems
- Working with finance to measure and improve the cash conversion cycle and the order-to-cash cycle time

As these points reveal, there is no shortage of ways to make improvements that affect the physical and financial inventory that a firm maintains.

DON'T MAKE DECISIONS WITH INCOMPLETE INFORMATION

It should come as no surprise to say that companies continue to make many purchase decisions based primarily on price. After all, price is easy to iden-tify and everyone knows how much they pay for something. Unfortunately, less known is the fact that unit price (i.e., what we think we paid) never equals total cost (i.e., what we actually end up paying). Basing decisions on price, although easy, is not always the right thing to do.

Making decisions with more complete information requires taking a total cost of ownership perspective. Total cost includes the expected and unexpected elements that increase the unit cost of a good, service, or piece of equipment.[13] The logic behind the development of total cost models is that the unit cost or price of something never equals its total cost. Understanding the size of the gap between a unit price and its true total cost must be an ongoing pursuit.

The reasons for measuring total cost are quite persuasive. It becomes next to impossible to select a higher price option (but a lower total cost option) without some way of supporting that decision. Total cost models also help companies identify the relative impact of different cost elements, allowing management to see what is driving total cost. These systems also track the impact of changes from a cost perspective. And, total cost systems help gain management's atten-tion regarding the areas where cost reduction efforts will have their greatest payback. Total cost data also support fact-based rather than subjective decision making, something that makes the quality purists quite happy. It would be a challenge to identify reasons why we would not want to capture total cost data, at least for the more critical or high cost items.

Regardless of where a company applies total cost models, each total cost model attempts to capture data beyond unit price. The reality is that total cost models, like forecasting models, almost always have some degree of unreliability. The question becomes how much unreliability is embedded in the model. Unreliability is largely a function of the type of data that comprises the model.

The cost elements (unit price and transportation costs are two examples) that populate total cost models can be segmented into four categories that start with the letter "A." The first "A" category—the one that provides the highest reliability—includes *actual data*. Unit price, transportation charges, and tariffs are examples of actual cost data. The second most reliable "A" category includes *approximations* or *averages*. The key feature here is that the data are at least based on figures derived from your own internal sources.

Moving down the spectrum, the next "A" category includes data based on *assumptions*. Assumptions come from external sources that form the basis for applying a total cost. Be careful not to develop total cost models that are loaded with external assumptions, something that will make the model highly suspect. A final data category that starts with "A" includes data that are *absent*. Why might data be absent? The challenge with any cost model is that, at times, the cost to collect data outweighs the value of the data. At other times, the sheer number of possible cost elements that could be part of the model is overwhelming. And, at times, a company simply fails to include a relevant cost.

A search of the total cost literature leads to several conclusions. First, a wide variety of cost elements are included in total cost models. Literally dozens of cost elements could populate a cost model, particularly when dealing with international transactions. Second, except for price and transportation costs, no clear consensus exists regarding what elements to include in the models. Total cost models are not standardized across companies or industries.

Types of Total Cost Models

Total cost models are part of a family of measurement systems called cost-based systems. No agreed-upon typology of total cost systems exists. As it relates to supply chain management, we often see the application of three different types of total cost models. This includes total landed cost models, supplier performance index models, and life-cycle cost models.

Total Landed Cost Models

A total landed cost model is often used when evaluating suppliers prior to making a selection decision; although that is not the only time they are used. Landed cost is the sum of all costs associated with obtaining a product—including acquisition planning; unit price; inbound cost of freight, duty, and taxes; inspection; quality; and material handling, storage, and retrieval. Some companies will also use landed cost models when they are evaluating whether or not to shift work from one supplier to another or when evaluating whether to insource work that was previously outsourced. Total landed cost models should also be used when doing business with suppliers on an ongoing basis.

It is best to start with unit price and build up the total cost as goods move from origin to destination when developing total landed cost models. Cost elements are often divided into categories that reflect a logical progression of material through the supply chain. The following list illustrates these categories along with examples of costs that fall within each category:

- *Within country of manufacture*: unit price, storage, labor, quality, overhead, obsolescence, packaging, risk or disruption, exchange rates, inventory carrying charges
- *In transit to country of sale*: transportation charges, fuel surcharges, insurance, port charges, handling, security, banking fees, broker fees, potential detention charges, duties, handling agency charges, inventory carrying charges
- *Within the country of sale*: local transportation and handling, storage fees, taxes, safety stock, inventory carrying charges, production yield, maintenance, quality, overhead allocation, payment terms

Spreadsheet software is ideal for developing total landed cost models. If your company does not base its important purchasing decisions on total landed cost, then it is time to assemble a team to change that shortcoming.

Supplier Performance Index Models

Various models attempt to capture the true cost of doing business with a supplier on an ongoing basis. Perhaps the best known of these models is something called the supplier performance index (SPI). SPI calculations are helpful when tracking supplier improvement over time, when quantifying the severity of performance problems, when deciding which suppliers should stay or exit the supply base, and when establishing minimum levels of supplier performance.

The SPI is a total cost model that presents its output in the form of a standardized index or ratio. It assumes that any quality or other infraction committed by a supplier increases the total cost of doing business with that supplier. If a company can track each supplier nonconformance and assign a cost to it, the calculation of a standardized SPI becomes relatively straightforward. The SPI calculation for a specific period uses the following formula:

$$SPI = (\text{cost of material} + \text{nonconformance costs}) / (\text{cost of material})$$

Let's say a supplier delivers $250,000 worth of parts to a company in the second quarter of a year. The supplier also commits three infractions that quarter—a late delivery, missing documentation, and some defective units with one of its shipments. The buying company assigns $20,200 in total nonconformance charges for these infractions. The supplier's SPI for the third quarter is 1.08, or (($250,000 + $20,200) / $250,000).

An SPI of 1.08 means the total cost of doing business with this supplier is 8% higher than the unit price, at least in terms of quality-related issues. If the unit price of a supplier's product is $100, then the estimated adjusted cost of that item is $108.80 ($100 × 1.08). Because the SPI is a standardized metric, it allows comparisons between suppliers. A supplier with a higher SPI has a higher total cost than one with a lower SPI. It is important to compare suppliers within the same commodity to ensure valid comparisons.

Unfortunately, the SPI is not as straightforward as just presented. The base SPI calculation has a built–in bias against suppliers that provide deliveries with a lower total value. We overcome this bias with the calculation of a quantity (Q) adjustment factor. The Q factor allows valid SPI comparisons by removing the inherent bias against suppliers with a lower total value of deliveries, which are often smaller suppliers. If we want to make our total cost models as accurate as possible, then we have to consider the Q adjustment factor. Please refer to Chapter 12 of the book *Supply Chain Financial Management* for a detailed presentation regarding how to calculate Q adjustments.

Tracking and calculating the SPI does not require a major IT effort. The challenge is to identify the nonconformance that occur and then assign a charge to those infractions. Failure to record nonconformance when it occurs results in an underspecified SPI model. Missing data means the supplier's SPI value is too low, which makes the supplier appear to be a better performer. The use of the SPI model requires discipline.

Life-Cycle Cost Models

Life-cycle cost models are usually what comes to mind when thinking about total costs analysis. This type of model is most often used when evaluating capital decisions that cover an extended period, often for equipment and facilities. Most life-cycle cost models are used to evaluate capital decisions rather than the purchase of everyday components and services.

Developers of life-cycle cost models often allocate their cost elements across four broad categories that reflect usage over time:[14]

- *Unit price*: This is the price paid including purchase terms
- *Acquisition costs*: This includes all costs associated with delivering equipment, such as buying, ordering, and freight charges to the customer

- *Usage costs*: Includes all the costs to operate the equipment, including installation, energy consumption, maintenance, reliability, spare parts, and yield and efficiency during production
- *End-of-life costs*: Includes all costs incurred when removing equipment from service less any proceeds received for resale, scrap, or salvage

The flow through a life cycle is essentially one of buying, shipping, installing, using, maintaining, and disposing. Life-cycle costs apply whether a capital good is sourced domestically or internationally. This type of model should not be a one-and-done type of thing. Companies should compare the assumptions made during the development of life-cycle estimates with actual data as they become available. This will help validate the life-cycle model.

CONCLUDING THOUGHTS

Combining supply management and financial management will take many supply professionals out of their comfort zone. For supply management to continue to mature as a discipline, it is essential to speak the language of business as well as to use the tools and techniques that finance professionals have developed over the last 100 years. This chapter summarized five key areas where financial thinking supports supply and supply chain management. Explaining the impact of lower negotiated prices on improved gross profit and net income, for example, and then showing how that improves ROA builds a powerful case regarding the importance of supply management. Demonstrating the value of supplier development initiatives by using financial investment techniques will certainly be better received than expressing these initiatives only in terms of expenses. And, you will find that making supply decisions based on total cost data is a much better way to go through life.

REFERENCES

1. From http://www.investopedia.com/terms/a/altman.asp.
2. S. Weaver and F. Weston, *Strategic Financial Management: Application of Corporate Finance* (Mason, OH: Thomson South-Western): 337.
3. Weaver and Weston, 382.
4. From http://www.investopedia.com/terms/h/hurdlerate.asp.
5. From http://smallbusiness.chron.com/assessing-projects-hurdle-rate-75860.html.
6. From http://www.investopedia.com/terms/i/irr.asp.
7. From http://www.investopedia.com/terms/r/returnoninvestment.asp.

8. From http://www.investopedia.com/terms/r/returnoninvestment.asp.
9. From   http://www.investopedia.com/terms/r/returnoninvestmentcapital .asp.
10. From   http://www.investopedia.com/terms/r/returnoninvestmentcapital .asp.
11. From http://www.cpapracticeadvisor.com/blog/10628023/why-extending -payables-is-a-really-bad-idea.
12. Smart suppliers will calculate the additional cost to them when buyers extend payment terms and then attempt to build that into their price. See *Supply Chain Financial Management* (page 235) for a discussion of how to calculate cost adders due to extended payment times.
13. This discussion of total cost is based partially on work by R. J. Trent and L. Roberts, *Managing Global Supply and Risk* (Fort Lauderdale, FL: J. Ross Publishing, 2010), Chapter 4.
14. R. M. Moncka, R. J. Trent, and R. H. Handfield, *Purchasing and Supply Chain Management* (Mason, OH: Thomson South-Western, 2005): 364–365.

9

WINNING THROUGH COLLABORATION

Pressure to improve performance across virtually every industry and company is relentless and severe. Given this pressure, a logical question centers around what will be the emerging business practices and processes that will support the next generation of improvements? For an increasing number of firms, their next game-changing advances will come from collaboration with suppliers.

This chapter explores the important topic of collaboration, a topic that promises to become increasingly important as companies search for their next source of competitive advantage. The chapter provides an in-depth understanding of collaboration, including the important role that trust plays within collaborative relationships. Leading-edge topics that are related to collaboration, including vested outsourcing and innovation sourcing, are also presented.

UNDERSTANDING COLLABORATION

Let's begin our discussion of collaboration with a tale of two enterprises that pursued similar projects but arrived at decidedly different end states. The first enterprise is a global logistics company with employees and operations located around the world. The second is the postal service of a major country. Although they are different organizations in terms of their businesses, they share some commonality. Each has thousands of employees who wear uniforms and interact with customers on a daily basis. Without question uniforms are an important part of each organization's brand image that also affects employee morale. Each operates across a variety of climates with a diverse workforce. And, each decided it was time to undertake a major redesign of its uniforms.

At this point, the similarities end. The logistics company, knowing that its expertise in uniform design was severely limited, asked its long-time uniform supplier to lead the redesign. This supplier met with employees to understand their diverse requirements, organized fashion shows to present potential designs modeled by employees, created online catalogs displaying the new uniforms, placed facilities outside the U.S. to respond quickly to local and regional uniform orders, and developed an online ordering system so that local sites could order uniforms easily. Simplified billing and automatic cross-charging against each location's operating budget also came with the package. The project resulted in uniforms that were well-received by employees, with the entire project requiring about half the time as the previous redesign. This project even strengthened the working relationship between the two companies. What is not to like here?

The postal service took a different and much less successful approach. It decided it would develop new uniforms internally without a supplier's help, even though it had no particular knowledge about that business. After a prolonged development process featuring minimal employee or supplier involvement, the new uniforms were rolled out to a decidedly unenthusiastic response. Besides not being stylish, the company specified fabrics that became quite revealing when wet, something that most of the letter carriers experienced at one time or another. The postal service humbly returned to the drawing board with a supplier's help to develop uniforms that were a bit more accepting and a bit less revealing.

What is the lesson here? Collaborating with an expert can mean the difference between success and failure. As this example illustrates, tapping into a supplier's expertise early can dramatically alter the outcome of a project. And it's important to know what you know and, perhaps more important, what you don't know. If what you don't know is important enough, relying on a third party through a collaborative relationship might just be your ticket to paradise.

What is Collaboration?

A connotation of goodness is associated with the word *collaborate*. And when something is widely perceived as good, how could it not be worthwhile and important? With that said, there is no guarantee that collaboration will lead to better performance any more than new product development using state-of-the art techniques guarantees product success. Collaboration, like so much that is presented throughout this book, is an activity that must lead to an accomplishment. That accomplishment is not guaranteed.

Collaboration, which was discussed in Chapter 2 as an overused and often misused term, involves *two or more enterprises working together to achieve shared strategic goals that produce greater value for all parties than could be gained by acting alone or by operating in a noncollaborative environment.* Some important characteristics define collaborative relationships between suppliers and buyers. Collaborative relationships feature deeper and richer interactions between parties than what occurs with basic cooperation. True collaboration is also characterized by shared processes, joint actions, mutual trust, executive-to-executive communication, and risk and reward sharing. It also features a joint commitment of people, processes, capital, information, facilities, and other resources as required. An easy way to think about collaborative relationships is to think of the three Rs—a true collaborative relationship features the sharing of risk, resources, and rewards.

While many interchange the terms cooperate and collaborate, others will argue (rightfully) that a collaborative relationship is the most intense and highest form of supply chain relationship. Recall that a cooperative relationship, which typically underlies longer term purchase contracts, features the open sharing of information. What they do not typically feature are more intensive forms of communication and the sharing of resources, risks, and rewards. An analogy between cooperative and collaborative relationships involves dogs. While all dogs are animals, not all animals are dogs. While all collaborative relationships are cooperative, not all cooperative relationships are collaborative.

Collaborative relationships are like a best friend—they should be special, unique, and relatively rare. If someone says he or she has 20 best friends, one of two things are likely true. Either this person does not understand the concept of a best friend—or this person is issuing a cry for help. When a company maintains it has 20 or more collaborative relationships with suppliers, it is likely mistaking collaboration with the cooperation that occurs with longer term contracting.

Collaborative relationships are true *win-win* relationships. Recall from Chapter 2 that win-win is also an overused term today. Like many terms, win-win does not come with a universally accepted definition. One way to look at win-win relationships is through a value lens. Win-win relationships feature a variable rather than fixed amount of value that is potentially available to the parties within a relationship. By working together, the parties can grow the amount of value they derive from that relationship. As value grows, each party has the opportunity to capture ever-increasing amounts of value.

Win-lose relationships feature a fixed amount of value that the parties compete over. No appreciable attempt is made to alter the size of the value pie through cooperative or collaborative efforts. Any gain by one party must come at the expense of the other, or what is described as a zero-sum game. Win-win relationships are about expanding the value pie; win-lose relationships are about dividing the value pie. The differences between win-win and win-lose relationships are not trivial. By definition, collaborative relationships are win-win relationships. To be otherwise contradicts what a collaborative relationship is all about.

At times the term *alliance* is used when describing supply chain collaboration. Without question, strategic alliances should be collaborative by design (some alliances are lower level and focus primarily on cost reduction). If a strategic alliance does not stress collaboration, then the alliance is likely suffering from some serious deficiencies. What, then, is an alliance? One company's perspective of an alliance is:

> *An alliance represents a long-term, mutually beneficial business relationship containing specific elements unique to the relationship—an agreement detailing performance requirements and conditions, structures to promote successful interaction between parties, organizational alignment, clear measures of success, and a high level of mutual commitment.*

While alliances are collaborative by design, not all collaboration is performed within the context of an alliance. Most, if not all formal alliances are expected to continue over an extended period (think of the Star Alliance in the airline industry). A great deal of collaboration has nothing to do with formal alliances. Collaboration is often aligned to specific projects that have a defined end date.

Many factors can affect the success or failure of collaborative relationships. Unfortunately, except for the need for trust, no single set of success factors is generalizable to all collaborative efforts. What affects the success of one collaborative relationship may not necessarily affect to the same degree the success of another relationship. Table 9.1 provides a listing of the more noteworthy factors that we know have the potential to affect collaboration success.

Table 9.1   Factors that affect the success or failure of collaboration

• Executive commitment, often at the highest organizational levels, supports the objectives and goals of the collaboration
• A rigorous selection process is in place to identify collaborative opportunities and candidates
• The collaboration features joint strategy development, problem solving, and continuous improvement efforts
• Goal congruency exists between parties to the collaboration
• Support mechanisms and documents define the strategic aims of the collaboration
• Ongoing collaboration features a continuous focus on win-win opportunities
• Extensive communication and open information sharing takes place between parties
• A high level of trust characterizes the relationship
• The parties commit resources specifically to the relationship
• The collaboration has clear measures of accomplishment rather than activity-based measures
• Internal education regarding the goals and expected benefits from the collaboration takes place
• The collaboration continues when personnel change
• The collaboration achieves success, which promotes further success
• Risk sharing is part of the collaboration

What Companies, Consultants, and Academics Are Saying About Collaboration

It is a challenge to find anecdotal accounts in the press concluding that collaboration does not work or that the future of collaboration is anything less than stellar. Most collaboration failures at the corporate level are not reported or publicized, at least by the companies involved.

Research studies offer conflicting conclusions regarding the value of collaboration. One source maintains that corporate alliances, which are collaborative by design, have no better than a 50% chance of yielding returns to each partner above and beyond their cost of capital.[1] Interestingly, a major issue concerns the widespread use of service agreements that emphasize what each side commits to delivering within the relationship rather than what each hopes to gain. These agreements emphasize operational performance rather than strategic objectives. A later section addresses this topic in more detail.

Research on supplier collaboration during product development has also produced contradictory results. Some studies show a positive relationship between collaboration and development success, other studies show no relationship with success, and still others indicate a negative relationship between supplier involvement and project success. A major study of supplier-buyer collaboration during product development concluded that collaboration positively affects product quality, adherence to product cost targets, adherence to development budgets, and adherence to development schedules.[2]

A longitudinal study of supplier-buyer collaboration (i.e., a study over time) concluded that collaboration with suppliers is worthwhile, with coordination efforts and investments leading to better profits and competitive advantages. This study also found that goal congruence and interpersonal trust facilitate coordination between the parties, and complementary capabilities between the parties facilitate joint effort and investments.[3]

A major conclusion from a review of what others are saying about collaboration is that collaboration does not guarantee success or better performance. Various factors can adversely affect collaborative efforts, including shutting out new ideas from suppliers that are not part of the collaboration as well as complacency over the life of the collaboration. The potential for opportunistic behavior, loss of control, incongruent goals that feature competition instead of cooperation, and incompatible cultures can also be inhibiting factors. And, do not forget the relationship costs that are part of a collaborative relationship, particularly when these relationships resemble alliances. Collaboration can bring its own set of risks.

Another research conclusion is that companies pursue value-chain collaboration within at least three domains. The first domain features collaboration defined largely in terms of demand planning and management, often enabled by Collaborative Planning, Forecasting, and Replenishment (CPFR) techniques and onsite supplier support. This collaboration occurs between producers and retailers, although collaboration can also occur with upstream suppliers and producers. A study involving the European grocery industry, an early adopter of demand planning collaboration, revealed that supplier-retailer collaboration can reduce the total cost of the grocery supply chain by as much as 2% of retail sales.[4]

Corporate case examples are available that describe the value of collaboration. Schering-Plough (now part of Merck) developed a collaboration framework for sharing supply chain information to and from suppliers. Cross-functional teams from suppliers and Schering-Plough participate in this process. Additionally, the company conducts annual executive-level planning meetings with key suppliers and monthly supplier collaboration meetings, largely within the context of a sales and operations planning process. Weekly meetings are conducted with suppliers to finalize short-term plans and schedules.[5]

IBM has pursued supply chain collaboration with its primary suppliers for a number of years. Its view of collaboration involves the integration of demand data, inventory data, and automated transactions into one overall process between IBM and its key suppliers. This is supported by collaboration with logistics services providers. IBM has pursued collaboration by starting with tier-one suppliers and then extending its collaborative efforts into sub-tiers and across its supply chain network.[6]

The second domain where supply chain collaboration often occurs involves technology and product development. Perhaps no company has received more attention for its collaboration efforts than Boeing during the development of the 787 Dreamliner. While the Dreamliner experienced technical hurdles and delays, the scale and scope of the collaboration is unprecedented. Suppliers now provide around 70% of the plane's content; they meet regularly with Boeing personnel to discuss engineering issues and solutions; they designed, built, tested, and verified entire subsystems for the 787; they engaged in project risk sharing by paying their own development costs; and they acted as integrators for tier-two suppliers.

Perhaps more important, Boeing's chairman's noted that a suite of technologies developed for the Dreamliner are being applied to Boeing's next generation of commercial aircraft—the 777X, 787-10, and the 737 Max. He states, "The kind of performance improvements that can be generated by the composite wing and new engines are pretty eye-watering."[7] These eye-watering advancements, which will have a technology shelf life stretching over the next 30 years, are the result of collaboration during product development.

The third domain involves collaboration designed to reduce costs outside of demand planning and management. There are many examples of collaboration involving process industries and suppliers, including onsite supplier representatives who work directly at a buyer's site to reduce facility operating costs. A final conclusion from the literature is that no single or agreed upon model of collaboration exists.

Collaboration and Culture

Do not underestimate the role that culture can have on the success of collaboration. At the country level, culture represents the set of norms, behaviors, beliefs, and customs that exist within a nation's population while corporate culture represents the set of shared attitudes, values, and practices that characterize that institution. Both can impact the ability to engage in a process as intensive as collaboration.

At one time, the prevailing business culture with U.S. companies featured arm's-length relationships. These relationships, best described as adversarial and at times even antagonistic, featured mutual mistrust between supply chain members. Fortunately, most companies have made major strides toward changing their attitudes about the effect that suppliers have on supply chain success. These changing attitudes support the belief that collaboration should be an important part of a firm's business model. Without trust and a culture that recognizes the value of collaboration, a process as intense as collaboration becomes problematic—if not impossible—to achieve.

Companies located in countries where collaboration is an accepted part of the national culture have shown a willingness to maintain that culture when locating their operations outside of the home country. In the U.S. auto industry, for example, studies reveal that the New Domestics (primarily Nissan, Honda, and Toyota) have shown a greater willingness to engage in cooperative and collaborative efforts when seeking cost reductions with tier-one suppliers, including suppliers located in the United States, compared with Ford, GM, and Chrysler.[8] The good news is that a culture that is incongruent with the objectives of collaboration can change over time.

Macro Trends Supporting Collaboration

A number of trends or forces are at work that supports the need for greater supply chain collaboration. These trends include the relentless pressure to improve, the growing importance of product development and innovation, higher level outsourcing, and the need to enhance customer value.

Relentless Pressure to Improve

It is difficult to identify an industry that has not experienced an increase in global competition over the last fifteen years—leading to ever-increasing pressure to improve. Customer and competitor pressure to reduce prices, improve quality, shorten cycle times, improve delivery, rapidly innovate, introduce new technology, and be responsive to change has become today's new normal. At some point, the current ways of doing business will not deliver the kinds of improvement that is demanded by the marketplace. When this occurs, the discussion should turn to a serious assessment of new practices and strategies—including supply chain collaboration.

Growing Importance of Product Development and Innovation

For most firms the development of innovative new products and services comprises a major part of their competitive business model. Something we have come to realize is that an increasing amount of features and technology that differentiate products and services now originates with suppliers. A logical question becomes how to gain differential advantage from the innovation and product development process.

Realizing differential advantages from product development will require suppliers that are willing to share their expertise and resources along with buyers who understand how to manage these special relationships. The ability to collaborate with suppliers during product development will increasingly make the difference between supplier innovations becoming a differentiating part of your product offering versus those same innovations becoming part of your competitor's offering. Increasingly, firms at least appreciate the importance of supply chain collaboration during product development. Chapter 10 discusses becoming the customer of choice to suppliers.

Higher Level Outsourcing

The last 20 years witnessed a growing focus on core competencies and capabilities. While these terms are often overused and misunderstood, the ideas they represent still guide the thinking of many executives. Although firms have always practiced some level of outsourcing, it is only recently that many have been willing to relinquish control over entire portions of their supply chain. While outsourced activities or requirements are presumably not part of a company's internal core capabilities or competencies, they are still critical to success.

As firms focus on those areas where they add the most value, they will invariably rely on a smaller set of suppliers to fill in gaps across the supply chain. As responsibility for entire parts of the supply chain is transferred to third parties, including the decision rights that go with that transference, anything less than a total commitment to strong relationships, including collaboration, will likely suboptimize supply chain performance.

Pressure to Enhance Customer Value

Whether it is from customer or competitors, most companies are experiencing pressure to enhance the value they provide through their product or service offerings. For original equipment manufacturers (OEMs), this often means a shift from providing a product solution to providing a product-service solution. The challenge for many firms is that they lack the full range of capabilities that customers demand. Increasingly, we should expect collaboration with suppliers to be an attractive option for meeting these demands. The time and cost required for formal acquisitions or the internal development of new capabilities is often simply too great from a time and financial perspective. This makes supply chain collaboration a likely response to support the continuous movement up the value creation stream.

It would be a challenge to identify a set of factors that suggest less of a need for collaboration. As an awareness of opportunities offered by collaboration begins to become more widespread, the need to better understand how to capitalize on this important topic becomes ever more critical.

Types of Supply Chain Collaboration

Figure 9.1 illustrates various types of collaborative relationships that, while not an exhaustive listing, does provide a representative set. When supply chain collaboration occurs, the most common type involves two-party collaboration. On the supply side, this may occur during product development or when forming a strategic alliance with a supplier. A significant portion of the two-party collaboration that occurs on the supply side involves working with a single supplier to gain access to technology that enhances the value of end products or services. Supply chain collaboration can also occur that supports the downstream portion of the supply chain. This will generally involve the marketing group collaborating with a specific customer.

More complex models of collaboration will emerge that move beyond the two-party model. As indicated in Figure 9.1, some of these models feature multiple tiers of suppliers and even networks of participants. In particular, we are witnessing a growth in the use of the collaboration featured in Types 3 and 5.

I worked with an OEM where this company successfully pursued a collaboration strategy for the first time. It bypassed the two-party model and instead pursued a multi-party model during the development of a new line of appliances. The OEM relied on a tier-one supplier to assume the role of designer and integrator for a critical electronic system, a role that was new to that supplier. The tier-one supplier (who is now acting as a systems integrator) then worked collaboratively with a tier-two supplier that now acted as an integrator

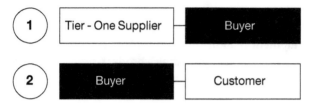

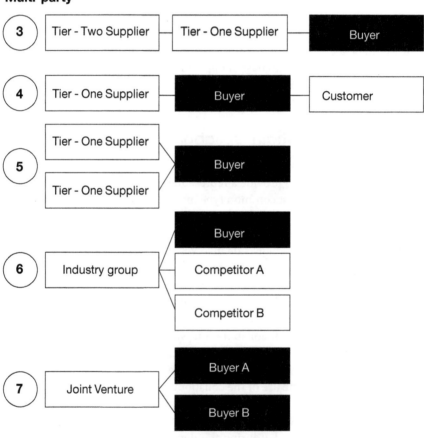

Figure 9.1 Types of collaborative arrangements

for component parts suppliers. This is Type 3 in Figure 9.1. For most companies supply chain collaboration is an evolving concept that takes many forms.

NO TRUST? NO COLLABORATION!

A major factor affecting the strength of any relationship, particularly collaborative ones, is the presence of trust, which is a deceptively simple sounding term. Studies involving trust have been conducted in at least four major areas: game theory, negotiation, interpersonal work relationships, and interorganizational relationships.[9] Disciplines where trust-based research occurs include management, marketing, philosophy, psychology, sociology, and economics.[10] Not surprisingly, as a result of this diversity the body of knowledge involving trust is not well integrated and often lacks coherence.

General perspectives of trust usually describe the concept in terms of the reliability, honesty, and ability of a person or thing. A common view maintains that trust is a belief that someone or something is good, honest, or effective while another perspective refers to a belief in the character, ability, strength, or truth of the party (or parties) within a relationship. In terms of trust with an individual, still another perspective argues that trust is a feeling of confidence in that individual. One source reiterates this perspective when he says that *simply put, trust means confidence in others.*[11] Still, another perspective defines trust as a willingness to be vulnerable to another party. Oftentimes, individuals will say they know trust when they see it—and that they inherently know when it is lacking.

An important conclusion is that three critical elements underlie various perspectives of trust—the potential for betrayal, the temporal aspects of trust, and confident expectations of performance. With this perspective, trust exists only when the potential for betrayal is present; trusting someone therefore creates a sense of vulnerability. Second, trust develops as individuals have the opportunity to demonstrate their trustworthiness over time. This relates to the temporal or longitudinal aspect of trust. Third, trust almost always involves a belief in the performance capabilities of the other party(s).

A widely cited perspective of trust defines three essential components that are necessary for trust-based relationships: the demonstration of ability, benevolence, and integrity.[12] Applied to supplier-buyer relationships, *ability* represents the supplier or buyer's likeliness to perform; *benevolence* represents a supplier or buyer's unwillingness to behave opportunistically toward the other party, particularly when the opportunity to do so presents itself; and *integrity* relates to a commitment to fairness, justice, and ethical behavior.

Central to the concept of trust is trustworthiness. Some researchers characterize the concept of trust as *perceived trustworthiness.* A person who aligns his or her words and actions with their behavior has the best chance of being perceived as trustworthy.[13]

While no single agreed-upon definition of trust exists, most perspectives maintain that trust can exist between individuals, between individuals and organizations, and between organizations. Trust can even exist between a person and an inanimate object (i.e., trust that your car will start in the morning). While differences exist in terms of defining trust, most knowledgeable observers are in agreement that trust, however defined, demonstrates a positive impact on the performance of a relationship.

A stream of research has focused on trust among members of organizational teams. This is critical as suppliers increasingly collaborate with customers by participating on various kinds of teams. Trust among team members indirectly increases team performance by motivating members to share information and work together. Trust also helps remove any emotional and interpersonal obstacles to effective team functioning.[14] Its presence allows team members the freedom to devote a greater proportion of their time toward team tasks.

The effect of team size on trust is also of interest. One overarching conclusion is that as size increases, the probability that distrust between members will increase becomes higher. A study cited in Chapter 4 revealed that just over 35% of members of larger teams (eight or more members) agree that distrust between members exists on their team while only 5% of members of smaller teams (three or four members) perceive that distrust exists.[15] Larger teams usually feature cross-functional members, where organizational trust issues may already be present, as well as greater opportunities for mistrust simply due to a larger number of members. Managers need to consider the effect of size on trust when forming organizational work teams.

Stephen M. R. Covey, an authority on this subject, has reached a set of conclusions regarding trust.[16] He maintains that trust is hard, real, and quantifiable; and affects both the speed and cost of a relationship. When trust is present, the cost to manage a relationship decreases while the speed or rate at which things are accomplished through the relationship accelerates. He maintains further that trust is a function of both character and competence; that it can be created as well as destroyed; that it can be effectively taught and learned; and that it can be leveraged to gain strategic advantage. And, when trust is lost it can be reestablished—albeit at a significant cost.

Covey also maintains that an absence of trust carries a tax, which is an economic burden that must be borne by parties as they discount and often must verify what they receive from another party. This tax is real, measureable, and often extremely high. Conversely, Covey puts forth the notion of a trust dividend. This dividend leads to improved communication and collaboration, better and faster execution of decisions, enhanced innovation and strategy development, and stronger engagement with the other party (or parties). Preferential treatment from suppliers is an important component of the trust dividend.

Few would argue with the notion that few relationships start with a foundation of trust. As parties work together, they form a perception about the trustworthiness of the other party. In this regard, trust is a learned outcome that is based on experience. But, once trust is an outcome, it also becomes an antecedent that must be present before relationships can evolve to the point where more collaborative and complex activities between parties can take place.

Trust at a National Level

The importance of trust has been linked empirically to the development of societies and markets. Without a belief that participants will follow through on their commitments, it would be impossible to have financial markets with sufficient liquidity and market breadth to operate. The notion of contracting is predicated on a belief that the parties will perform according to a contract's terms and conditions, thereby avoiding a condition known as breach of contract.

Trust is a major part of a nation's culture. Trust at a macro level is higher in countries with a relatively higher per capita income, less income inequality, higher political stability, and greater legal security.[17] Furthermore, a lack of trust increases transactions costs, presumably as individuals take steps to protect themselves from the risks associated with lower trust. Countries with cultures that feature low trust also often feature lower investment, lower growth, and corruption—conditions that constrain economic development. In this sense, trust and country risk are closely related.

Trust Between Suppliers and Buyers

Most industrial firms recognize that achieving the next generation of performance advantages will increasingly require collaborative relationships with select suppliers. As mentioned, collaborative relationships feature the sharing of risks, resources, and rewards between parties. They also feature the sharing of confidential or proprietary information. Not surprisingly, trust is a major factor affecting these sought-after, but relatively rare relationships. It is the basis upon which competitive advantage is built, driven by a collaborative culture that supports teamwork, open and honest communication, and innovation between companies.[18]

Companies with the most trusting supplier relations tend to have the most financially rewarding relationships.[19] This supports two important conclusions. First, building trusting relationships with suppliers is a financially responsible activity that every company should undertake. Second, by working to create trust-based relationships with suppliers, the opportunity to achieve meaningful supplier-provided benefits that are not necessarily available to other companies is maximized.[20]

The level of trust that one party has with another likely affects important processes and outcomes, which should lead directly to tangible benefits. Although a significant amount of research examines trust as a construct, much less attention is given to examining ways that trust actually translates into tangible benefits, particularly between buyers and sellers.[21] Something that is missing from most research is an attempt to quantify the quantitative impact that trust has on financial performance or preferential treatment. One exception involves work by Hencke, who calculated the value lost by a major automotive company over a ten-year period because of the company's deteriorating relationships and loss of trust from suppliers.[22] A key conclusion by Hencke is that trust equals profits, and lower trust means profits foregone.

Trust clearly forms the foundation of successful business relationships. Most individuals have an intuitive belief about its importance. Part of why we have this belief has been gained through experience and even hard-wired through evolution. We inherently recognize the importance of trust when interacting with others. It is hard to imagine a collaborative relationship that does not feature trust leading to the kinds of outcomes that create differential advantages. The next chapter will explore the important linkage between trust-based relationships and becoming the customer of choice. The bottom line is that when trust is absent, the chances of developing a collaborative relationship are almost nonexistent.

VESTED OUTSOURCING—A SPECIAL KIND OF COLLABORATION

In traditional outsourcing, one party usually tells another party what it needs to do, usually through a detailed contract. The customer (i.e., the buyer) wants to receive the best service at the lowest cost per activity. The outsource provider (i.e., the supplier) wants the highest margin possible with many activities to perform (and charge for) to maximize revenue and profits. The problem is that while each party may give their best effort individually, the overall solution is often far from optimal. Even though the parties within the contract presumably are working together, their objectives are often misaligned and in conflict. Two major issues include unclear expectations and conflicting interests over time. This results in negative or subconscious behaviors that drive unintended consequences. Is there a better way to tap into the benefits of true collaboration?

Vested outsourcing, a concept articulated in a book with the same name, combines four influential concepts that are affecting today's business environment: outsourcing, collaboration, innovation, and measurement.[23] The premise is to create a business model where both the company that outsources and the company that is outsourced to are able to maximize their profits (win-win) rather than one gaining at the expense of the other (win-lose). This approach encourages the companies that are involved in an outsourcing relationship to work collaboratively toward an optimized solution, even if it means that the parties to the relationship have to accept some trade-offs.

Underlying the vested-outsourcing approach are five important rules. These rules are designed to counter the various flaws associated with traditional outsourcing arrangements:

- *Rule 1: Focus on an outcome-based versus transaction-based model.* Instead of being paid for transactions, the service provider is paid for achieving mutually agreed upon desired outcomes.
- *Rule 2: Focus on* what *and not* how. The outsourcing company specifies what it wants and then moves the responsibility of determining how it is achieved to the provider—who presumably is the expert. The outsource provider determines the best way (*how*) to achieve the *what*.
- *Rule 3: Agree on clearly defined and measurable outcomes.* These outcomes are expressed in terms of a limited set of usually no more than five high-level metrics.
- *Rule 4: Optimize pricing model incentives for cost/service trade-offs.* The pricing model must balance risk and reward for the organizations and the agreement should specify that the service provider will deliver solutions, not just activities.
- *Rule 5: Governance structure should provide insight and guidance, not merely oversight.* This avoids the tendency to *go overboard* and micromanage outsource providers. A properly designed governance structure should provide insight and guidance rather than layers of supervisory oversight.

In vested outsourcing, the primary objective is for organizations to work together from a foundation of trust where there is mutual accountability for achieving a set of desired outcomes rather than adhering to a strictly defined set of transactions or activities. An important belief is that the service provider is the expert and, as such, should understand the best way to deliver a set of expected outcomes. Vested outsourcing aligns well with a central tenet of strategic supply management, which is that, at some point, activity must yield to accomplishment.

PURSUING TOP-LINE GROWTH THROUGH INNOVATION SOURCING

Innovation sourcing involves the process of capitalizing on external innovation and capabilities with the explicit goal of growing top-line revenue. This differs from an environment where supply personnel focus their efforts almost exclusively on reducing costs. The idea of supply managers being held account-able for increasing revenue growth is often difficult to swallow. Welcome to our brave new world.

An example that illustrates innovation sourcing involves Gulfstream, a maker of premier business jets. During the design of a new jet, Gulfstream's de-velopment team worked at the onset with a group of critical suppliers that were capable of providing technologies and features that differentiated the aircraft. Honeywell provided major advancements in cockpit avionics; Kollsman de-signed state-of-the-art poor weather and night visioning systems; Rolls-Royce created a new, more powerful engine; and Vought Aircraft Industries developed new wing structures. Innovation sourcing is a crucial capability for a company such as Gulfstream.

The logic behind innovation sourcing is relatively straightforward.[24] With-out question, smart people work at other companies as well as your own. And, external research and development (R&D) at those companies can create con-siderable value, particularly when a third party is a technical specialist, while internal R&D works to capture that value. It is myopic to believe that innovation has to originate internally in order for a company to profit from it. Companies should develop a business model where they profit as others use their intellec-tual property, while at the same time they pursue others' intellectual property when it advances their own business needs.

A logical question becomes how to gain an advantage from innovation sourcing. Perhaps the most powerful way is to engage suppliers and custom-ers in something called *early involvement*. Early involvement is the process of relying on suppliers and customers, physically or virtually, to provide support early during strategic planning; demand and supply planning; continuous im-provement projects; project planning; and new product, process, and technol-ogy development.

Early involvement often involves external participation on teams. This involve-ment offers a powerful way to tap into the expertise of third parties. Research findings are clear that teams that rely on supplier input and involvement when the task warrants involvement are more effective in their task, on average, than teams that do not involve suppliers. We also know that teams that include suppliers as participants report a variety of improvements that support better performance.

Identifying the right suppliers to involve early can be a challenge. Figure 9.2 presents a simple but effective tool (simplicity is a virtue here) for assessing early involvement candidates. Since early involvement opportunities are usually lim-ited, special care must be taken to manage this process along with any related is-sues. An example of one such issue is how to manage intellectual property that is developed jointly.[25] Table 9.2 summarizes the issues that may require attention when pursuing early involvement—particularly during product development.

	Limited		Moderate		Extensive
Performance improvement potential due to early involvement	1	2	3	4	5
	Adversarial		Cordial		Cooperative
Relationship between the buying company and the supplier	1	2	3	4	5
	Not Willing		Somewhat		Very Willing
Willingness of the supplier to participate in early involvement	1	2	3	4	5
	Not Capable		Moderately		Very Capable
Capability of the supplier to support early involvement activities	1	2	3	4	5

Figure 9.2   Evaluating early involvement candidates

Table 9.2   Early involvement questions

• Should early involvement be ad hoc or continuous?
• How can we motivate suppliers to participate?
• How can we gain internal acceptance to early involvement?
• How can we protect proprietary information?
• What kinds of projects or activities should involve suppliers?
• What will be the effect on other suppliers who are not invited as early participants?
• Do we compensate suppliers for their early involvement support?
• Which suppliers should be involved?
• Who should have internal ownership of the early involvement process?
• What if we are inexperienced or do not understand how to manage early involvement?
• Should involvement be physical, virtual, or a hybrid approach?
• Which personnel from the suppliers should be involved?
• How can we share learning across the organization after each early involvement engagement?

As companies search for new growth, they also cannot ignore the importance of what is largely an untapped opportunity—the receipt of preferential treatment from suppliers. (Chapter 10 addresses how to become the customer of choice.) Oftentimes, this treatment is specific and not available to other firms, particularly competitors. Make no mistake, preferential treatment, like trust and respect, is earned rather than given. How an industrial customer engages with its suppliers can mean the difference between receiving game-changing innovation that leads to top-line growth versus watching from the sidelines as others prosper.

As presented in Chapter 4, one way to ensure that a customer becomes preferred is to use reverse scorecards to measure supplier attitudes. Reverse scorecards involve the customer (i.e., the buyer) asking the supplier to rate the customer's performance. Recall from Chapter 4 that one such reverse scorecard is the *Supplier Satisfaction Survey*. The premise of a reverse scorecard is to identify ways to improve a buyer's performance as a customer with the objective of earning preferred customer status. The reality is that few firms routinely survey their suppliers, making this an untapped opportunity.

The bottom line is that a need to tap into innovation that supports top-line growth is best supported by relationships that are trust-based, collaborative, and explicitly consider a supplier's needs. Innovation sourcing is a new and largely undeveloped frontier for most companies. For that reason alone, it is worth understanding.

CONCLUDING THOUGHTS

Most industry and academic observers have concluded that supply chain collaboration will become a more important part of the corporate business model. And, without question, the scope and kinds of collaboration that companies pursue will become increasingly complex and varied. As mentioned, most supply chain collaboration features the interaction between a single buyer and a single seller (two-party collaboration). While this model will remain popular, more complex collaboration models are emerging. Some of these models feature multiple tiers and networks of participants working jointly toward a common goal.

As a concept, supply chain collaboration is in a growth rather than maturity stage. A deeper understanding of this topic should move the transition of collaboration along the concept life cycle toward great acceptance and maturity. Most experts would agree that collaboration, in general, is a rational, even strategic response to the demands brought about by hyper-competitive markets. If this is correct, and we have no reason to believe it not to be, the need to better understand what supports successful collaboration becomes quite important.

REFERENCES

1. R. Kaplan, D. Norton, and B. Rugelsjoen, "Managing Alliances with the Balanced Scorecard," *Harvard Business Review*, 88, nos. 1–2 (January/February 2010): 114–120.
2. M. Hoegl and S. Wager, "Buyer-Supplier Collaboration in Product Development Projects," *Journal of Management*, 31, no. 4 (August 2005): 530–548.
3. S. Jap, "Pie-Expansion Efforts: Collaboration Processes in Buyer-Supplier Relationships," *Journal of Marketing Research*, 36, no. 4: 461.
4. M. Walker, "Supplier-Retailer Collaboration in the European Grocery Industry," *Logistics Information Management*, 7, no. 6 (1994): 23.
5. "How Schering-Plough Uses Collaboration to Boost Supplier Relations," *Supplier Selection and Management Report*, nos. 2–3 (February 2003): 1.
6. T. Fleck, "Supplier Collaboration in Action at IBM," *Supply Chain Management Review*, 12, no. 2 (March 2008).
7. M. Mecham, "With 777X, Boeing Looks to Partnering," *Aviation Week & Space Technology*, (October 29, 2012): 14.
8. M. Anderson, "The Ebb and Flow of Supplier-Customer Collaboration," *Automotive Design and Production*, 124, no. 1 (January/February, 2012): 8.
9. D. Ferrin, M. Bligh, and J. Kohles, "Can I Trust You to Trust Me? A Theory of Trust, Monitoring, and Cooperation in Interpersonal and Intergroup Relationship," *Group & Organization Management*, 32, no. 4 (2007): 465–499.
10. F. Schoorman, R. Mayer, and J. Davis, "An Integrative Model of Organizational Trust: Past, Present, and Future," *Academy of Management Review*, 32, no. 2 (2007): 344–354.
11. S. M. R. Covey, *The Speed of Trust: The One Thing that Changes Everything*, (New York: Free Press, 2008).
12. R. Mayer and H. Davis, "The Effect of the Performance Appraisal System on Trust for Management: A Field Quasi-Experiment," *Journal of Applied Psychology*, 84, no. 1 (1999): 123–136.
13. Ferrin, Bligh, and Kohles, 465–499.
14. S. deJong, G. Van der Vegt, and E. Molleman, "The Relationships Among Asymmetry in Task Dependence, Perceived Helping Behavior, and Trust," *Journal of Applied Psychology*, 92, no. 6 (2007): 1625–1637.
15. R. J. Trent, "Understanding the Many Factors that Affect the Success of Organizational Work Teams," *Journal of Business*, 1, no. 3 (2016): 1–14.
16. S. M. R. Covey, *The Speed of Trust: The One Thing that Changes Everything*, (New York: Free Press, 2008).
17. P. Zak and S. Knack, "Trust and Growth," *The Economic Journal*, 111, no. 470 (2001): 295–321.

18. B. Keith, K. Vitasek, K. Manrodt, and J. Kling, *Strategic Sourcing in the New Economy: Harnessing the Potential of Sourcing Business Models for Modern Procurement* (New York: Palgrave MacMillan, 2016).

19. J. Henke, T. Stallkamp, and S. Yeniyurt, "Lost Supplier Trust: How Chrysler Missed Out on $24 billion in Profits over the Past 12 Years," *Supply Chain Management Review*, (May/June 2015): 24–32.

20. B. Keith, K. Vitasek, K. Manrodt, and J. Kling, *Strategic Sourcing in the New Economy: Harnessing the Potential of Sourcing Business Models for Modern Procurement*.

21. K. Dirks and D. Ferrin, "The Role of Trust in Organizational Settings," *Organization Science*, 12, no. 4 (2001): 450–467.

22. J. Henke, T. Stallkamp, S. Yeniyurt, 24–32.

23. Material in this section is adapted from K. Vitasek, M. Ledyard, and K. Manrodt, *Vested Outsourcing—Five Rules that Will Transform Outsourcing* (New York: Palgrave Macmillan, 2010).

24. J. R. Carter, P. L. Carter, R. M. Monczka, and T. V. Scannell, "Innovation Sourcing—The Suppliers' Perspective," *Supply Chain Management Review*, (November 2011): 18–19.

25. For a fuller discussion of the many issues associated with early involvement, see R. J. Trent, *Strategic Supply Management—Creating the Next Source of Competitive Advantage* (Fort Lauderdale, FL: J. Ross Publishing, 2008): 230–231.

10

BECOMING THE CUSTOMER
OF CHOICE

In the early 2000s, Boeing made a decision to develop long range (LR) and extended range (ER) versions of its highly successful twin-engine 777. Boeing designated GE as the sole engine provider for the new 777, something that was not typical in the aerospace industry (airlines usually have a choice of engine providers). In exchange, not only did GE commit its own resources to develop a radically new engine exclusively for Boeing, the company provided support to develop the new planes. The 777ER and 777LR were so well received by airlines that Boeing's primary competitor, the four-engine Airbus 340, ended production due to a lack of orders. The 777LR and 777ER, due partly to performance improvements attributed to GE's engines, changed the economics of an entire industry.

Several years later Airbus publicly accused GE of favoring Boeing during the development of engine technology for the next generation of commercial aircraft, a market estimated to be worth several hundred billion dollars. An Airbus executive complained, "The problem we have with GE is they go to Boeing and say, 'What kind of engine should we design for your airframe?' Then they come to Airbus and say, 'Here is the kind of airframe you need to build to fit our engine.'" Complicating matters is the fact that the largest version of Airbus' A350 XWB competes directly with the largest version of the Boeing 777 where GE is the sole engine supplier. GE officials have commented they will not build a new engine for an Airbus plane that competes against a Boeing plane where GE is the sole supplier.[1] Extending this relationship even further, Boeing has designated GE as the sole engine provider for the next generation 777X. As these examples illustrate, receiving preferential treatment from suppliers can be a real game changer.

This chapter addresses the important topic of becoming the *customer of choice*. Operating from the premise that satisfied suppliers are more willing to provide preferential treatment to their most favored customers, the chapter addresses topics that help us understand how to become the customer of choice, including the importance of trust and translating what we know about this topic into a set of managerial actions.

BECOMING THE CUSTOMER OF CHOICE— WHAT DO WE KNOW?

As part of a research project called *Beyond the Horizon*, APICS, working in conjunction with a major university, identified some recurring themes regarding how supply chains will evolve and create future value.[2] In particular, the APICS-sponsored research describes five actions that are necessary to create value and enhance the impact of procurement and sourcing. Receiving preferential treatment from suppliers is one of those necessary actions. This research highlights the importance of becoming the customer of choice to suppliers.

Recall that a measurement instrument called the *Supplier Satisfaction Survey* was introduced in Chapter 5 as a reverse scorecard where suppliers evaluate a customer (rather than the more customary approach where buyers evaluate the supplier). Insights from data that were collected from hundreds of suppliers that completed this survey support some important findings regarding how to become the customer of choice. The following summarizes these findings:

> *A supplier's satisfaction with a customer (i.e., the buyer) relates directly to that customer's performance and behavior rather than demographic or other attributes.*

Supplier satisfaction with a customer correlates highly with factors that relate to a customer's behavior toward that supplier (i.e., pay on time, share relevant information, ethical treatment, etc.) rather than factors such as supplier size or the size of a contract. Interestingly, a negative, though not strong, relationship exists between the total years a supplier has worked with a customer and lower supplier satisfaction with that customer. In other words, as a supplier works with a customer for longer periods of time, the probability increases that the supplier will indicate lower satisfaction with that customer. Other research has also revealed declining satisfaction within relationships as longevity increases.[3]

No statistical relationship exists between the size of a supplier in terms of sales and supplier satisfaction with the buying customer. Supplier satisfaction with a specific customer is no different for smaller suppliers as compared with larger suppliers. Furthermore, no statistical relationship exists between the size of the contract relative to the supplier's total sales and supplier satisfaction with the buying customer. Many companies offer progressively larger volumes to suppliers with the expectation that higher volumes will lead to more satisfied suppliers and hence preferential treatment. While that may happen to some degree, supplier satisfaction shows no statistical correlation with contract size. Satisfaction relates directly to customer performance and behavior rather than the volume of sales that the customer represents. This is a welcome finding because customers can change their behavior, thereby affecting supplier satisfaction.

A strong relationship exists between a supplier's satisfaction with a customer and viewing that customer as preferred.

An unusually strong correlation exists between the level of a supplier's satisfaction with a customer and how that supplier views that customer. A clear conclusion is that becoming a preferred customer will likely not occur if a supplier is dissatisfied with its customer (i.e., the buyer). Logic suggests that a sequence occurs where supplier satisfaction leads to preferred customer status. And, a link between preferred customer status and a willingness by suppliers to provide preferential treatment is well supported by data. The statistical linkages between supplier satisfaction, preferred customer status, and preferential treatment are unambiguous.

Suppliers indicate agreement regarding the top customer performance attributes that are most important to them.

Aggregating data from hundreds of suppliers reveals the performance items that are most important to them. The items where suppliers show convincing agreement about what they want from their customers include earning a fair financial return, receiving payment in a reasonable time, opportunities for longer term business relationships, and ethical and respectful behavior. When supplier executives ask themselves what they want most from a customer, these four items will likely be at the top of most lists.

These findings are similar to a European survey of automotive suppliers that investigated why suppliers like or dislike an industrial customer. A supplier's willingness to do business with a customer correlates closely with satisfying a supplier's expectations in four areas—the supplier's return on investment, the customer's longer term support of the supplier, the customer's willingness to reward cost-saving ideas, and the customer's ability to protect proprietary technology (something that has clear ethical implications).[4] The increasing power of suppliers and their willingness to shift business away from less favorable customers was also noted.

A supplier that is satisfied with a customer is more willing to provide that customer with different kinds of preferential treatment.

A central question underlying supplier-buyer relationships is whether satisfied suppliers are more willing to provide preferential treatment to their most preferred customers. Specific types of preferential treatment fall into three broad groups—a supplier's willingness to make direct investments that only benefit a specific or limited number of customers, a supplier's willingness to provide internally developed innovation to a customer, and a supplier's willingness to provide certain types of favorable treatment to a customer. Table 10.1 identifies the supplier-provided outcomes that suppliers can potentially deliver to their customers.

The bottom line is that satisfied suppliers are more willing to provide valuable kinds of preferential treatment, as compared to less satisfied suppliers. Preferred customer status brings with it a set of benefits that are not available to typical customers—benefits that can provide a hard-to-duplicate source of competitive advantage.

A supplier that is satisfied with a customer is much more likely to perceive it has a positive relationship with that customer, perceive that the relationship has improved over the last three years, and expect the relationship to improve further.

Table 10.1   Examples of supplier provided preferential treatment

Supplier-Provided Favorable Treatment	• Shorter quoted lead times • Preferential scheduling of orders • Early insight into future technology plans • More favorable payment terms • Performance improvement ideas • More frequent deliveries	• Access to the supplier's executive level personnel • Access to market information that the supplier may possess • Better pricing • First allocation of output if supplier capacity is constrained • Early warning to potential supply problems
Supplier-Provided Direct Investment	• Personnel to work directly at the customer's facilities • Capacity dedicated to the customer • Engineers to support customer's product development needs • Investment in new equipment that benefits only the customer	• Exclusive use of new technology developed by the supplier • Inventory held to support the customer's needs • Direct financial support if needed • Information technology systems unique to business with the customer
Supplier-Provided Innovation	• Product innovation • Production process innovation • Process innovation involving nonproduction processes	

Suppliers are consistent in their belief that a higher satisfaction with their customer correlates strongly with cooperative and collaborative relationships. And, those suppliers that indicate higher satisfaction with their customer tend to agree that their relationship with that customer has improved over the last several years (and will continue to improve). A direct link exists between supplier satisfaction and relationships that are cooperative or even collaborative. Customers must recognize the importance of supplier relationship management.

> *Over 90% of all suppliers indicate that it is critical for the personnel they deal with at their customers' facilities to be knowledgeable about the specifics of the suppliers' products, processes, businesses, and industries.*

Almost all suppliers say they have assigned an individual to be their primary contact with a particular customer. Furthermore, almost every supplier indicates they are aware that a specific individual who is responsible for managing the supplier relationship had been assigned by the customer. When tasking specific individuals with the responsibility of working with a supplier, it is not sufficient to simply assign that responsibility. In the eyes of suppliers, that individual must be highly qualified.

These findings provide guidance regarding how a company can position itself to become a preferred customer to its suppliers. While becoming a customer of choice does not appear anywhere on a financial statement, it is an intangible asset that can provide differential advantages. Understanding what causes supplier satisfaction with a customer, which in turn links to a willingness by a supplier to provide preferential treatment to a customer, is an essential part of strategic supply management.

IMPORTANCE OF TRUST-BASED RELATIONSHIPS

An important part of becoming the customer of choice centers on the presence of trust-based relationships. An unusually strong correlation exists between the trust that a supplier indicates it has with a customer and the supplier's satisfaction with that customer. Chapter 9 provided insight into the concept of trust. Here, we will extend this by discussing a set of research findings that link trust and supplier-buyer relationships. Understanding what relates to trust will help us develop and manage trust-based relationships. Table 10.2 provides a summary of research findings involving trust.

We know that supplier trust with a customer relates directly to specific areas of a customer's performance. Part of the *Supplier Satisfaction Survey* discussed in Chapter 5 asks suppliers to compare their customer's performance against a

Table 10.2 Summary of trust-based findings

• The trust that a supplier has with its customer does not relate statistically to any demographic variable studied
• Supplier trust with the customer relates directly to satisfaction with that customer: furthermore, suppliers that have higher satisfaction with the customer are likely to say that customer is a preferred customer
• Supplier trust with a customer relates directly to specific areas of customer performance
• A belief that the customer will protect the supplier's confidential information relates directly to the supplier's trust in that customer
• Trust relates strongly to the perception that the personnel the supplier deals with at the customer are knowledgeable and qualified
• A strong relationship exists between the trust a supplier has with its customer and the quality of the communication that takes place with that customer
• Higher trust with the customer correlates highly with positive views the supplier has about negotiating with that customer
• Trust relates strongly to the kind of relationship the supplier perceives it has with that customer
• Trust with a customer relates to a greater willingness by the supplier to provide preferential treatment to that customer

best or ideal customer for 25 performance areas. Items that correlate the highest with a supplier's trust in that customer include the customer's ability to:

- Exhibit ethical and respectful behavior
- Develop effective supplier-buyer relationships
- Pursue efficient negotiating and contracting practices
- Provide tangible support if problems arise
- Provide clear channels of communication
- Be receptive to the supplier's improvement ideas
- Be knowledgeable about the supplier's business and industry
- Offer longer term business opportunities to the supplier
- Commit to continuously improving the supplier-buyer relationship
- Respond to supplier inquiries in a timely manner

Customers who perform well across these areas are tapping into the behaviors that affect a supplier's perception of trust. Ethical behavior, open and frequent communication, tangible support when problems arise, continuous relationship improvement, and offering longer term relationship opportunities convey an appreciation by the customer of a supplier's business needs. It is not difficult to conclude that if a customer performs well across these areas, higher trust should result.

Strong correlations also exist between trust and the confidence the supplier has that the customer will protect proprietary or confidential information, which relates to the integrity dimension of trust. This includes protecting the integrity of the supplier's information and data submitted in quotations and/or proposals, internal cost data, product and process improvement ideas, current product designs, future product development plans, and supply chain improvement ideas.

A popular perspective of trust involves a party's willingness to accept vulnerability based upon positive expectations of the intentions of the other party. Here, the presence of trust allows a supplier to reduce its vulnerability regarding the misuse, misappropriation, and sometimes even theft of the supplier's intellectual property and confidential information.

A number of years ago a major automotive original equipment manufacturer (OEM) asked suppliers to submit design ideas, without compensation, related to the development of a new vehicle. The OEM subsequently shared these ideas with Chinese suppliers, a clear ethical lapse on the part of the OEM. The OEM then informed its Western suppliers they had to match or beat China pricing if they expected to win new business.

This OEM has had relationship issues with suppliers for many years. According to a 2014 survey, it had a reputation as one of the worst automakers to work with. Suppliers have rated this company low on all kinds of key measures, including trustworthiness, communication skills, and protection of intellectual property. Suppliers also say this company is the least likely to allow them to raise prices to recoup unexpected material cost increases. As a result, this company has not been the customer of choice. Interestingly, since 2014 this company has made a concerted effort to improve its relationships with suppliers. The company now scores toward the middle of the pack in terms of supplier satisfaction, compared with other companies in its industry.

Trust also relates strongly to the perception a supplier has regarding whether its customer's personnel are knowledgeable and qualified. This finding highlights the important role that individuals play within supplier-buyer relationships. It also taps into the ability dimension of trust. A strong correlation exists between supplier trust and the belief that the personnel at the customer's facility are knowledgeable about the supplier's business.

It is logical to conclude that qualified personnel affect a supplier's perception of customer trust and performance. Saying that a customer's personnel are qualified means these personnel have a solid understanding of the purchase contract; the economic changes and trends, including emerging technology, affecting the supplier's industry; the supplier's cost and operating structure; and the supplier's production processes, delivery processes, quality management systems, and capacity constraints and limitations. These personnel must also act in an ethical manner, a theme that comes out repeatedly when surveying suppliers.

This finding raises some questions regarding how a firm manages its human talent. It is not unusual for supply and supply chain personnel to rotate frequently between positions, sometimes every 12 to 18 months. When this is the case, the relationship learning curve may regress as newly assigned individuals work to rebuild a supplier-buyer relationship. The important role that individuals play within trust-based relationships cannot be understated.

A strong relationship also exists between the trust that a supplier has with its customer and the quality of communication that takes place. It is hard to envision a trust-based relationship that does not feature open and direct communication. Communication is a multidimensional construct that includes the timeliness of responses when the supplier contacts the customer with concerns or questions, the accuracy of those responses, the completeness of responses, and the courteousness of personnel when contacted with concerns or questions. The ability of the customer to perform positively on each of these items correlates highly with the suppliers' perception of trust.

Higher trust with a buying customer correlates directly with the views that a supplier has about negotiating with that customer. Few would argue against the notion that negotiation is a process of communication. Progressive companies view negotiation as an opportunity to enhance a relationship and to search jointly for new opportunities rather than as a means to punish or coerce another party. Positive communication put forth during the negotiating process should enhance the strength of a relationship as well as the trust that underlies it.

Higher trust also correlates with a supplier's belief that a customer's personnel take supplier concerns and questions seriously. And, trust also correlates strongly to a supplier's belief that personnel at the customer's facility are willing to work with the supplier to resolve any performance issues or misunderstandings. Finally, suppliers that indicate higher trust with their customer are also more likely to say they are confident that the customer will not be punitive or seek retribution if presented with less than desirable news. This relates to the benevolence dimension of trust.

Suppliers that say they trust a customer are more likely to say they have a cooperative or collaborative relationship with that customer. Higher supplier trust also correlates at an unusually high level with a belief that personnel at the customer are committed to improving the business-to-business relationship. In all likelihood the presence of trust has enabled the parties to evolve to a level that features the open sharing of information, resources, risk, and rewards—all of which characterize relationships that are toward the higher end of the relationship continuum.

Finally, trust with a customer, like satisfaction, relates directly to a greater willingness by a supplier to provide preferential treatment to that customer. This is an important finding because it links trust and a supplier's willingness to provide preferential treatment to the customer. A primary objective of trust-based relationships should be the receipt of benefits that are not readily available from relationships that feature lower trust.

Why are these findings so important? A supplier's willingness to provide benefits, some of which are mandated coercively by the customer, ebb and flow with the level of trust that a supplier has with its customer.[5] Conversely, supplier-provided non-price benefits almost always outweigh, sometimes dramatically, the dollar value received from mandated supplier piece-price concessions. The challenge is to create an environment where suppliers willingly provide non-price benefits that are not readily available to other customers, some of whom may be your direct competitors.

BECOMING THE CUSTOMER OF CHOICE

The primary premise of this chapter is that a clear linkage exists between a customer's behavior, the satisfaction and trust that a supplier has with that customer, and a supplier's willingness to provide preferential treatment. The following builds on this by presenting a set of actions that will help a customer benefit from the kinds of preferential treatment that satisfied suppliers potentially offer.

Understand How Suppliers Perceive Your Company as a Customer

Given the effort required to obtain objective data from suppliers, it should come as no surprise that relatively few buying customers understand how their suppliers regard them as a customer. Yet, how else will a buying company improve its relationships and receive preferential treatment from suppliers if it does not know in what areas it is doing well and where it is falling short? Gaining this insight requires a commitment from the highest levels of the supply organization to obtain and then act upon supplier-provided feedback. Shortly after receiving the results of its supplier satisfaction study, supply executives at a company on the East Coast identified ways to incorporate the findings directly into its planning process. Supplier-provided feedback quickly influenced the strategic direction of the entire supply organization.

Recognize the Importance of Knowledgeable Personnel and a Stable Workforce

As mentioned, almost unanimous agreement exists among suppliers that it is important for the personnel they deal with directly at their customer's facility to be knowledgeable. Maintaining supply knowledge will be a challenge as the baby boomer generation leaves the workforce. This exodus of talent requires strategies that focus on acquiring and then retaining personnel with the right capabilities, including knowledge about how to manage critical supplier relationships.

Avoid Relationship Entropy

Research findings suggest the satisfaction that suppliers have with their industrial customer tends to decline the longer the supplier has worked with that customer. The inflection point for this downward shift occurs around the seven-year point of the relationship. This downward shift could be due to complacency between the parties, a wearing down of the relationship as years of continuous improvement demands affect the relationship, or myriad other reasons. The challenge becomes one of recognizing that this downward shift is a real possibility and then taking steps to reenergize the supplier-buyer relationship.

Request Preferential Treatment

We know that satisfied suppliers are often willing to provide preferential treatment to their most preferred customers. A challenge becomes one of understanding how to obtain that treatment. One way to pursue preferential treatment is during contract negotiations—particularly when crafting a supplier's statement of work. Another way is to address this topic during annual review meetings with suppliers—meetings that suppliers view as extremely valuable. Suppliers also indicate a willingness to engage in various forms of executive-to-executive engagement—one of the most logical situations in which to have discussions about preferential treatment. Progressive companies will have established buyer-supplier councils that feature executive-level contact between the customer and its key suppliers. Each of these approaches offers the opportunity to address the topic of preferential treatment.

Tap into Supplier Innovation

An important finding surrounds the willingness of satisfied suppliers to share innovation with their most preferred customers. Fortunately, a variety of ways exist to tap into that innovation. This includes early supplier involvement during product development; technology demonstration days where suppliers are encouraged to showcase their new ideas to engineers and supply personnel; and supplier participation on a buying company's improvement teams. If innovation is the lifeblood of growth, then it becomes necessary to tap into sources of innovation wherever they exist.

Promote Trust-Based Relationships

As explained earlier, powerful linkages exist between trust and important elements of the supplier-buyer relationship. The presence of trust, however, is not the result of happenstance. Building trust-based relationships is so important that ways to achieve this receives special attention here.

Create a Culture that Stresses Supplier-Buyer Relationships

Corporate culture refers to the philosophy, values, and behavior that together constitute the unique style and policies of a company. Culture is often implied rather than expressly defined, and it is something that develops gradually over time from the cumulative traits of executive leaders as well as the people that a company hires. Some might argue that a corporate culture reflects the personality of an organization.

Executive leadership has the opportunity to create an environment that stresses the importance of supplier-buyer relationships or they can create an environment that seeks to extract every concession possible from suppliers. Enlightened leadership at the customer's facility will appreciate the linkage between trust-based relationships and preferential supplier treatment and convey the importance of this linkage throughout the organization. Making trust a central part of a corporate culture reflects a conscious decision, just as taking an adversarial approach with suppliers represents a conscious decision.

The pursuit of supplier-buyer trust must be systemic rather than idiosyncratic. It must permeate the thinking of an entire organization rather than being unique to a particular group, individual, or relationship. A belief regarding the importance of trust-based relationships must become an embedded part of an organization's culture, and as a result of this embedded belief, employees will act accordingly.

Don't Discount the Role of Individuals

The important role that individuals play within trust-based relationships is without question. The ability of a customer's personnel to protect proprietary information, demonstrate competency (particularly about a supplier's business), act ethically in all dealings, and engage in constructive communication each contribute to a supplier's perception of trust and trustworthiness. The bottom line is that hiring intelligent, ethical individuals to interact with suppliers, supported by the right corporate culture, will promote trust-based relationships.

Engage in Trust-Building Activities

Many straightforward ways exist that should result in greater trust between parties, including collocating personnel to encourage direct and frequent communication, following through on promises and commitments, acting legally and ethically in all dealings, acting on the behalf of the relationship rather than narrow self-interests, publicizing success stories and personal narratives—particularly those that enhance the standing of the other party, and protecting the confidentiality of the information and data gathered within the relationship. These tactics, each of which requires few resources, will affect the trust that exists between parties.

Demonstrate Ethical Behavior at the Corporate and Individual Level

The relationship between ethical behavior and a supplier's perception of trust with a customer is extremely strong. Ethics deal with questions related to the fairness, justness, rightness, or wrongness of an action and include the moral principles or values that guide behavior. Ethical behavior is a primary antecedent of trust and trust-based relationships. One certainty is that the risks of unethical behavior can be devastating to supplier-buyer relationships (not to mention possible legal ramifications). Ethical behavior contributes to greater trust; trust does not cause ethical behavior.

Say What You Do, Do What You Say

A basic principle that underlies trust-based relationships is that actions speak louder than words. Nothing builds trustworthiness better and faster than when words and actions align.[6] Building trust is not about telling another party what they want to hear—rather, it is about being open and honest in a manner that demonstrates confidence, consistency, and predictability. Suppliers that perceive that a customer is not following through on its commitments (and vice versa) should have an efficient way to address any concerns.

Understand What Is Important to Suppliers—and Then Perform

Industrial customers will find it useful to have an objective third party assess the many aspects of their supplier-buyer relationships, including the supplier's perception of customer performance and the level of trust that exists. This assessment will help a customer understand what a supplier values most from a relationship.

Gaining insight into what is important to suppliers increases the likelihood that a customer can direct its behavior in ways that will provide the greatest return. While certain behaviors are obvious (i.e., treating the supplier ethically or paying in a reasonable time) other behaviors, depending on the setting, may be more nuanced. Those customers that put forth the effort to understand the needs of their suppliers should be better off because of that effort. The challenge becomes one of replacing anecdotal or subjective analysis of what suppliers want with an objective understanding of what suppliers want.

Communicate, Communicate, Communicate

Communication increases knowledge of the other party and therefore understanding, which strengthens the bonds of trust. Frequent communication directly affects the trust that exists between parties. Parties within a relationship should welcome opportunities to communicate, and when they do, the communication should be open, accurate, timely, frequent, and complete.

These guidelines are designed to strengthen the relationship that exists between suppliers and buyers. A relentless pursuit of better relationships with key suppliers will help transform an aspiration (i.e., the desire for better relationships) into an accomplishment (i.e., the attainment of preferential treatment).

CONCLUDING THOUGHTS

It should come as no surprise that a commitment to stronger relationships offers the potential to help meet the demands of a rapidly changing marketplace. The challenge becomes one of ensuring that suppliers view the buying company as a preferred customer. Being the customer of choice offers advantages that are not as readily available to other customers, advantages that could lead to longer term competitive advantage.

As mentioned, preferential treatment from suppliers is not something that appears on a financial statement or as an accounting line item. This does not mean that buying companies should ignore the importance of preferential treatment—nor should they ignore the risk when others receive supplier-provided benefits. An objective of becoming the customer of choice should be a strategic imperative.

REFERENCES

1. D. Michaels and K. Kranhold, "Engine Spat Could Slow Airbus," *The Wall Street Journal*, July 10, 2007, A10.

2. D. J. Frayer, J. M. Whipple, and P. Daugherty, "Creating Value in Integrated Supply Chains," *APICS Magazine*, (March/April 2016): 18.
3. See S. Jap, and E. Anderson, "Testing a Life-Cycle Theory of Cooperative Inter-organizational Relationships: Movement Across Stages and Performance," *Management Science*, 53, no. 2 (February 2007): 260–275; G. Bell, R. Oppenheimer, and A. Bastien, "Trust Deterioration in an International Buyer-Supplier Relationship," *Journal of Business Ethics*, 36, no. ½ (March 2002): 65–78.
4. J. Snyder, "European Suppliers Play Favorites," *Automotive News*, May 16, 2005.
5. J. Henke, T. Stallkamp, and S. Yeniyurt, "Lost Supplier Trust: How Chrysler Missed Out on $24 Billion in Profits over the Past 12 Years," *Supply Chain Management Review*, (May/June 2014): 24–32.
6. B. Keith, K. Vitasek, K. Manrodt, and J. Kling, *Strategic Sourcing in the New Economy: Harnessing the Potential of Sourcing Business Models for Modern Procurement* (New York: Palgrave MacMillan, 2016).

11

MANAGING THE INEVITABILITY
OF RISK

Launching rockets is without question a high-risk endeavor. Even the slightest glitch can cause a failure so profound that it is hard for mere earthlings to grasp. One company that knows this firsthand is SpaceX, a company founded by Elon Musk. After an impressive record of successful launches, SpaceX experienced two catastrophic failures. Besides the financial loss associated with the lost rockets and their payloads, the company suffered a setback in its effort to demonstrate to NASA and other potential customers that it deserves to be a preferred launch provider, including launches that involve humans. Trust in the company was shaken.

A review after one of the failures revealed the explosion was caused by a defective strut that broke free during the rocket's ascent. The failure of this relatively insignificant item caused a helium canister to break loose, which set off a chain reaction that resulted in a big boom. The review noted that SpaceX allowed its strut supplier to self-test the strength of the struts it supplied to SpaceX and to self-certify quality. SpaceX has since announced plans to stress test every strut that it receives from the supplier, something that was not done previously. The company now appreciates that even relatively unimportant items can be critical to quality when they fail. Risk is real, and it is costly.

This chapter addresses the important but still evolving topic called supply chain risk management (SCRM). The first part of the chapter provides an essential understanding of SCRM, while the second part highlights ways to manage supply chain risk, presents predictions about the future, and develops an action plan for moving forward. The chapter also includes examples that show how susceptible supply markets are to risk. The main premise of this chapter is that supply managers must also become risk managers.

UNDERSTANDING RISK MANAGEMENT

What exactly is meant by the term *risk*? One perspective maintains that risk is a situation involving exposure to danger or loss. Another perspective takes this further by saying that risk is the probability or threat of damage, injury, liability, loss, or other negative occurrences that are caused by external or internal vulnerabilities, and that may be avoided through preemptive action.[1] Risk can also be viewed, at least partly, as the inability to capitalize on an opportunity. A preferred way to look at risk is to define it as the probability of realizing an unintended or unwanted consequence that leads to an undesirable outcome such as loss, injury, harm, or missed opportunity. Table 11.1 summarizes a set of important terms and concepts that are associated with risk management.

Most supply managers believe that when a risk becomes a reality, bad things usually happen. Not surprisingly, supply and supply chain managers almost always look at risk in terms of something to be avoided. However, Aswath Damodaran, a professor at NYU, writes that risk is an essential part of a society's

Table 11.1   Important risk concepts

• *Risk event*: a risk event is a risk that has become a reality; formally defined, a risk event is a discrete, specific occurrence that negatively affects a decision, plan, firm, or organism
• *Risk exposure*: the quantified potential for loss that might occur as a result of a risk event.
• *Risk vulnerability*: susceptible to harm or injury; usually not as quantified as risk exposure
• *Risk resilience*: the ability to recover from or adjust to misfortune or change; the ability to *bounce back* from a risk event
• *Risk appetite*: the degree of risk that an organization or individual is willing to accept or take in pursuit of its objectives; also referred to as risk tolerance or risk propensity
• *Risk analysis or assessment*: the process of qualitatively and quantitatively assessing potential risks within a supply chain
• *Risk response plan*: a document that defines known risks and includes descriptions, causes, probabilities, or likelihood of risk occurrence, costs, and proposed risk management responses; can also be a risk continuity plan
• *Risk compliance*: includes the internal activities taken to meet required or mandated rules and regulations, whether they are governmental, industry-specific, or internally imposed
• *Risk governance*: includes the frameworks, tools, policies, procedures, controls, and decision-making hierarchy employed to manage a business from a risk management perspective

advancement. He argues that every major advance that civilizations have made involves someone who is willing to take a risk by challenging the status quo.[2] The single-minded view that risk is primarily about avoidance is narrow and constraining. It can also be paralyzing as individuals and companies become excessively risk averse.

A review of the risk literature reveals some broad conclusions. First of all, while some risk definitions focus strictly on the probability of an event occurring, a richer perspective extends this to incorporate a valuation of the consequence of that event. A second conclusion is that in some disciplines, a clear distinction is made between a risk and a threat. With this perspective, a threat is thought to be a lower probability event, while risk is regarded as a higher probability event. Finally, some definitions of risk focus only on the downside of risk, whereas other perspectives are more expansive and consider all variability as risk, including lost opportunities. The challenge today is one of not allowing a fear of risk to paralyze us from pursuing opportunities that are important to our personal and professional advancement. Risk is something that needs to be managed as well as respected.

What Are Enterprise Risk Management (ERM) and SCRM?

It is important to differentiate between two important concepts—ERM and SCRM. Almost all corporate executives are aware of ERM. According to the Aberdeen Group:

> *"ERM is the process for effective identification, assessment, and management of all significant risks to an entity. This includes not only the traditional areas of financial and hazard risk, but also larger operational and strategic risks. ERM refers to the people, tools, systems, and structures that are part of a broader framework of governance, risk, and compliance."*

Corporate executives have been concerned with enterprise risk for years. The Securities and Exchange Commission (SEC) requires publicly traded companies to identify corporate-level risks in Section 1A of their company's 10-K report. Failure to identify these risks can create risk if shareholders claim the company did not adequately warn them of potential risks.

Risk identification within the 10-K reporting requirements is an important part of the ERM process. Historically, the vast majority of risks identified in the 10-K report relate to financial and legal risks. Operating and other supply chain risks often were not thought to be important enough to be addressed at the ERM or 10-K level.

ERM is traditionally the corporate responsibility of finance, treasury, insurance, and legal groups. A survey by Accenture revealed that at the corporate level, 98% of organizations have what they consider to be a chief risk officer. And, according to Accenture, 96% of risk management owners report to the CEO.[3]

What, then, is SCRM? The perspective taken here is that SCRM is the *implementation of strategies to manage everyday and exceptional risks along the supply chain through continuous risk assessment with the objective of reducing vulnerability and ensuring continuity.*[4] One way to view SCRM is to think of it as the intersection of supply chain management and risk management.

Some SCRM Observations

Most observers have concluded that supply chain risk has increased over the last 15 to 20 years. A survey by the American Productivity & Quality Center revealed that 75% of responding companies said they had experienced a major supply chain disruption over the last two years from when the survey was taken. Another survey revealed that almost 75% of risk managers say that supply chain risk levels are now higher than in 2005. Over 70% say the financial impact of supply chain disruptions has also increased.[5] And, there is no question that supply markets have become more volatile.

It is easy to conclude that too many firms are not prepared to handle the supply chain risks that may come their way, even though most managers understand that supply chain risk is a concern. A study by *Industry Week* revealed that for firms with less than $500 million in annual revenue (which is the vast majority of companies), only 25% take a proactive approach to risk management.

The reasons why many firms are not prepared to manage risk effectively are varied. We cannot ignore what is perhaps the most likely reason of all—risk management has simply not been a part of the supply management and supply chain domain. Why would we focus on something that is not considered all that relevant? It is also easy to view the efforts put forth toward risk planning as an exercise in busy work. This may not be the kind of work that gains recognition and promotions. A study by the Supply Chain Council identified a set of barriers that affect the practice of SCRM:

- Senior management has a tendency to focus on risk management only during times of crisis.
- SCRM requires many functions to work together—something that is challenging even on a good day.

- SCRM responsibilities are typically added to existing staff responsibilities, making it just another task.
- The increasing complexity of products, divisions, regions, and supply chains makes a coordinated SCRM effort more of a challenge.
- A partial effort to SCRM dilutes the perceived need for a real and sustained risk management effort. A close-enough-is-good-enough attitude toward SCRM often prevails.

Although SCRM may not receive the attention it deserves, a study by the Aberdeen Group identified various reasons why a company should make SCRM an embedded part of its corporate culture. Perhaps most important, the need to protect an organization's brand is a strategic necessity. In late 2015, Chipotle customers became ill due to food poisoning from tainted ingredients. The effect on the company's financial performance was profound. Chipotle's net income in 2016 was $23 million compared with $475 million in 2015. And, revenue declined from $4.5 billion to $3.9 billion in that period. Consider how stories on social media, whether true or not can impact the value of a brand. The day after a video showed police dragging a United Airlines passenger off a plane, the company's stock lost $10 billion in market value.

A second reason to stress SCRM is that the increasing volatility of the global markets—something the International Monetary Fund has documented—is creating greater risk exposure. Third, corporate mandates to institute and/or improve risk management and governance programs are only going to increase. Fourth, a growing need to comply with changing regulatory requirements is forcing a greater emphasis on managing risk. Finally, a constant pressure to improve shareholder value may create greater risk exposure as companies search for opportunities—on the buying and selling side—in regions that take them out of their comfort zone.

We tend to see the same set of standard approaches for mitigating or lessening the impact of risk events that fail to reflect bold or innovative thinking. While stressing the fundamentals of risk management will always be important, it is time to see more creativity and sophistication within the SCRM arena, particularly within supply management. Table 11.2 presents a set of research-based conclusions regarding the current state of SCRM.

While various frameworks categorize the domain of supply chain risk, no standard agreement exists regarding what should make up these categories. Any categorization scheme should identify broader risk categories and then place specific risks within those categories. While some risk category schemes are quite involved and even complex, a more simplified approach might better suit our needs. Table 11.3 summarizes four categories of supply chain risk.

Table 11.2   The current state of SCRM

• SCRM is an evolving discipline and will remain so for the foreseeable future
• Many companies have developed their risk management tools internally due to an absence of third-party applications
• The financial impact of supply chain disruptions can be devastating but are often not understood until after a risk event takes place
• Supply chain strategies driven primarily by cost and delivery improvements are no longer comprehensive enough to manage today's supply chain risks, some of which are strategic
• Reactive risk heroics and reaction must give way to risk prevention and anticipation wherever possible
• Organizations need to take an end-to-end (i.e., sub-tier) rather than narrower view of SCRM
• Supply chain risks are becoming enterprise-level risks, as they increasingly appear on SEC mandated 10-K reports
• Showing a hard return for risk management initiatives is a difficult task, making the use of traditional investment analytic techniques to justify risk initiatives a challenge
• Social media (such as Twitter) is an unpredictable risk wildcard
• Global supply chain risk is increasing, on average, rather than decreasing worldwide
• The risk ledger has two sides—risk presents an opportunity to some while others see it as the potential for loss
• The supply chain management profession has become too comfortable with deterministic models and tools (such as traditional forecasting) over the last 35 years, making a need to develop probabilistic risk models that utilize scenario planning a greater priority

Table 11.3   Categorizing supply chain risk

• *Strategic risk*: Strategic risks are those risks that are most consequential to an organization's ability to carry out its business strategy, achieve its corporate objectives, and protect asset and brand value.
• *Hazard risk*: This category pertains to random disruptions, some of which involve acts of God. This category also includes fires and malicious behavior such as accidents, product tampering, theft, and terrorism.
• *Financial risk*: Financial risks relate to the internal and external financial difficulties of the participants within a supply chain. We categorize a risk as financial when the primary and immediate effect of the risk, rather than a subsequent or secondary effect, is financially related.
• *Operational risk*: A disproportionate set of supply chain risks will be categorized as operational since this category includes internal and external quality problems, late deliveries anywhere in the supply chain, service failures due to poorly managed inventory, problems related to poor forecasting, and many other events related to operational failures.

SUPPLY CHAIN RISK CAN REALLY HURT

We could fill an entire book with stories that show how fragile most supply chains are today. Far too many companies are a single disruption away from bankruptcy. The following provides three examples of risk that caused many people a great deal of hurt.

The 100-Year Flood

Industries are often clustered into geographic regions. A prime example of the risk of locating suppliers and producers within a geographic cluster involves the massive flooding that occurred in Thailand, a region that accounted for almost half of the world's computer hard drive production. And, more recently, the energy industry clustered around Texas suffered major losses due to Hurricane Harvey. While clusters have redeeming economic and supply chain qualities, their dark side is less mentioned. One only has to look at the Thailand flooding that wiped out a large portion of the electronics hard drive industry. Before profiling the financial impacts of the flood, let's understand the back story.

At some point, multi-national companies concluded—after taking into account labor, taxes, freight, logistics, and government incentives—that Thailand was an appealing location for operations. If someone had taken the time to develop a supply chain map, he or she might have noticed that many suppliers, particularly those in the hard drive industry, were located in a 100-year flood plain. Some companies must have recognized this, since some facilities were built 6–10 feet above the flood plain. While those plants did not get damaged as badly, the flood made it impossible to move material in and out of these facilities.

The impact from this flood was depressing in its scale. Over 660,000 people were forced out of work and almost 10,000 factories shut down. In the auto industry, 6,000 automobiles per day could not be built. In the camera industry, Nikon eventually lost $786 million in sales; Canon had $604 million in lost sales; and Sony had recovery costs of $107 million in a single quarter. In the hard drive industry, iMac launches were delayed and hard drive prices skyrocketed by 100%. Many foreign companies, having witnessed firsthand the risk of clustering too much of their production and supply chain in one location, have since shifted production outside of Thailand.

What the Heck Is Guar?

Guar, a bean-like vegetable grown mainly in India is used in a diverse group of products including ice cream, fertilizer, cattle feed, chocolate milk, explosives, hair conditioner, peanut butter, kitty litter, and cranberry sauce. It is a ubiquitous item—it shows up just about everywhere. The real shock to the guar market occurred when oil and gas companies began using it as a key ingredient in their fracking solution. A single oil or gas well requires hundreds of acres of guar production. During the fracking process guar is mixed with water to thicken the fluid that is forced into the fractures of energy-bearing rock, thereby allowing oil and gas to seep out.[6] Needless to say, the guar market became volatile after the energy industry became a major guar buyer. Many companies that use guar did not even know about the pending commodity market disruptions until it was too late.

An analysis of the guar market reveals several important points that supply managers should understand. First, guar is primarily grown in India, a region where crop statistics are hard to come by. Relying on a single region is risky in itself, particularly one where the infrastructure for bringing crops to the international market are less developed. Second, no commodity market exists where buyers and sellers can hedge their risk. And third, the U.S. government does not offer crop insurance for guar, making it risky for U.S. farmers to grow. A relatively insignificant crop called guar suddenly became quite significant. The significance and the volatility that came with it exposed many companies to increased risk.

When Half the World's Supply Disappears in the Blink of an Eye

Nylon-12 is a critical resin for producing fuel lines and other automotive components. Unfortunately, Nylon-12 was essentially produced in a single facility in Germany. What is even more unfortunate is the explosion that removed half of the world's output in the blink of an eye. Within hours of the explosion, automotive original equipment manufacturers had established crisis management teams to scour the globe for new supply sources. This example provides some real-world lessons in SCRM.

After the explosion, users of Nylon-12 needed to ask some important questions, some of which should have already been answered during previous risk management exercises:

- How much Nylon-12 is currently available in inventory?
- How long will any supply that is available last, given short-term requirements?
- Is any Nylon-12 currently in transit?
- Does anyone else produce Nylon-12, or can anyone else ramp up and make it quickly?
- Is there an approved substitute for Nylon-12 and, if so, who provides the substitute?

The answers to the latter two questions should be known before a risk event even occurs, particularly for items that have limited supply availability. These examples reveal how susceptible supply chains can be to risk. At times, we can predict or even prevent risk events from occurring—at other times, a lack of planning limits our ability to mitigate the impact of a risk event.

RISK MANAGEMENT TOOLS AND APPROACHES

The following tools, techniques, and approaches all offer the opportunity to manage some aspect of supply chain risk. They appear here because they are not fully developed or implemented at most firms. Other approaches that have clear risk management implications—including becoming a preferred customer, developing a flexible supply chain, and assessing the financial condition of suppliers—appear elsewhere in this book.

The War Room

Imagine a room where risk management information is collected, categorized, analyzed, prominently displayed, and widely disseminated to the right people at the right time. Imagine dedicated staff who are tasked with the responsibility for monitoring supplier health, collecting and analyzing third-party data, spotting disruptive weather patterns, tracking material movement around the globe, updating in real time a dashboard of risk-related metrics, following political and business news and trends, responding to specific risk-related information requests from internal customers, and sending early risk warnings to those who would benefit from that information. This room would also allow users to flag supplier names or commodities for alerts when noteworthy information becomes available. A central role of the war room is to act as a repository for gathering, storing, interpreting, and disseminating, as needed, risk-related intelligence.

Several trends make the war room an attractive option for managing supply chain risk. First of all, we are witnessing a general movement toward greater centralization and centrally led leadership within supply chain management. It is time for risk management to join the list of activities that would benefit from a central leadership focus. Second, widely dispersed supply chains are making risk more rather than less critical as a topic. Finally, technology is available that can search and capture data and information in real time around the world.

Part of the war room can be outsourced to risk-event specialists. One such specialist is NC4, a California company that provides detailed and real-time threat intelligence to clients about global risks and changing conditions.[7] The company scans databases and newsfeeds around the globe 24/7 to provide a real-time assessment of global incidents and assigns a magnitude or priority on a global situation map (along with other risk-related services). This information is available graphically at the company's command centers as well as at each client location. The combination of in-depth global risk analysis, tracking of employee worldwide travels, and real-time incident alerts can provide predictive intelligence to those responsible for the well-being of employees and company assets.

Risk Management Heat Maps

As the concept of SCRM began to solidify into a body of knowledge, several major tenets evolved that resulted in the development of questions-of-discovery. As these questions became more refined, a mechanism to review, evaluate, and position a company's risk management maturity took shape in the form of a *spider diagram*. This diagram profiles a company's supply chain maturity, which highlights risks across ten areas that are related to supply chain management. This analysis has evolved into a supply chain risk awareness and readiness *heat map*. The resulting output of this analysis, the heat map superimposed over a spider diagram, provides a relative profile of red (high), yellow (medium), and green (low) levels of risk within the ten areas.

The heat map is an awareness technique that supports a valuable dialogue about risk readiness. Since many companies do not maintain an integrated view of their supply chain, this tool helps establish, with input from multiple disciplines, an enterprise-wide view of a company's supply chain risk profile.

Supply Chain Maps and Mapping

A supply chain map is a graphical representation of a firm's tier-one and sub-tier suppliers for any purchased item or service, whether it is a finished product, service, system or assembly, or component. Better maps will also include the downstream (the customer) portion of the supply chain. Mapping is an attractive risk-management technique, since most firms are unaware of what transpires past their tier-one suppliers. Those that do map their supply chain usually map only a small portion of it.

No standard nomenclature exists regarding what a supply chain map should contain or look like. This is in contrast to project management or lean management where the tools and techniques are well established. A mapping technique that is probably the most frequently used is the links and nodes approach. Links and nodes is a fairly common approach when designing or modeling a supply chain network. Nodes are the entities within a supply chain, such as suppliers, distributors, customers, other channel members, and the focal company. Links represent flows and are represented by solid or dotted lines. Flows typically include material, services, funds, and information.

The growth of supply chain mapping faces various challenges. For companies with a large supply base or complex product structures, the maps become complex very quickly. A supply base with hundreds of tier-one suppliers will have thousands of tier-two and tier-three suppliers. The same holds true for the downstream supply chain entities.

Another challenge is that many companies are not that concerned with what transpires past their first-tier suppliers. This is due partly to benign neglect as well as the fact that supply chain mapping is an intensive work process. A third challenge is that some suppliers are not willing to release their bill of material (BOM) data to customers or reveal their supply sources, making it difficult to identify sub-tier suppliers.

A fourth challenge involves determining the right kind of maps to develop. Some maps are so high level, such as industry level maps, that they lack the insight required to use them effectively for risk management. At the other extreme, a supply chain map may contain so many connections, nodes, and information that they become difficult to understand. A final challenge is that supply chains constantly evolve so the maps must be kept up-to-date.

Although supply chain maps are challenging to develop, they play an important role when conceptualizing risk. As a picture tells a thousand words, so do supply chain maps. Table 11.4 presents some guidelines when developing supply chain maps.

Table 11.4 Supply chain mapping guidelines

The following guidelines will help when developing supply chain maps, regardless of the mapping technique used: • *Don't forget the demand chain*: Most supply chain maps focus on suppliers because the supply group is often responsible for developing supply chain maps. The mapping process should include the supply and demand sides of the supply chain since risk can appear anywhere along a supply chain.   • *Include geographic locations*: It is difficult to come up with a logical reason why companies should not include the geographic locations of supply chain entities.   • *Suppliers and sites should be different entities in supply chain maps*: When supplier corporate locations and shipping locations are different entities, special designations should be treated separately from the corporate entity. Logistical providers and their sites should also be part of the map.   • *Insert hyperlinks in the map to connect to additional information and data*: Hyperlinks will help simplify maps while providing access to detailed data and information about supply chain entities.   • *Use a product's BOM as a guide when developing supply chain maps*: BOMs provide an excellent platform from which to begin developing a supply chain map.

- *Include more than material flows in the map*: Maps should also consider information, financial, and service flows. This can be accomplished by different designations that represent the flows within the supply chain.
- *Don't ignore interrelationships among firms*: A supply chain entity may be part of a supply chain map for another product or business unit within your company. Or, your customer's customer may also be a critical supplier. These interrelationships are what turn supply chains into supply networks.
- *Gain visibility to sub-tier supply chain entities*: Insisting on visibility to a tier-one supplier's suppliers should be a contracting requirement. World-class companies would never relinquish their understanding of the origin of components or other items that make up their final product.
- *Share the work burden*: Part of the evaluation process of tier-one suppliers can be an assessment of how well these suppliers map their supply chain. And, if tier-one suppliers insist that their tier-one suppliers (your tier-two suppliers) map their supply chain, you will gain visibility well downstream into your supply chain.

External Intelligence Capabilities

External intelligence consists of the data, information, and knowledge that originate outside of your company, including macroeconomic changes, legal and regulatory changes, industry trends and changes, supplier and competitor actions, social and labor force trends, customer expectations, technology innovations, and risk factors. Two challenges that are associated with external intelligence are that we either have information overload or that we simply fail to grasp what is happening around us.

A concept related to external intelligence is a company's external intelligence quotient (EIQ). EIQ represents how well your firm collects, assesses, and acts upon relevant external data, information, and knowledge. If an operating location senses that a significant event is about to happen (or has just happened), how quickly is it brought to the attention of a much broader audience? We can divide external intelligence into two primary groups—market intelligence and supply market intelligence.

Market intelligence deals with everyday information about developments in the external marketing environment. It is oriented toward the customer and the downstream part of the supply chain. A market intelligence system is a set of procedures and sources that is used to obtain that intelligence. Most firms rely on market intelligence systems and marketing research to gain external knowledge about their markets. Companies can take a variety of steps to improve the quality of their market intelligence including toll-free numbers or web-based customer feedback tools; customer advisory boards made up of key customers; market intelligence purchased from outside providers; automatic news alerts; sales force insights regarding marketplace developments; mechanisms to share information across your company; intelligence from distributors, retailers, and other intermediaries to forward important market intelligence; competitive and market benchmarking; trade shows and journals; competitor brochures and websites; and marketing research.

Supply market intelligence is the output from obtaining and analyzing information that is relevant to a company's current and potential supply markets. Its primary purpose is to manage risk and support effective decision making. There are four levels of supply market intelligence:

- *Macro-environment*: This includes information about market dynamics and global economic conditions, world trade, demographics, political climate, environment, and technology.
- *Country-level*: This category includes economic topics specific to a country, such as the location of free trade zones, the tax environment, labor availability, population size and trends, and regulatory bodies. It also includes information about cultural issues, political climate and stability, and national holidays.[8]
- *Industry and commodity*: This relates to the size and relative strength of industries and the worldwide users of commodities.
- *Supplier*: This category relates to the number of suppliers that exist; the products and services they provide; and their size, capabilities, and location.

Much of this information will come from reliable and objective websites.

De-cluster the Clusters

Anyone who follows the work of Michael Porter appreciates the connection between business or industry clusters and competitive advantage. Porter defines a cluster as geographic concentrations of linked businesses that enjoy unusual competitive success in their field. Compared with market transactions among dispersed buyers and sellers, the repeated exchanges between firms in a cluster promote trust, interdependence, coordination, innovation, and communication.[9] In the supply chain space we also have logistics clusters, which are defined as communities that bring together a broad range of supply chain services and deep expertise.[10] Examples of clusters are not hard to find—movie production in Hollywood; high-technology companies headquartered in Silicon Valley; the domestic U.S. automotive industry in Detroit; business process service providers in India; and financial services in New York City. And, as mentioned, Thailand was a cluster for the computer hard drive industry.

From a risk management perspective, it makes sense to think about de-clustering the clusters. De-clustering requires knowledge of the location of the most important entities in your supply chain, including sub-tier suppliers. One approach is to color code the different nodes in a supply chain. Sub-tier supplier, first-tier suppliers, internal manufacturing sites, contract manufacturers, ports and other logistical centers, and distributors will each have a color assigned. Next, create a color-coded global map. Are your imported items arriving through a single port? Do your exports all move through the same logistical network? Are a large number of your suppliers clustered together geographically? Are you relying on a single distributor location? Are your clusters located near areas known for hazard risk, including fault lines, tornadoes, flood plains, or hurricanes? A buying company may have its own clusters simply because it relies on suppliers that are located in the same vicinity.

The next step in the de-clustering process is to develop risk management plans that address any cluster-related risks. This can involve creating flexible supply chains (a concept discussed in the next chapter), requiring suppliers to have multiple production locations, qualifying multiple suppliers, and relying on more than a single logistical center or provider for processing imports and exports.

Two other approaches for managing risk presented in earlier chapters offer tremendous potential for managing supply chain risk. The first is supplier performance measurement systems (supplier scorecards) and reverse scorecards. The second approach involves the use of big data and predictive analytics.

WHAT DOES THE FUTURE LOOK LIKE? 12 PREDICTIONS YOU CAN TAKE TO THE BANK

Something that we should have concluded by now is that the world is not suddenly going to become a kinder and gentler place. The future will be kind to those companies that recognize the importance of risk management. It will be even kinder to those that understand how to anticipate, prepare for, and manage risk. The following is a set of predictions that will likely affect the future of SCRM. Keep in mind these predictions are relevant to supply managers as they operate within the context of an integrated supply chain:

- *Prediction 1: Attitudes toward risk will shift from avoidance to more thoughtful risk taking.* A common view among managers is that risk is something most closely associated with loss. As companies become confident in their risk management capabilities, risk attitudes should shift. This newfound confidence will lead to a greater willingness to engage in thoughtful risk taking. Companies will become more comfortable taking on risk as they develop their ability to manage risk, although hopefully not to the point of recklessness.
- *Prediction 2: Risk management will become an embedded part of supply and supply chain management.* Supply chain risk initiatives have largely

been handled separately from the normal responsibilities of supply and supply chain managers. As companies become better regarding their understanding of risk, we expect that risk initiatives will become a more routine part of the supply management process. Supplier selection teams, for example, will consider not only a supplier's operating capabilities; they will routinely assess a supplier's financial condition as well as its risk management plans and capabilities. Selection teams will also consider geographic location to ensure that a supply base is not overly clustered or located near known hazards. And, commodity management teams will include risk management plans when they develop commodity strategies. The bottom line is that a supply manager's job description will increasingly include risk management responsibilities.

- *Prediction 3: Companies will emphasize risk management initiatives past tier-one suppliers.* Most risk management initiatives stress (and usually stop at) first-tier suppliers. A *CAPS Research* study revealed that while 75% of participants report they have good risk management visibility regarding critical tier-one suppliers, only 30% report having visibility to their critical tier-two suppliers.[11] The need to focus on what is happening at the sub-tier levels of supply chains has never been greater. The question becomes how to manage sub-tier suppliers from a risk perspective. One way is to evaluate a potential supplier's risk management capabilities during supplier selection visits. When evaluating a supplier, why not also assess how well that tier-one supplier manages its suppliers (which are your tier-two suppliers)? Another approach that will gain in popularity is mapping supply chains past the tier-one level. There are few good reasons today for not knowing what the world looks like past tier-one suppliers.

- *Prediction 4: Supply chain risk metrics will increasingly stress real-time predictive indicators.* Far too often risk management decisions rely on historical or a batch data approach that is backward looking. Companies will increasingly search for ways to update the timeliness of their supply chain data and information. Rather than knowing what has happened, predictive analytic approaches will emerge that anticipate risk events before they occur or before an event results in a more serious loss.

- *Prediction 5: A pockets-of-excellence risk management model will shift toward an enterprise-wide risk management model.* An interesting phenomenon occurs as philosophies such as quality management, lean, and risk management evolve from concept to maturity. We often see internal sites or units display a capability that is not shared across the enterprise. The challenge becomes one of extending these pockets of excellence to an entire enterprise and supply chain. As a concept gains widespread attention, these pockets will become more widespread. The cross-fertilization of risk management abilities will be a clear indicator that risk management is maturing as a discipline. The evolution of risk management will likely be no different than other important processes we have seen over time.

- *Prediction 6: Total cost of ownership modeling will become a more routine part of SCRM.* Several factors will ensure that total cost models become a more routine part of the risk management process. First, making important supply chain decisions with limited data presents too much risk. Second, a global strategy based on sourcing in emerging markets demands better data upon which to base decisions. We fully expect a movement away from sourcing decisions based primarily on price and toward decisions based on total cost. To not do so exposes a company to excessive risk.
- *Prediction 7: Third-party risk solutions will increasingly replace home-grown solutions.* Risk management tools and applications are still in their infancy. As with most evolving concepts, the early tools are developed internally simply because external tools are not yet available. Or, the tools that are available don't quite fit a company's requirements. Third-party risk management tools and applications should proliferate as providers develop risk management tools that respond to marketplace needs. Most companies, even those with well-recognized supply chain management capabilities, are still progressing along a risk management maturity curve. As they become more sophisticated, so too will the tools that are available to manage risk.
- *Prediction 8: Risk categories and specific risks will continue to evolve and change.* The risks that companies face are dynamic rather than static, particularly since many companies expect to expand geographically away from their home borders. Global expansion creates supply chain complexity, which correlates directly with increased risk. Evolving risks often differ across companies and industries. Companies that rely on raw materials are increasingly concerned about the impact of rules addressing the sourcing of minerals as well as commodity market manipulation. Other companies are concerned about evolving risks regarding greenhouse gases, workplace conditions, labor issues, and the use of toxic materials. Everyone sees risk through a slightly different prism, and that prism will continuously evolve and change.
- *Prediction 9: Risk management approaches will rely increasingly on anticipation and less on reaction.* Most companies recognize their proficiency at responding to risk events. Most would say, however, that they would

like to be recognized for their proficiency at sensing and preventing risk events rather than reacting to and mitigating them. Risk anticipation will receive greater attention during product development and supplier selection, although preventive actions could lead to their own set of risks. A company that is working to simplify its product designs may rely more heavily on suppliers as design partners. This arrangement could raise concerns about intellectual property (IP) ownership and becoming overly dependent on suppliers for product design. Conversely, some suppliers are concerned about turning over their IP to customers during the design process or being asked to provide customers exclusive use of new technologies or innovations. Risk management requires an objective assessment of first- and second-order risks, even those risks that occur when trying to become more preventive or anticipatory.

- *Prediction 10: Risk management awareness will increasingly affect corporate culture.* The affect that risk management has on a company's culture can be a positive or negative force. On the positive side, as the language and practice of risk management become an embedded part of an organization's culture, personnel at all organizational levels and within all functional groups will consider risk implications when formulating strategies. On the negative side, risk awareness can lead to risk obsession, resulting in a culture that becomes excessively risk averse. Risk paralysis can prevent a company from pursuing the kinds of activities that lead to future growth.

- *Prediction 11: Supply chain risk will increase as companies source and sell in emerging markets.* Part of the reason that supply chain risk will likely increase is that companies will continually search for low-cost suppliers and selling opportunities in emerging countries. The result of sourcing and selling in emerging markets is that supply chains will continue to become longer, more complex, and inevitably riskier. Within supply chain management, this increases the need for external intelligence.

- *Prediction12: SCRM will increasingly become part of ERM.* ERM, which most companies have practiced at the corporate level for decades, and SCRM, which is relatively new, will increasingly be viewed as interdependent rather than independent. Part of this is due to the strategic implications that are associated with supply chain risks, particularly supply disruptions. As public companies fulfill their SEC reporting requirements, supply chain participants are increasingly part of this corporate reporting process; and supply chain executives will increasingly become part of executive risk committees. Supply chain risk and enterprise risk will increasingly overlap.

WHAT DO WE DO NOW? NEXT STEPS IN THE RISK MANAGEMENT JOURNEY

Supply chain stability and success depends partly on a company's risk management capabilities. A key question becomes how to use our knowledge regarding risk management to craft an action plan for moving forward. The following should be part of any company's strategy for managing supply chain risk.

Recognize the Importance of Risk Leadership

Becoming a risk management leader will not happen without individuals who demonstrate leadership, knowledge, and are willing to make the investments necessary for effective risk management. A continuous challenge concerns how to develop a generation of leaders who understand how to make risk management an organizational competency.

One way to link leadership and risk management is to make responsibility for risk an important part of executive steering committees. Leading companies usually have in place executive committees that are responsible for setting the strategic direction for their supply groups. Wherever leadership teams exist in the corporate hierarchy, the opportunity presents itself to embed risk management responsibilities.

Leadership is not the exclusive domain of executive leaders. Whether we are dealing with buyer-planners, commodity team leaders, supply chain managers, or vice presidents, each must demonstrate risk leadership at the appropriate level.

Establish Risk Crisis Teams

When thinking about risk, the question is not whether a risk event will occur, but when it will occur and how severe that event will be. During a crisis, every second matters—making preassigned crisis teams something that should be part of every supply organization. These teams, staffed with professionals who have access to real-time data and information, are an indispensable part of the risk management process.

Build the Risk Management Foundation

In addition to superb leadership, creating a risk management foundation entails emphasizing the four enabling areas featured in Chapters 3–6. These enablers include a supportive organizational design, information technology (IT) systems that provide real-time or near real-time data and information, risk-related measures and measurement systems that provide insight into the effectiveness of risk management efforts, and capable human resources. Developing more advanced risk management approaches is unlikely if an organization lacks the foundation upon which to build a sophisticated risk management competency.

Assess the Current State of Risk Management Preparedness

As SCRM evolves, a mechanism mentioned earlier to evaluate a company's maturity is a risk spider diagram. This diagram, which profiles a company's supply chain maturity, has evolved into a risk awareness heat map. The heat map provides insight into the exposure to supply chain risk by assessing a company's current state of preparedness. It is an awareness technique that starts a dialogue about supply chain risk. Effective risk management requires a solid understanding of the current state of risk management capabilities as well as identifying areas of opportunity.

Perform Risk Assessments and Develop Risk Management and Business Continuity Plans

A risk analysis or assessment is the process of evaluating potential risks within a supply chain. The objective of the assessment is to identify and categorize risks. The development of risk management strategies and business continuity plans should occur after performing the assessment. A risk plan is a document that considers known risks and includes descriptions, causes, probabilities or likelihood of risk occurrence, costs, and proposed risk management responses. It should be updated regularly and include reporting updates. Business continuity planning is the process for planning for and implementing procedures that are designed to ensure the continuous operation of critical business processes and functions when the most severe risks become a reality.

Gain Visibility Across the Supply Chain, Including Supplier and Customer Sub-Tiers

It is hard to imagine effectively managing risk without visibility to what is occurring across the supply chain. The logical question now is, "In which areas do we require visibility?" A partial visibility listing includes:

- Changes to the demand and supply side of supply chains
- Location and performance of sub-tier suppliers
- Current and predicted operational performance of suppliers
- Updates of supplier and customer financial health

- Real-time location of materials and transportation assets that are in transit
- Employee location and travel movements worldwide
- Hazard risks such as conflicts and weather
- Real-time identification and assessment of events to determine potential impact

It is hard to underestimate the role that IT systems play when pursuing supply chain visibility as an objective.

Benchmark Risk Management Practices Against Industry Leaders

Benchmarking is the continuous process of measuring products, services, processes, and practices of a firm against world-class competitors or those companies that are recognized as industry or functional leaders. The reasons for benchmarking risk management practices are not a mystery. The process accelerates the development of best practices from any industry; motivates those who must implement benchmarking findings; breaks down ingrained resistance to change; identifies technological breakthroughs from other industries; and provides valuable professional contacts. Benchmarking is also a way to create a corporate culture that understands the importance of external intelligence.

Organizations that do not benchmark tend to be reactive to change while pursuing internal, evolutionary change based on historical performance. They also tend to demonstrate a *not-invented-here syndrome*. On the other side, organizations that actively benchmark tend to be forward thinking, proactive, and receptive to new ideas—and they continuously search for industry best practices.

Build Resilience and Flexibility

Resilience is a hot topic in SCRM. At a basic level, resilience refers to the ability to recover from or adjust to misfortune or change.[12] It represents the ability of a company and supply chain to bounce back after an event. While the concept of resilience has been studied scientifically in the development of psychology and ecosystems for many years, it is still an emerging topic in the supply chain arena. Even in well-developed disciplines, the definitions of resilience are often contradictory and confusing.[13] Using a boxing metaphor, resiliency means being able to take a punch and still be standing. Companies that are resilient will have well-thought-out contingency plans in place that address any risk events that occur. This includes preapproved backup suppliers, approved substitutes, and system redundancy, to name but a few areas. Creating a flexible supply network and chain, the subject of the next chapter, will also be a key part of resiliency.

CONCLUDING THOUGHTS

Accounts of why SCRM must become a primary concern of supply managers are not hard to come by. For a variety of reasons, supply chain risk seems to be increasing rather than decreasing, making an appreciation of this topic an essential part of the supply management journey. While natural disasters like hurricanes and floods will always get the headlines, the reality is that supply chains face a whole range of risks that can ruin your day.

A culture that appreciates the importance of risk management, supported by supply managers who have access to a set of tools and techniques and can quantify the value of risk management, will be well positioned to face the realities of a less-than-friendly world. When the right culture is supported by tools, techniques, measures, and skills, supply managers can engage in thoughtful risk taking rather than being paralyzed by an irrational fear of risk.

REFERENCES

1. From http://www.businessdictionary.com/definition/risk.html.
2. From http://people.stern.nyu.edu/adamodar/pdfiles/valrisk/ch1.pdf.
3. E. Teach, "The Upside of ERM," *CFO*, (November 2013): 44.
4. A. Wieland and C. M. Wallenburg, "Dealing with Supply Chain Risks: Linking Risk Management Practices and Strategies to Performance," *International Journal of Physical Distribution & Logistics Management*, 42, no. 10 (2012).
5. F. Donovan and J. McCreery, "Coming to Grips with Supplier Risk," *Supply Chain Management Review*, 12, no. 6 (September 2008): 26, citing statistics from Marsh, Inc. and *Risk & Insurance* magazine.
6. R. Dezember, "Farmer Says: Hitch Your Wagons to Some Guar," *The Wall Street Journal*, November 25, 2011, C1.
7. M. W. Tobias, "Names You Need to Know: NC4 Situational Readiness," *Forbes*, from http://www.forbes.com/sites/marcwebertobias/2011/05/01/names-you-need-to-know-nc4-situational-readiness/.
8. R. Handfield. *Supply Market Intelligence* (Boca Raton, FL: Auerbach Publications, 2006): 175.

9. T. DeWitt and L. C. Giunipero, "Cluster and Supply Chain Management: The Amish Experience," *International Journal of Physical Distribution & Logistics Management*, 36, no. 4 (2006): 289–308.
10. B. McCrea, "Best Practices in Global Transportation and Logistics," *Supply Chain Management Review*, (December: 2012): 8.
11. "Supply Risk Blind Spots," *Inside Supply Management*, (November/December 2013): 34.
12. From www.merriam-webster.com.
13. S. Ponomarov and M. Holcomb, "Understanding the Concept of Supply Chain Resilience," *The International Journal of Logistics Management*, 20, no. 1 (2009): 124–125.

12

MEET FLEXIBILITY, YOUR NEW
BEST FRIEND

Close your eyes and imagine that you are walking along a deserted beach. During your walk you come across a bottle that has washed ashore. After picking up the bottle you remove its cap, which magically releases a genie. The genie informs you that you have one and only one wish that he will grant (your immediate wish for 50 more wishes only serves to irritate the genie). So, what is your wish? If you are a good supply manager you will wish that your company demonstrates a level of supply chain flexibility that other companies can only dream about. While this does not sound glamorous or exciting, it will make your life more comfortable. Plus, we know that the other things you would have wished for would eventually bore you or get you into trouble.

Why is flexibility so important that you would use your only wish to obtain it? In a now classic example of the effects of supply chain disruptions, a fire destroyed a supplier that had been providing Nokia and Ericsson with critical phone components. The response to this event showed the strategic implications of flexibility as a means to manage supply chain risk. Nokia's ability to secure components quickly from other sources compared with Ericsson's inability to respond to this event resulted in a dramatic industry shift. Ericsson's disruption not only cost the company several hundred million dollars in lost sales, it essentially ended the company's position as a player in the growing wireless phone business. (Apple's eventual introduction of the iPhone essentially did to Nokia what the fire did to Ericsson.) Ericsson's poor business continuity planning and lack of supply chain flexibility turned a hazard risk into a strategic risk.

The previous chapter addressed the still emerging topic of supply chain risk management. This chapter builds on that topic by exploring a construct called flexibility, a construct that will only grow in importance as risk management becomes a more intense focus of corporate planners. As a major player within the supply chain, supply managers must appreciate the role they play in creating a flexible supply chain, particularly since suppliers affect many types of flexibility. This chapter also presents some ways to embed flexibility into a company's culture and thinking.

WHAT IS FLEXIBILITY?

As the search continues for new and improved ways to manage supply chain risk, a capability called flexibility will be a sought-after approach to risk management. Flexibility is a concept that is receiving increased attention in the popular press as well as from supply chain professionals. A *Global Supply Chain Survey* conducted by PwC concluded that almost 65% of respondents plan to implement greater flexibility to better respond to supply chain challenges. This makes flexibility a top supply chain priority, just behind maximizing delivery performance and minimizing supply chain costs.[1] Table 12.1 summarizes a set of factors that are driving the need for greater supply chain flexibility.[2]

Most perspectives look at flexibility in terms of adjusting volumes in a manufacturing environment—a perspective that is not only limiting but also dangerous. Consider one definition of flexibility from a business dictionary: *flexibility is the ability of a system, such as a manufacturing process, to cost effectively vary its output within a certain range and given time frame.*[3] Supply chain flexibility involves so much more than what these limited perspectives convey. Managers need to view the domain of supply chain flexibility broadly rather than narrowly.

If our view of flexibility tends to be narrow, then what might be a better view? Flexibility represents the ability of an organization to be agile, adaptable, and responsive to change—particularly changes brought about by demand changes

Table 12.1   Factors driving the need for supply chain flexibility

• Emerging economies are expanding at double-digit rates, bringing a need to respond to growth and global shifts in sourcing and demand patterns
• Companies face increased scrutiny by activists, media, and social media-savvy consumers to uphold labor conditions and sustainability practices across dispersed supply chains
• Global growth requires changes in physical footprints and material flows, as well as a need to produce tailored products with faster order-to-delivery times
• Competitive factors, often resulting from competition worldwide, related to cost, speed-to-delivery, and customers are increasing the complexity of supply chains
• Supply chain risk is becoming a major corporate concern
• Supply chains are increasingly vulnerable to disruptions caused by natural disasters, political unrest, and labor unrest such as port strikes
• Commodity markets are more volatile compared with 20 years ago

and risk events. The opposite of being flexible is being rigid, resistant to change, or unable to modify a course of action. Companies should view flexibility as an important supply chain objective that we strive to achieve.

Another perspective views flexibility in terms of a micro and macro perspective. Micro flexibility refers to how fast a supply chain detects and responds to issues and opportunities in the short term, including time horizons as short as one day or even hours. Examples where micro flexibility may come into play include a late truck delivery, a special packaging request, or a sudden change in demand. Micro flexibility deals with how fast and how effectively a company can respond to these kinds of short-term events.[4]

Macro flexibility refers to the speed at which a company's supply chain can adapt and execute new strategies and programs to support changes in overall company strategies or market changes. A traditional retailer may want to establish an online retailing capability, or conversely, an online retailer may want to distribute its products through traditional brick and mortar outlets. Macro flexibility pertains to how fast the company can respond to achieve its goal of a new supply chain channel or the development of a new product.

Let's look at several examples that link flexibility and resiliency, one of today's hot supply chain topics. A good example of enhancing resiliency through flexibility comes from the utility industry. As utilities work to storm-harden their networks (a form of risk prevention), some are also investing in technology to recover faster from outages (mitigate the risk) through an approach called the *smart grid*. New systems use advanced technology to pinpoint problems, reroute power around problem areas, and identify where repair crews need to go first to get the most customers restored the fastest.[5] One emerging technology cuts off power at the spot where a tree falls into a power line and then reroutes electricity so nearby customers still retain power. This is all done to bounce back after a risk event.

A second example involves offshore oil exploration in the Gulf of Mexico. It became obvious that following the 2010 explosion at BP's Macondo well, new and complex regulations would emerge addressing offshore drilling safety. Some observers predicted that drilling in the Gulf of Mexico would not recover for years, if ever. But that does not seem to be the case. In the words of one analyst, "Bottom line—Gulf of Mexico oil production is in considerably better shape than even the most ardent optimists envisioned following Macondo."[6] Part of the reason for such optimism is the oil industry's flexibility in adapting to a new regulatory environment that features stricter safety oversight and slower permit reviews. Estimates indicate that by 2022 oil output from the Gulf of Mexico will be 28% higher compared to previous levels. The energy industry, at least in this case, has shown its resiliency.

Perhaps the most important aspect of flexibility is that it provides choices. Resilient supply chains are able to adapt quickly to changes while maintaining customer service levels.[7] The point here is that effective supply chain management demands the ability to respond quickly to changes and events, sometimes within minutes. The primary objective of flexibility is to provide that ability.

Let's consider some examples that highlight the risks of inflexibility. A derailment of an eastbound passenger train in Connecticut and subsequent collision with a westbound train severely affected the busiest passenger rail corridor in the U.S.[8] Part of the reason the impact was so severe was that construction in the area of the accident reduced the number of active tracks from four to two over a seven-mile stretch. The result was a complete lack of routing flexibility that prohibited the diversion of trains to other tracks with the predictable gridlock resulting. Thousands of commuters were forced to shift from rails back to roads in a part of the country that already experiences traffic nightmares.

Another example reveals the risks of inflexibility in a lean production environment. In 2007, an earthquake with a magnitude of 6.8 struck central Japan. One of the companies affected was a supplier named Riken Corporation, surely a name that is not familiar to most readers.[9] Because this company could not supply a $1.50 piston ring after the earthquake, 70 percent of Japan's auto production shut down within days of the quake. Japan's supply chain simply had no buffer inventory. Companies affected by the supply disruption included Toyota, Honda, Nissan, Mazda, Fuji Heavy Industries, Mitsubishi, and Suzuki. Just about any company that made a product with wheels and an engine attached to it was affected. Toyota temporarily shut down production at all 12 of its Japanese assembly plants.

Why would a low-cost item such as a piston ring cause so many problems? Most Japanese firms rely on one supplier for a purchase requirement, making the fallback to another supplier difficult in the short term. To further complicate matters, each customer specified its own custom designed piston rings and maintained little to no safety stock. A lack of standardization with something as basic as a piston ring contributed to bringing an entire industry to its knees. After the earthquake, Toyota's president said the company was going to examine its risk management policies. It was clear the current policies limited the company's flexibility and resiliency.

CATEGORIZING FLEXIBILITY

Flexibility is a complex construct, particularly since so many kinds of flexibility exist. As mentioned, we often see this concept presented as if it were generic or one dimensional, which is far from the truth. Table 12.2 presents 15 dimensions or types of supply chain flexibility along with possible ways to achieve that flexibility. Supply managers play an important role in developing flexible supply chains, particularly since suppliers affect a fair number of the items in this table. The following subsections describe, with examples, various kinds of flexibility. Space limitations prohibit addressing each type of flexibility that is presented in Table 12.2.

Table 12.2 Types of supply chain flexibility

Type of Flexibility	The Ability to . . .	Supply Chain Tactics
Order lead time flexibility	Request variable rather than fixed lead times with suppliers as required by customer demands	• Request shorter lead times from suppliers • Select suppliers with capabilities that allow flexible rather than rigid lead time requirements
Job scheduling flexibility	Adjust production and delivery dates internally and with suppliers as conditions change	• Real-time data visibility and dynamic scheduling • Close information linkages with customers • Work to secure preferential scheduling treatment from suppliers
Product configuration and variety flexibility	Modify the design of a base product, including adding new varieties or features	• Develop platform products that allow re-configurability and modification • Practice mass customization • Develop quick changeover capabilities and flexible production processes
Supply chain design flexibility	Adjust or tailor supply chains to satisfy specific requirements or customer segments	• Create multiple supply chains to match product and customer segment requirements
Logistics flexibility	Reroute or adjust movement through logistical networks; shift modes of transportation or carriers	• Preapprove secondary carriers • Have multiple port options • Preapprove modal choices • Control title to goods to enable rerouting
Source/location flexibility	Shift production from one internal or external supplier or site to another supplier or site	• Qualify multiple internal production sites • Qualify alternate suppliers • Use suppliers with multiple production sites
Capacity flexibility	Modify the internal and external capacity levels of supply chain members	• Reconfigure work cells to shift according to product mix requirements • Use overtime and weekend production • Approve secondary supply sources and contract manufacturers • Reserve capacity slots with suppliers • Evaluate capacity flexibility during supplier selection

Design flexibility	Modify product designs quickly	• Computer-aided product designs • Virtual simulation and testing • Use standard components wherever possible • Integration between engineering and supply chain/operations personnel
Internal routing flexibility	Alter how a product flows internally through a facility	• General rather than specialized workers and equipment • Preapproved alternate routing • Use of flexible work cells
Volume flexibility	Adjust order volumes internally and with suppliers in response to demand changes	• Overtime and weekend production • Access to temporary labor • Contract manufacturers and secondary suppliers • Use of safety stock inventory
Physical facility flexibility	Change the structure or layout of physical processes or sites	• Use modular facilities that can be modified for new uses • Build in future expansion and re-configurability capabilities during facility design
Workforce flexibility	Assign or reassign workers as needed	• Simplify labor work rules and job classifications • Utilize temporary labor • Cross-train employees
Energy flexibility	Shift seamlessly between energy sources	• Purchase flex-fuel vehicles and equipment • Consider energy flexibility as a decision variable when specifying new equipment and facilities
Material flexibility	Shift from one material to another with relative ease	• Consider material flexibility during product design • Test and preapprove material substitutes • Qualify substitute material suppliers or distributors
Production mix flexibility	Ability to produce more than one product line within a facility or work area	• Flexible assembly lines and processes • Cross-trained workers who can produce more than one type of product • Use of IT systems to provide assembly instructions and guidance

Design Flexibility

Design flexibility allows a company to modify product designs quickly. Why would designs need modifying? A product design could have a flaw that requires correction, a component suddenly becomes unavailable, new or better components or materials become available, or cost pressures lead to product simplification. At times, designs are changed simply in the name of continuous improvement.

Companies can pursue design flexibility in many ways. Computer-aided product design systems enable rapid changes to design; rapid prototyping allows design changes to be tested quickly; and using standard components wherever possible helps avoid locking in designs that are difficult to change due to excessive customization. Working with suppliers that are able to make modifications quickly also enhances design flexibility.

The following example highlights the advantage of design flexibility. Common wisdom would say that it is not feasible to build servers in the U.S. Someone should have told that to SeaMicro (which eventually became part of AMD), a company located in Santa Clara, California. The company relied on a contract manufacturer located one mile away from its engineering center to build a radically different kind of server. SeaMicro says that manufacturing locally has helped it compete successfully against much larger rivals. The company's engineers are constantly experimenting with new components and designs in a bid to reduce energy consumption and quicken the performance of their servers. Engineers take their design changes a mile down the road to the contract manufacturer and test them in new systems almost immediately. Design flexibility, which SeaMicro calls lean engineering, saves weeks and even months compared with using contract manufacturers located in China or Taiwan.[10]

Capacity Flexibility

Capacity flexibility refers to the ability to modify relatively quickly the available capacity levels of internal and external supply chain members. Usually, but not always, capacity flexibility refers to upward adjustments in output, although downward revisions do occur. Dozens of reasons exist why a company may need to modify supply chain capacity levels. Unexpected orders, demand growth, product recalls that require replacements, or a need to buffer a supply chain with more inventory due to uncertainty can all result in a need for changes in output.

Capacity flexibility can be achieved in a variety of ways. Work cells can be reconfigured to accommodate shifting product requirements, companies can use overtime and weekend production to respond quickly to changing requirements; and a company can preapprove secondary supply sources and contract manufacturers to handle unusual demand requirements.

One innovative way to gain access to capacity involves pursuing longer term contracts with suppliers that feature reserved capacity that is not committed to any particular product. As demand becomes better known these capacity slots are replaced with actual orders. This approach provides greater flexibility, shorter lead times, assurance of supply, and, of course, reduced supply chain risk. The medium- to longer term forecasts that are used to reserve capacity slots usually involve an aggregate number rather than forecasts of specific products.

Energy Flexibility

Energy flexibility is not what usually comes to mind when we think about supply chain flexibility. This type of flexibility allows a company to shift between energy sources, whether it is energy to power vehicles or entire facilities. Various ways to achieve this flexibility include flex-fuel vehicles and dual energy options when designing new equipment and facilities.

Nowhere is energy flexibility more prominent than in the utility industry. An increasing number of utilities now operate power generating facilities that use coal, natural gas, or renewable energy sources. As market prices shift between these various energy sources, some utilities take advantage of these shifts by switching their fuel source. The primary shift has been between coal and natural gas. One observer notes that "natural gas prices can't really shoot much more above a certain level because then utilities will pile back into coal."[11]

Of course, the reverse is true. Coal prices cannot rise too high because utilities will shift to gas. Historically, utilities have been such large consumers of coal and gas that industry observers expect coal and natural gas prices to generally move inversely rather than in unison as utilities adjust their usage in response to market prices. Energy flexibility helps provide a natural hedge against the financial risk of rising energy costs (or, in the case of coal, against governmental and environmental pressures). We expect shifts in market share between energy sources as utilities adjust their raw material usage based on various factors.

Product Configuration and Variety Flexibility

John Deere manufactures products that are known for more than just tearing up dirt. While a number of factors contribute to this company's success, something we cannot ignore is the Deere's ability to offer an unbelievable variety of product configurations. Farm equipment is not a product that is generally standardized country to country, like aircraft, for instance. In a recent year, Deere built almost 8,000 variations of its popular 8R tractor line. Product configuration flexibility allows Deere to serve the needs of diverse farm markets using a single product platform. This reduces the risk of lacking the right product for a particular geographic market.

Companies that excel at flexible product configuration are taking advantage of a production model called mass customization. Mass customization is the process of delivering goods and services that are modified to satisfy specific customer needs. It is a technique that combines the flexibility and personalization of custom-made with the lower unit costs associated with mass production.[12] In a mass customization environment, make-to-stock (push) production strategies are replaced by make-to-order (pull) production strategies.

Physical Facility Flexibility

One of the key objectives of supply chain management is the effective matching of supply with demand. For companies that make multiple products, particularly in the same facility, the ability to quickly and easily reconfigure physical space as market demand changes has obvious benefits. A way to do this is to create physical processes that can be changed or expanded easily. Capacity flexibility and physical flexibility have some obvious overlap.

How does this work in practice? When Stryker, a leading medical technology company that designs and manufactures orthopedic products, planned its Mahwah, NJ facility, it did so with physical flexibility as a primary objective. The facility includes work cells that can quickly be reconfigured from one product line to another, a capability that allows the company to better match demand and supply across its numerous products. Furthermore, the building was constructed so it could be physically expanded if more square footage was required. This compares with facilities whose square footage is fixed due to the proximity to other structures, roads, railroad tracks, waterways, etc. Physical flexibility was a primary focus affecting the development of the facility.

Supply Chain Design Flexibility

Supply chains are rarely as neat and tidy as presented in academic models. In fact, they often feature a multitude of forms as firms pursue a variety of customer segments as well as different sourcing and distribution channels. Supply chain design flexibility means that an organization has designed or can adjust its supply chain to satisfy specific requirements. A one-size-fits-all supply chain rarely meets the needs of a complex organization.

Dell Computer, a company that faced strategic risk as customers shifted from PCs and laptops to tablets and other devices, realized that the supply chain it established to support make-to-order online sales was not necessarily the right supply chain to support its expansion into retail sales and other market segments. Dell has since developed four supply chains, each dedicated to a different customer segment, that give the company added flexibility to respond to a broader array of market opportunities. The build-to-order supply chain supports Dell's online customer segment; the build-to-plan supply chain supports the retail segment; the build-to-stock supports the online/popular configurations segment; and the build-to-spec supply chain supports the corporate segment.[13]

Logistics Flexibility

Logistics flexibility means being able to adjust the route, carrier, or even the mode of transportation used to move goods between points. This kind of flexibility allows shipments to be rerouted when natural hazards occur, roads are closed due to accidents, a strike occurs at a port or a carrier, or a mode of transportation becomes less viable.

The benefit of logistics flexibility is increasingly evident in the U.S. oil industry. A proposed $2 billion pipeline (a fixed, inflexible mode of transportation) designed to take plentiful crude oil from West Texas to California has failed to generate interest among large California refiners because of the flexibility offered by rail cars. Relying on rail shipments to transport oil allows refiners to source from different locations around the U.S. and route the oil to their California refineries, something that is not feasible with a fixed pipeline. A growing supply of North American crude oil is coming from locations where prices fluctuate, allowing refiners to use different routes and modes of transportation to make opportunistic purchases for their crude supply.[14]

Material Flexibility

Material flexibility allows producers to shift from one material to another with relative ease, which enables substitutability. Unfortunately, this type of flexibility is not always easy. A major U.S. food producer found that it had to change an ingredient in one of its key products due to a safety concern at its supplier. The producer was forced to spend thousands of hours validating a new ingredient and a new supplier to verify the change did not alter the taste or quality of the food product. This inflexibility severely limited this company's ability to respond quickly to a problem. The guar and Nylon-12 examples from Chapter 11 revealed the importance of material flexibility.

Industries that rely extensively on raw materials should value material flexibility. Recall from Chapter 1 that if you think commodity price fluctuations have been a bit volatile over the last decade or so, you are right. The size of fluctuations in commodity prices has more than tripled since 2005 compared to 1980–2005 based on International Monetary Fund data. When markets become volatile, the ability to pursue material flexibility (as well as some other types of flexibility) would offer welcome alternatives to simply accepting that volatility.

Increased market or commodity volatility should make material flexibility a sought-after capability, which some users of nickel have come to appreciate. In the not too distant past the price of nickel soared, making it a cost prohibitive item for companies that rely on stainless steel 318, an industry standard item that contains nickel. One industry that was hit particularly hard includes companies that manufacture vehicles to carry food products. Fortunately, material engineers at some companies were able to shift quickly to *lean duplex*, a type of stainless steel that offers material properties that are anywhere from 30 to 200% better than traditional alloys with only a fraction of the nickel contained in other stainless steels. Lean duplex also offers higher yield strength, making it less susceptible to cracking and corrosion.[15] Material flexibility has helped the producers of tank trailers avoid risk due to the volatility associated with nickel.

Product Mix Flexibility

Product mix flexibility means having the ability to produce multiple items or products in the same work cell or facility. The logic behind this flexibility is that as demand for one product declines, demand for another product in that facility may be increasing, thereby allowing the company to maintain a balance between supply and demand. Product mix flexibility is what allows a facility to maintain an even balance of work that is less susceptible to the volatility that may affect a facility that produces a single or limited product portfolio. The bottom line is that supply chain planners do not like volatility. The ability to adjust the production mix offers one way to offset the detrimental effects of demand volatility at the stock keeping unit level.

Let's look at a case where product mix flexibility did not exist. When Toyota expanded its truck making capacity in North America, it built a facility in Texas that could only produce a single type of vehicle. This contrasts with Toyota's Japanese plants that produce up to six different vehicles. As gas prices began to rise, this reduced the demand for the trucks that the Texas facility built and increased the demand for smaller cars, which the company could not fill at other facilities due to capacity constraints. Product mix inflexibility affected Toyota in two ways. It increased the company's costs due to an underutilized assembly plant; and it limited revenue growth because of an unsatisfied demand for smaller cars.

While Table 12.2 includes other kinds of flexibility, the types elaborated upon here should have created an awareness of the depth of this construct. A discussion of supply chain flexibility must not ignore the fact that many of the actions taken to enhance flexibility will come with some sort of cost. As it pertains to risk management, some of these costs will be hard to quantify or justify with traditional investment analysis techniques.

EMBEDDING FLEXIBILITY INTO THE SUPPLY CHAIN

One important issue focuses on how to transition from a conceptual understanding of flexibility to making this concept an embedded part of an organization's thinking and culture. Four areas where flexibility should be an embedded part of our thinking are during the development of business continuity plans, development of new products and services, development of commodity strategies, and supplier evaluation and selection. This section operates under the premise that building a flexible supply chain is one of the most powerful ways to manage supply chain risk.

Incorporate Flexibility into Business Continuity Plans

The objective of a business continuity plan is to assure the availability, reliability, and recoverability of business processes that service a company's customers, partners, and stakeholders. Business continuity formalizes a company's overall approach to effective risk management, and should be closely aligned to a company's incident management, emergency response management, and information technology disaster recovery. The great sage Warren Buffet once observed that risk comes from not knowing what you are doing. Business continuity planning helps ensure we know what we are doing when bad things happen.

A key part of a business continuity plan involves the recovery strategies that are put in place to mitigate specific risks that have been identified during a risk assessment. This is where various kinds of flexibility come into play. Data gathered from a business impact analysis and risk assessment (two important subparts of the continuity planning process) will lead to recovery strategies that mitigate potential risks. Recovery strategies and the associated estimated costs for implementation are then developed and presented to a business continuity governance board (i.e., executive board) for review. Increasingly, different kinds of flexibility will be part of the continuity plan.

Make Flexibility an Important Part of New Product and Service Development

A typical feature of new product development projects, particularly at higher technology companies, involves engineering teams that are working as fast as possible to develop new products or technologies. Then, at some later point, supply chain professionals become involved and suppliers are selected to support a design. Unfortunately, this approach limits a company's ability to consider the impact of risk.

It is a challenge to find examples of companies that consider product development, risk, and supply chain flexibility simultaneously. While integrated product and process development is well understood, the integration of supply chain flexibility within the development process is not. The opportunity to think about flexibility during product development is severely limited with models that fail to consider risk issues early on.

What are the characteristics of a process that brings together product developers and supply chain risk managers who understand the importance of flexibility? First, supplier selection must happen early rather than later in the design process. This gives those responsible for supplier risk management time to identify supplies that have certain kinds of flexibility (among other things). Next, each cross-functional team involved in product development, with the help of supply chain managers, will have responsibility for identifying a set of supply chain risks, including logistical risks that may affect the project. These risks are then collected and categorized for easy access. Development team members will then meet regularly to review not only product development progress but also the actions taken to address potential risks. Increasingly, these actions will incorporate supply chain flexibility.

Taking this a step further, the product development team will estimate the probability of each risk and its impact on product launch. Priority is then given to evaluating the higher risks to determine what action can be taken to reduce their probability and impact, including approaches that provide supply chain flexibility, thereby turning a higher risk into a lower risk prior to launch.

Make Risk Plans Supported by Flexibility Part of Commodity Strategies

As mentioned in Chapter 7, one indicator of an organization's maturity is the presence of well-thought-out strategies, which in supply chain management includes commodity or category strategies. A purchase commodity or category is simply a grouping of like items or services. Something that should increasingly be required is for commodity or sourcing teams to include risk assessment plans as part of their proposed commodity strategies. This forces commodity teams to assume the responsibility for risk management rather than shifting it to another party. This also helps embed risk management thinking into the corporate culture.

A risk assessment plan is an extension of a risk analysis. This plan documents known risks and includes descriptions, causes, likelihood of risk occurrences, costs, and proposed risk management responses. The plan can easily be included as part of a formal commodity strategy. Again, many of the risk management responses proposed in the plan will relate directly to actions that enhance supply chain flexibility.

Consider Supplier Flexibility During Evaluation and Selection

Supplier evaluation and selection is one of the most important business processes that firms undertake today. The consequences of making a wrong decision can have long and lasting consequences, particularly when suppliers receive longer term contracts. Referring back to Table 12.2, suppliers affect a fair number of the kinds of flexibility that affect risk management and corporate resiliency. In particular, suppliers affect a firm's order lead time, job scheduling, logistics, source/location, capacity, design, volume, and material flexibility. The list could be shorter, depending on the kinds of flexibility that suppliers affect directly. It is probably safe to conclude that most selection teams fail to evaluate explicitly the kinds of flexibility that suppliers affect. This should change as a focus on risk management becomes a progressively larger part of supply and supply chain management. Chapter 14 discusses the importance of supplier selection as an organizational process.

CONCLUDING THOUGHTS

A commitment to risk management will logically include a focus on supply chain flexibility. When the ingredients are present that allow a company to create a flexible supply chain, that company can more confidently engage in thoughtful risk taking rather than facing an irrational fear of risk. Within the domain of supply chain management, flexibility might just become your company's newest source of competitive advantage. And, unlike the story at the beginning of this chapter, you really do not need a genie to achieve it.

REFERENCES

1. A. Sun and G. Goldbach, "How a Flexible Supply Chain Delivers Value," *Industry Week*, (April 5, 2013), accessed from http://www.industryweek .com/procurement/how-flexible-supply-chain-delivers-value.
2. Adapted from the PWC Global Supply Chain Survey 2013 and A. Sun and G. Goldbach, "How a Flexible Supply Chain Delivers Value," *Industry Week*, (April 5, 2013).
3. Accessed from http://www.businessdictionary.com/definition/flexibility .html.
4. D. Gilmore, Editor-in-Chief, *Supply Chain Digest*, March 4, 2010, http:// www.scdigest.com/assets/FirstThoughts/10-03-04.php.
5. R. Smith, "Getting 'Smart' on Outages," *The Wall Street Journal*, November 8, 2012, B6.
6. T. Fowler, "After Spill, Gulf Oil Drilling Rebounds," *The Wall Street Journal*, September 21, 2012, B1.
7. M. Stevenson and M. Spring, "Flexibility from a Supply Chain Perspective: Definition and Review," *International Journal of Operations Management*, 27, no. 2 (2007): 713.

8. T. Mann, "Rail Corridor Hit with Major Outage." *The Wall Street Journal,* May 20, 2013, A3.

9. This example is adapted from A. Chozick, "A Key Strategy of Japan's Car Makers Backfires," *Wall Street Journal,* July 20, 2007, B1 and A. Chozick, "Toyota Sticks by 'Just in Time' Strategy after Quake," *The Wall Street Journal,* July 24, 2007, A2.

10. A. Vance, "Stars and Stripes and Servers Forever," *Business Week,* (February 28, 2011): 33.

11. D. Strumpf, "Headwinds for Rally in Natural Gas." *The Wall Street Journal,* October 8, 2012, C5.

12. Adapted from http://www.investopedia.com/terms/m/masscustomization .asp.

13. D. Simich-Levi, "When One Size Does Not Fit All," *MIT Sloan Management Review,* (Winter 2013): 15–17.

14. B. Lefebvre, "Trains Leave Pipeline in Lurch," *The Wall Street Journal,* May 24, 2013, B1.

15. D. Rondini, "Less Nickel Was Worth the Savings," *Transport Topics,* April 29, 2013, 19.

13

GLOBAL SUPPLY, RESHORING, AND OTHER WORLDLY TOPICS

Sourcing in an era of change and disruption requires an ability to adapt and innovate. As we think about how to respond to an extensive list of competitive demands, the development of global strategies becomes an increasingly attractive but potentially risky option if not implemented well. The potential for high rewards from globalization makes the case for global supply management a strong one.

This chapter presents a variety of topics that are relevant when sourcing across the world. The first section explores international trade and purchasing. The next section explains the differences between international purchasing and global supply management. Following that, an analysis of reshoring is discussed, and in particular, addresses why a shifting of work back to the U.S. from overseas has been a trickle rather than a deluge. The chapter concludes with some predictions and trends regarding the future location of suppliers as companies develop worldwide supply networks.

UNDERSTANDING INTERNATIONAL TRADE

A discussion of international purchasing and global supply management will benefit from stepping back and looking at a broader picture called international trade. The growth in worldwide commerce over the last 35 years, which includes buying and selling across borders, has been nothing short of astounding. Since the late 1980s, international trade has accelerated rapidly and the U.S. has played a major role in this growth.

Without meaning to insult anyone's intelligence, international trade is made up of the goods and services that enter (imports) and exit (exports) a country. For reporting purposes, the U.S. government divides imports and exports into six primary categories—foods, feeds, and beverages; industrial supplies, including petroleum and petroleum-based products; capital goods; automotive vehicles and related items; consumer goods; and other goods. Other countries also segment their trade statistics in some logical manner. For example, the U.S. imports several hundred billion dollars a year in automotive vehicles and parts. It's not hard to see what makes up a major part of U.S. trade.

While we hear a great deal about the trade deficit that the U.S. maintains with the rest of the world—and this roughly $750 billion annual deficit in goods is not trivial—what is often overlooked is the dramatic increase in exports over the last several decades. (The U.S. has a roughly $250 billion positive balance of trade annually in services.) Since 1980, the total value of goods that are exported from the U.S. has increased over 547% (from $224 billion in 1980 to almost $1.45 trillion in 2016). The value of services exported from the U.S. for this same period increased almost 1,500% (from $47.5 billion in 1980 to over $750 billion in 2016).[1] While manufacturing is still a major part of the U.S. economy, the growth in services supports the contention that the U.S. is becoming a services and knowledge-based economy.

Is it possible that these figures increased simply because prices have also increased? After all, higher prices will inflate the value of the goods and services that are moving across borders. While inflation explains some of the changes in the gross domestic product (GDP) and trade figures, the consumer price index in 1980 averaged 82.4 while the index averaged 240 in 2016, representing an increase of 191%.[2] The producer price index also showed similar restraint over this period. Factors besides price increases are clearly responsible for the dramatic export and import growth. What other reasons might explain the growth in trade? Perhaps first and foremost is the overall growth in the world economy. In 1980, the U.S. GDP, which represents the total value of goods and services produced in the country, was $2.8 trillion. By 2016 this figure climbed to $18.6 trillion, or an increase of 564%.[3] The percentage growth in GDP coincides with the percentage growth in imports and exports. In fact, faster economic growth in the U.S. compared with some other industrialized countries, particularly during the latter 1990s and early 2000s, combined with a strong dollar that made imports relatively cheap, were largely responsible for the widening gap between exports and imports.

Other factors affect the amount and pattern of global trade. The end of the Cold War resulted in increased trade in emerging markets in Eastern Europe and Russia, although a sometimes tenuous relationship with Russia could cause a reversal of this trend. And of course, the formerly closed country known as China became receptive to international commerce and the money that came with it. The 1990s also witnessed a growth in trade agreements that lessened import and export restrictions. World Trade Organization rules, the General Agreement on Tariffs and Trade, and the North American Free Trade Agreement all promoted a dramatic increase in worldwide trade. Various other free-trade agreements between countries (which are too numerous to review here) have also helped to reduce trade restrictions.

The last 35 years was clearly an era that favored the dismantling of trade barriers between countries, although some will argue this dismantling has not always been equitable. Interestingly, we appear to be entering a period in which free trade is not as welcomed as it was during the 1990s. Some will argue that free trade is not necessarily fair trade, particularly given the persistent trade deficits that the U.S. has with certain countries. An analysis by the *Wall Street Journal* and the U.S. Department of Commerce revealed that China imposes higher tariffs compared with the U.S. for 20 of 22 major goods categories. The European Union imposes higher tariffs compared with the U.S. for 17 of 22 categories. Many countries, particularly China, also impose non-tariff barriers that make it difficult to export goods from the U.S.[4]

Something that most observers probably do not realize is that a large part of international trade consists of transactions between subsidiaries or units of the same company. The U.S. government calls this *related-party trade*, which includes trade by U.S. companies with their subsidiaries abroad as well as trade by U.S. subsidiaries of foreign companies with their parent companies. While this fluctuates year to year, related-party trade accounts for almost 50 percent of imports and almost 30 percent of exports.[5] Related-party trade currently comprises around 40 percent of the dollar value of all exports and imports in the U.S.—a percentage that has remained fairly consistent over the years. As companies become more global in their operations, we should expect to see an increase in international trade due to related-party trading.

International Purchasing Growth at the Company Level

The number of U.S. companies that source internationally has increased dramatically over the last 35 years. While precise data are hard to come by, the percentage of U.S. companies purchasing internationally between 1973 and 1975 doubled from around 20% to 45%. The oil embargo of the 1970s coupled with shortages of other basic materials forced purchasers to search worldwide for sources of supply. During this time, many foreign producers were beginning their ascent as quality, cost, and even technology leaders. The most sought-after import items by U.S. companies in the mid-1970s were production machinery and equipment followed by chemicals and mechanical and electrical components.

By 1982, the percentage of U.S. companies that engaged in international purchasing increased to just less than 60%. This growth reflected the continuing inability of domestic suppliers (and original equipment manufacturers) to compete in terms of price, quality, and even delivery performance. The early 1980s were a difficult time for many U.S. companies as they adjusted to new worldwide competition. Foreign suppliers often provided higher-quality goods at a lower total cost compared with their U.S. counterparts. The survival of many companies demanded that they source from the same suppliers that supported their foreign competitors.

The early to late 1980s witnessed a sharp increase in the number of companies that pursued international purchasing. One study concluded that just over 70% of U.S. companies engaged in foreign sourcing by 1987. Part of this growth is attributable to a dramatic increase in the value of the U.S. dollar against other major currencies. Imports became less expensive while exports from the U.S. became costlier to foreign trading partners. U.S. producers found it difficult to compete in world markets, leading to (then) unheard of trade imbalances. A stronger dollar coupled with a relative lack of competitiveness made life difficult for many within the U.S.

Probably a better way to look at the growth in international purchasing is the percentage of total purchases that are sourced from outside the U.S. Again, while precise numbers are hard to come by, total purchases from non-U.S. sources by U.S. companies have increased from under 10% of total purchases on average in the early 1990s to over 25% in 2000. The current figure most likely averages around 30%.[6]

A report by the *Center for Advanced Purchasing Studies* noted that the percentage of total direct purchases that are sourced on a worldwide basis has increased dramatically since the year 2000, growing from between 21 and 30% of total purchases to between 31 and 40% currently. Furthermore, companies expect to eventually increase this figure to between 41 and 50% of total purchases.[7] A rapid growth in foreign sourcing has surely been a contributing factor in the large trade deficits the U.S. maintains with much of the world. While currency adjustments and other cost factors, such as labor and transportation, will constantly tweak the volume of goods and services that are sourced worldwide, the emphasis that U.S. producers place on international purchasing is not going away. It is safe to say that international purchasing, even with its associated risks and uncertainties, is a permanent part of the sourcing landscape.

Why Do Firms Engage in International Purchasing?

Why do supply organizations engage in international purchasing? After all, it is probably easier to work with a supplier down the street than one located around the world. Long distances make planning and logistics more difficult, currency fluctuations can change the economics of a transaction, different cultures and languages can lead to misunderstandings, and the documentation that comes with international transactions can be cumbersome. Why go through this hassle? Regardless of the study or survey conducted, the primary reason to source on a worldwide basis is to obtain lower prices. In fact, one could say that supply managers have a solid reputation for chasing lower labor costs and goods around the globe. For most supply managers, international purchasing is about price, price, and then price. Other reasons include gaining access to new sources of product or process technology, higher quality, or introducing competition to the domestic supply base.

An obvious but often overlooked reason why supply organizations buy internationally is because some simply do not have a choice. Some commodities are only available from certain regions, such as central Africa, Australia, or South America, making worldwide sourcing a necessity when those items are required. Some capital equipment suppliers, such as those in the automation and robotics industry, are located primarily in Germany and Japan. Finally, some industries have largely disappeared from a country and are not coming back anytime soon (think textiles in the U.S.).

While cost reductions usually result from the crafting of international agreements, there is also the risk of hidden costs, particularly for less experienced buyers. As a rule of thumb, at least a quarter of the unit cost savings from international purchasing disappears, on average, when estimating the total cost of purchase ownership. This is due to hidden costs associated with longer cycle times, lengthened supply chains, and increased administrative and budget costs that are incurred during global strategy development and execution. The time required to analyze and execute a global agreement is usually months longer than the time required for domestic or regional agreements. While international purchasing can offer attractive cost-saving opportunities, it also requires supply managers to address a wider range of issues in terms of cost, time, and complexity.

UNDERSTANDING GLOBAL SOURCING AND SUPPLY MANAGEMENT

At some point supply organizations mature beyond basic international purchasing and take a more coordinated view of their worldwide operations. The distinction between international purchasing and global supply management, or what some also call global sourcing, is meaningful to our discussion here. Technically speaking, let's view global sourcing, which focuses more on global buying and contracting, as a subset of a broader process called global supply management.

To show how confusing the terminology surrounding this topic can be, various terms that describe the international domain include worldwide sourcing, international sourcing, international buying, international purchasing, offshoring, foreign sourcing, worldwide buying, foreign buying, and global sourcing. Few sources provide any meaningful differences between the terms.

For our purposes, international purchasing relates to a commercial purchase transaction between a buyer and supplier that are located in different countries. This type of purchase is typically more complex than a domestic purchase. Organizations must contend with lengthened material pipelines, increased rules and regulations, currency fluctuations, customs requirements, increased supply chain risk, and a host of other variables such as language and time differences. Do not ever minimize the complexities of international purchasing—they are very real.

Global supply management is not just about buying or contracting on a worldwide basis, although that clearly is part of this construct. Global supply management is a process that proactively integrates and coordinates common items and materials, processes, designs, technologies, and suppliers across worldwide purchasing, engineering, and operating locations. It is supply management performed at the highest worldwide level. Even within the same company, we often see different levels of progress. A supply group may be effective at developing global contracts but is less effective at developing process consistency across its worldwide buying centers. Another may be proficient at developing process consistency but has done little to coordinate its indirect purchase requirements. A third may be effective at managing direct items globally but has done an incomplete job of managing capital investment items. Improvement opportunities always exist somewhere within complex organizations.

It is difficult to discuss an evolution from international purchasing to global supply management without some framework underlying this progression. Figure 13.1 presents international purchasing and global supply management as a series of evolving levels or steps along a continuum. An internationalization of the sourcing process takes place as companies evolve or progress from domestic

Figure 13.1   Continuum of worldwide sourcing

purchasing to the global coordination and integration of common items (including services), processes, designs, technologies, and suppliers across worldwide locations. As will become clear, global supply management involves more than simply buying goods or services from foreign suppliers. In many ways it represents the pinnacle of supply strategy.

Companies that operate at Levels II and III exhibit behaviors that are characteristic of international purchasing. Those that operate at Levels IV and V practice global supply management. It is getting harder to find companies that do not engage directly in any international purchasing. This does not mean that Level I companies do not use goods produced in countries other than their own. Many of these companies use distributors that provide items that are sourced internationally.

Supply organizations progress, usually reactively, toward a basic level of international purchasing because they are confronted by some scenario, such as a lack of suitable domestic suppliers, or because competitors are gaining an advantage from their international practices. Level I participants may also find themselves being driven toward higher levels because of events in the supply market. Such events could be a supply disruption, rapidly changing currency exchange rates, a declining domestic supply base, or the sudden emergence of worldwide competitors. International purchasing in this level is usually limited or performed on an ad hoc or reactive basis. Most supply organizations begin to learn the fundamentals of international purchasing as they evolve to this level.

Strategies and approaches that are developed in Level III begin to reveal that properly executed worldwide buying strategies can result in major improvements. In fact, most of the price reductions that often drive a search for international sources are gained in this level. However, strategies at this level are not well coordinated across different buying locations, operating centers, functional groups, or business units. Each unit is operating essentially as a stand-alone or decentralized buying center. Many of the benefits that are available from global supply management are not as readily available to those that practice international purchasing.

At some point, supply organizations begin to realize that it might be in their best interest to begin integrating and coordinating their sourcing activities on a worldwide basis. Level IV, which is the first of two global supply management levels in this model, represents the integration and coordination of sourcing strategies across worldwide buying locations. Operating at this level requires worldwide information systems, personnel with sophisticated knowledge and skills, extensive coordination and communication mechanisms, an organizational structure that promotes central coordination of global activities, and executive leadership that endorses a global approach to sourcing. While worldwide integration occurs in Level IV, which is not the case with Level III, the integration is primarily cross-locational rather than cross-functional. Level IV also features an extensive focus on global contracting.

Organizations that operate at Level V have achieved the cross-locational integration that those operating at Level IV have achieved. The primary distinction is that Level V participants integrate and coordinate common items, processes, designs, technologies, and suppliers across worldwide purchasing centers and with other functional groups—particularly engineering. This integration occurs during new product development as well as during the sourcing of items or services to fulfill continuous demand or aftermarket requirements. Furthermore, design, build, and sourcing responsibilities are often assigned to the most capable units around the world.

A desire to pursue the highest levels of global supply management is not a matter of hoping good things will magically happen. Extensive research reveals a set of factors that characterize companies that are proficient at global supply management. This listing is important because it helps explain how to engage in global sourcing and supply management. While almost 90% of larger companies expect to operate at Level IV or V, the reality is that many will fall short. Table 13.1 summarizes a set of factors that characterize effective global supply organizations. Notice how many of these items relate to the four key enablers of strategic supply management that were presented earlier in this book.

Benefits of Global Supply Management

Companies pursue global supply management because they expect to capture benefits that are not as readily available from less sophisticated practices. Based on the results of several research projects, interesting differences exist between firms in terms of what they have realized from their worldwide efforts. Companies that

Table 13.1 Global supply management success factors

Success Factors
• Qualified talent that can operate globally
• A well-defined process that guides the development of global strategies
• Supportive organizational design features, such as centrally led sourcing, a global executive steering committee, and cross-functional strategy development teams
• Ability to measure savings from global agreements
• Real-time communication tools, particularly among strategy development teams
• IT systems that provide critical information
• Availability of suppliers with global capabilities
• Operations, manufacturing, and internal customer buy-in to the global supply strategy
• On-site supplier visits prior to selection

engage in global supply management achieve a desirable set of benefits at higher levels compared with companies that take a less sophisticated approach.

Companies that engage in global supply management indicate they realize an impressive set of benefits at a statistically higher level than those that engage in international purchasing. In fact, the overall average across all benefit areas is 30% higher for companies that practice global supply management compared with the overall average for the international purchasing segment. Table 13.2 segments a set of benefits across firms that engage in global supply management

Table 13.2   Comparing benefits: global supply management vs. international purchasing

Benefit	Global Sourcing/ Supply Segment	International Purchasing Segment	Difference
Better management of total supply chain inventory	4.29	2.74	1.55
Greater supplier responsiveness to buying unit needs	4.47	3.08	1.39
Greater standardization or consistency of the sourcing process	4.25	3.01	1.24
Greater access to product technology	4.69	3.49	1.23
Improved supplier relationships	4.61	3.46	1.15
Greater access to process technology	4.54	3.46	1.08
Improved sharing of information with suppliers	4.10	3.04	1.06
Greater supplier involvement during product development	3.86	2.80	1.06
Lower purchase price/cost	5.98	5.04	.94
Shorter ordering cycle time	3.61	2.76	.94
Higher material/component/service quality	4.16	3.25	.91
Improved delivery reliability	3.90	3.04	.86
Improved environmental compliance	3.24	2.39	.85
Greater appreciation of purchasing by internal users	4.25	3.44	.81
Lower purchasing process transactions costs	3.67	2.87	.80
Higher user satisfaction with purchasing	4.10	3.36	.74

Global Sourcing/Supply Segment = Levels IV and Level V firms; International Purchasing Segment = Levels II and III firms.

1 = benefit not realized, 4 = benefit moderately realized, 7 = benefit extremely realized

Average across all benefits = 3.2 average for Level II-III Segment; 4.23 average for Level IV-V Segment and those that engage in international purchasing. The benefits are ranked by the numeric difference between the two segments. The performance differences between the two segments are revealing.

If global supply management can be as rewarding as the data suggest, why aren't all firms pursuing the highest sourcing levels? First, many supply managers do not understand global supply management as a concept, making implementation a problem. The second reason is that supply organizations and leaders may lack the vision, leadership, resources, or sophistication to coordinate their activities globally. Far too many procurement organizations are still reactive or maintain a lower position within the corporate hierarchy. Finally, not every company needs to pursue global supply management. The appropriate sourcing level does not necessarily have to be the most advanced level. Larger companies pursue global supply management because they are more likely to have worldwide operations and buying centers.

Differences Across the Segments

One way to appreciate how to operate at the highest sourcing levels is to explore the differences between companies that practice international purchasing and companies that practice global supply management. The following is the result of statistical comparisons between a group of companies that practice international purchasing and a group that practices global supply management. Besides differing in the benefits that each receives from their efforts, the two segments differ along some important fronts:

- *Difference #1: Companies that engage in global supply management are larger and more likely to have competitors that are multiregional compared with international purchasing companies.* While this finding should come as no surprise, companies that pursue global supply initiatives are clearly larger in terms of sales compared with those that engage in international purchasing. Larger companies are more likely to have worldwide production facilities, design centers, and marketing and sales activities. The pursuit of global supply management opportunities becomes a fundamental extension of a larger company's sourcing philosophy.
- *Difference #2: Companies that engage in global supply management perceive their strategy implementation progress to be further along compared with international purchasing companies.* An interesting question involves the perception that each segment has about the progress of its worldwide strategies. The implementation progress for the international purchasing segment averages 4.5/10, while the global supply management segment averages 6.23/10 (where 1 = no progress and 10 = total

implementation). Companies that practice international purchasing recognize that they have a ways to go in terms of advancing their sourcing capabilities.

- *Difference #3: Companies that engage in global supply management believe that cost and performance improvement opportunities are more widely available compared with international purchasing companies.* This difference highlights the mindset that respondents have regarding worldwide improvement opportunities. The global segment is more likely to rate the improvement opportunities that exist from worldwide sourcing as being more extensive than the international purchasing segment. Companies that engage in global supply management are larger, which may indicate they have greater worldwide experience in general. They are also likely to be predisposed to believe that performance improvements are more readily available from globalization. Another explanation is that global organizations are more likely to have experienced firsthand the improvements that are available from global supply management.

- *Difference #4: Companies that engage in global supply management indicate that the development of global strategies is more important to their executive management compared with international purchasing companies.* It should come as no surprise that centrally led leadership is critical to a process as organizationally complex and important as global supply management. And it should come as no surprise that participants involved with global supply management believe that developing global supply strategies is important to their executive management. Global supply management does not happen without strong executive support. It is likely that global organizations have an executive steering committee that oversees the process. This committee reflects the importance that executives have regarding the global process.

- *Difference #5: Companies that engage in global supply management indicate that they face more rapid changes to product and process technology compared with international purchasing companies.* Companies engaged in global supply management indicate that they face greater competitive and customer pressure to introduce new product and process technology. While cost improvements will always remain a primary driver behind worldwide sourcing activities, the need to search globally for product and process technology will cause some to elevate their sourcing levels.

- *Difference #6: Companies that engage in global supply management rely on a wider array of communication tools to support their worldwide efforts compared with international purchasing companies.* Geographic complexity and extensive coordination requirements demand that global supply organizations rely more heavily on an extensive array of communication tools. This includes a reliance on groupware, video conferencing, web-based tools, and phone conferencing at higher levels compared with the international purchasing segment. Global coordination requires these companies to manage their activities and share information across worldwide purchasing and design locations, something that is not an issue in a less coordinated environment.

- *Difference #7: Companies that engage in global supply management have in place more organizational design features to support their worldwide efforts compared with international purchasing companies.* A critical difference between the international purchasing and global supply management segments relates to how extensively each segment has put in place certain features to support their efforts. Global organizations conduct regular strategy review and coordination sessions with worldwide procurement and other functional managers on a regular basis. Another differentiating feature is the greater likelihood that global supply organizations will have access to the services provided by international purchasing offices. And, effective global supply management benefits from a centrally led or centralized structure.
- *Difference #8: Companies that engage in global supply management rate certain factors as more critical to their success compared with international purchasing companies.* The international and global supply management segments rate a set of factors differently in terms of their importance, which was summarized in Table 13.1. These factors help define what a global supply organization looks like. Any company hoping to elevate their game on a worldwide basis is urged to review these factors carefully.

Succeeding in an era of change and disruption demands continuous improvement and new ways to compete. Most executives will say that responding to competitive, customer, and financial pressure requires steady and even dramatic improvements in all performance areas. The development of global strategies should become an increasingly attractive option for responding to a never-ending need to improve. The business case for global supply management is powerful.

RESHORING, NEAR SHORING, AND OTHER KINDS OF SHORING

Starting in the latter part of 2011, the Boston Consulting Group (BCG) released a series of papers addressing the resurgence of U.S. manufacturing due to reshoring.[8] BCG predicted that millions of manufacturing jobs would return to the U.S. due to a variety of factors, including rising wages in China, the increasing cost of logistics, and a resurgence of the U.S. energy industry. These factors would combine to create an influx of manufacturing jobs back to the U.S., the likes of which we have never before witnessed.

In reality this predicted deluge has been more like a trickle. Unfortunately, much of the work that came back to North America went south of the Rio Grande River straight to Mexico. This is not to say that some jobs have not returned. The Department of Commerce reported that between 2009 and the end of 2014, U.S. manufacturing output grew by 45 percent with 646,000 jobs added between February 2010 and May 2014. Another 243,000 positions were waiting to be filled. This growth did not compensate, however, for the losses realized during the 2008–2009 recession. The challenge when talking about job growth is separating growth due to reshoring, growth due to an expanding economy, growth due to foreign direct investment, and growth that did not occur because of automation and other efficiencies.[9] Reshoring and foreign direct investment led to a net gain of 27,000 manufacturing jobs during a recent year, according to data compiled by the Reshoring Initiative.[10]

Some simple definitions are in order here. Offshoring is the process of shifting sourcing or internal manufacturing/operations from a home country (such as the U.S.) to a foreign country. Reshoring is the process of bringing sourcing or manufacturing/operations back to the home country that was previously outsourced to a foreign country. Some refer to this as home shoring. Near shoring is the process of bringing work closer to the home country. For example, within the U.S., near shoring might involve shifting work from China to Mexico.

A major industrial state in the United States conducted an executive roundtable with companies that have or are considering moving some operations or sourcing out of or back to the U.S. The objective of the roundtable was to better understand why companies may or may not consider reshoring work back to the U.S. that was previously sent offshore. A secondary objective was to learn what it would take for companies to not move work to another country. Industries represented at the roundtable included advanced materials, steel, confectionary, industrial machines, children's educational products, performance apparel, mineral processing solutions, and plastic components. The insights from this roundtable explain, in part, why the influx of work back to the U.S. continues to be a trickle. The following summarizes some key points and themes surrounding reshoring.

Reshoring Is Real and Not Something Being Hyped by the Media and Consultants

Corporate executives feel the reshoring discussion is a serious one. Certain trends are supporting this viewpoint. First, the growth in energy production in the U.S. is a potential game changer. The potential benefit of lower cost natural gas is a major consideration for companies that are energy intensive. Several participants voiced concerns that the U.S. still lacks an adequate pipeline and distribution system to fully take advantage of lower-cost natural gas, something that remains a challenge as new pipelines face a host of legal challenges. Second, participants are acutely aware of changing economic factors in China (discussed further in the following subsection). A thought leader with extensive reshoring experience maintained that consumers want items that are *Made in America*. Furthermore, the *Made in America* label can be a factor that supports increased exports from the U.S.

China Is Becoming Less Competitive in Terms of Cost Savings

Executives recognize that China is becoming less competitive in terms of cost savings. Labor rates in many industries across China are increasing at well over 10% per year. The decreasing cost advantage of China is also supported by extensive research by groups such as BCG. Executives note that it is almost an imperative to have an expatriate assigned to oversee the Chinese manufacturer, something that adds significant costs. Issues relating to long order-lead times, the cost of carrying supply chain inventory, deficient supplier quality, poor logistics networks, and the risk to intellectual property (IP) are also factors making China less attractive as a sourcing location. Almost every participant had a story about sourcing in China that was less than positive. One commented that *the China experience is complex, unpredictable, and unreliable, but the quality has been good*. Participants noted that in the ongoing search for lower labor rates, Vietnam is now undercutting China in terms of labor costs. Vietnam, however, still lags China in worker productivity.

Interestingly, executives did not voice significant concern over currency issues, even though the Chinese currency (known as the yuan or renminbi) now floats more freely against the U.S. dollar. A lack of concern over this issue is likely due to the fact that most U.S. manufacturers, particularly smaller ones, insist on contracts priced in U.S. dollars. This approach to currency management transfers risk to the supplier.

One executive maintained that unless China is 30% cheaper than the U.S., his company believes it makes commercial sense to keep work in the U.S. This is due partly to the presence of hidden or qualitative factors that are difficult to quantify. These hidden costs chip away at the potential savings from sourcing in China. One source has identified nine hidden costs that are rarely, if ever, included in outsourcing or reshoring analyses when evaluating Chinese supply options. Table 13.3 identifies some of these costs. Failing to account for these costs under specifies total cost models, which makes Chinese suppliers appear more attractive.

Table 13.3   Hidden costs of offshoring

• *Internal expenses*: The higher skills, communication, and time required to evaluate and work with foreign suppliers are not free.
• *Supplier health*: Gaining visibility into the financial stability of foreign suppliers is not always easy.
• *Post-contract lull*: Failing to monitor supplier and contract performance after signing an agreement can result in cost creep.
• *Duty and tariff changes*: Employing resources to determine correct duties and monitor changes adds to total cost.
• *Contract noncompliance*: Internal noncompliance with a foreign contract reduces the total anticipated savings.
• *True inventory costs*: While longer pipelines increase inventory carrying charges, few companies fully account for these charges in their cost models.
• *Logistics volatility*: Managing the rapid changes in shipping costs adds an element of complexity.
• *Technology*: Extended supply changes require greater tracking capabilities.
• *Quality breakdowns*: Managing quality problems offshore can be more costly and complex to resolve, including the impact on corporate brand equity.
• *Intellectual property*: The cost to protect a company from intellectual property theft is real but hard to quantify. The financial effects of IP theft are also real.

Partly adapted from D. Hannon, "9 Hidden Costs of Global Sourcing," *Purchasing*, March 2009.

A Broad Set of Factors Can Inhibit Reshoring

Roundtable participants identified a set of factors that potentially hold them back from reshoring work back to the U.S. Examples of factors that can have an inhibiting role in reshoring include:

- Corporate and tax structure and burden (recent tax law changes in the U.S. have likely mitigated this factor)
- Lack of a U.S. supply chain
- Skill gaps in the workforce
- Accessibility and volatility of commodity markets
- Shifting exchange rates
- Lack of incentives to support capital equipment purchases (again, recent tax changes have likely altered this concern)
- Shifting away from the metric system
- Excessive government rules and regulations
- Unwillingness to reverse offshoring decisions
- Higher U.S. labor rates

A divergence of opinion exists regarding the raising of the minimum wage and the affect this might have on reshoring efforts. One school of thought argues that raising the minimum wage would increase labor costs. A secondary effect is that all wage levels will likely increase as the minimum wage increases. A second school of thought argues that it is vital to have a strong middle class so that consumers can afford the products that American companies are producing. The group as a whole recognizes the importance of labor costs in the reshoring equation.

An issue affecting some industries is a skill gap in the workforce. Bollman Hat Company, the maker of Kangol hats, found that a lack of employees with the right skills has hampered the company's reshoring efforts. Finding American workers as fast and skilled as their Chinese counterparts has proved challenging. Even with investments in training, some jobs at the company have remained unfilled. The lack of skilled workers who are interested in manufacturing is a massive concern according to another apparel manufacturer that reshored work from China to New Jersey.[11]

Some Work Will Never Leave the Home Country, Some Will Never Come Back

The executive roundtable group agreed with the BCG conclusion that some industries will likely not be returning outsourced work to the U.S., some industries will likely never leave the U.S., and some industries could make a location change given the right set of economic conditions. Readers are urged to consult the BCG reports referenced at the end of this chapter to get more insight into these industries.

Supply Chain Issues Are a Critical Part of the Reshoring Equation

Participants were clear that reshoring does not simply involve bringing an item or scope of work back to the U.S. In many cases it involves establishing or reestablishing an entire supply chain, which for some companies is a major task. For simple items, such as items that are made by plastic extrusion, this may be relatively simple. For complex items, the supply chain presents a significant barrier. Participants were also clear that issues pertaining to the supply chain cannot be ignored. The subject of supply chains, along with tax issues, was one of the most frequently cited topics by the executives.

As an example of the complexities involved with reestablishing a supply chain, a company at the roundtable reshored a complex gearbox after experiencing quality and delivery problems with its Chinese supplier. A year of planning and work was required to complete this reshoring initiative. This included rebuilding the company's supply chain by locating and qualifying domestic suppliers. A lesson learned from this company's experience is that reshoring a complex item can involve an entire supply chain.

The Importance of Total Cost Modeling Is Well Understood but Not Widely Practiced

Executives recognize the value of framing decisions from a total cost perspective. Total cost includes the expected and unexpected elements that increase the unit cost of a good, service, or piece of equipment. Total cost systems—and there are a variety of them—attempt to capture these cost elements. The logic behind the development of total cost systems is clear since unit cost or price never equals total cost. Our objective should become one of trying to understand the size of the gap between unit price and its corresponding total cost. We also want to know in some detail what makes up that gap.

Unfortunately, while the importance of total cost modeling is well understood, for a variety of reasons the use of total cost models is far from routine. The obvious costs of global sourcing, which can alter the savings realized from global sourcing, are only part of the equation. As mentioned, most experts acknowledge that sourcing offshore contains a variety of hidden costs that are difficult to quantify.

Other reasons help explain why total cost analysis is not a routine part of supply chain decision making. Some companies lack visibility to supply chain data; some do not know how to construct total cost models; and some lack the discipline required to carry out total cost analyses. And, some may not even be aware of the importance of making a decision from a total cost perspective.

Exchange Rates Are a Reshoring Wildcard

Part of the reason that the optimistic projections surrounding the return of work to the U.S. never materialized at predicted levels is due to changing exchange rates. Many of the predictions about reshoring occurred when the dollar was relatively weak against other major currencies. A trade weighted currency index of the U.S. dollar against a basket of major currencies, for example, had a value as low as 69 in 2011. Over the next six years or so this index climbed to over 90. A higher index means the dollar has gained in relative strength compared to the basket of currencies. As the dollar strengthened, the cost to purchase from foreign countries became less expensive (and, conversely, made it more difficult to export from the U.S.). Part of the reason to relocate sourcing or operations back to the home country suddenly disappeared. Exchange rates continue to be a wildcard for companies that cannot easily shift sourcing or operations as exchange rates shift.

Offshoring Sometimes Occurs to Support Local or Regional Requirements

A CAPS research study on emerging global supply strategies found that locating manufacturing and research and development facilities close to customers is rapidly becoming a key strategy for achieving worldwide growth and profits. Explanations for locating locally include understanding local customer needs, achieving flexibility and responsiveness to changing tastes and demand, enhancing the company's image as a good citizen, meeting economic goals in terms of lower costs or compliance with government regulations requiring local content, and taking advantage of preferential lending policies by countries.[12]

Anecdotal evidence suggests that major companies are establishing operations in the regions where they sell their products. It makes sense that local suppliers will also be part of this equation, making this of interest to supply managers. The next subsection discusses this important topic in further detail.

Companies Believe that *Made in America* Is Good for Marketing and Sales

Part of the reshoring movement is based on a belief that consumers prefer products from their home country. And, there is some support for this notion. *Consumer Reports* maintains that almost 8 in 10 American consumers say they would rather buy an American-made product than an imported one. Furthermore, more than 60 percent say they are willing to pay 10 percent more for it.[13] Two-thirds of Americans say they check labels when shopping to see if they are buying American goods.[14]

The executives at this roundtable provided some solid insights regarding reshoring. In the final analysis, executives must consider a set of factors that may discourage or promote an action. The decision process will vary from company to company and industry to industry. One thing is certain. The decision to offshore or reshore can be complex.

EMERGING LOCATIONS AND TRENDS

An earlier discussion in this chapter presented the factors that define an effective global supply organization. This helps us better understand how to pursue global supply management. What follows here is a set of emerging supplier location trends and strategies as identified during a CAPS Research study.[15] These observations pertain more to the *where* rather than the *how* of global supply management:

- Market penetration and growth plans are helping to shape sourcing location decisions

- Regional sourcing is becoming a preferred strategy
- Energy costs and logistics considerations are driving many sourcing decisions
- Companies are encouraging existing suppliers to locate in new growth markets
- An emphasis on low-cost country (LCC) sourcing continues, but concerns exist about diminishing returns, particularly in China
- Certifying supply sources in LCCs remains a key hurdle in industries with stringent safety requirements
- Government policies in emerging markets continue to encourage industrial development in those regions
- Sourcing decisions are dynamic and subject to change as factor conditions change
- Buyers still have minimal involvement in or influence over the location of sub-tier suppliers
- Africa as a source of supply is not on the immediate horizon for most companies

Supplier location strategies continuously evolve as requirements, opportunities, and market and economic conditions change. While LCC sourcing is still relatively popular, supply managers are also looking at a mix of global strategies, regional strategies, and reshoring as part of their strategy portfolio.

CONCLUDING THOUGHTS

The logic behind global supply management should not be in question today. Research clearly shows that global supply organizations realize a set of benefits at a higher level compared with firms that engage primarily in international purchasing. While making a business case for global supply management is relatively easy, understanding the differences between international purchasing and global supply management as well as understanding how to evolve beyond basic international purchasing is a more complex matter. Today, there is no excuse for not understanding what characterizes an effective global organization.

REFERENCES

1. From www.census.gov.
2. From www.bls.gov.
3. From www.bea.gov.
4. W. Ross, "Free Trade is a Two-Way Street," *The Wall Street Journal*, August 1, 2017, A15.

5. From www.census.gov, foreign trade statistics.
6. R. M. Monczka and R. J. Trent, "Purchasing and Supply Management: Key Trends and Changes throughout the 1990s," *International Journal of Purchasing and Materials Management*, 34, no. 4 (Fall 1998): 2–11.
7. R. M. Monczka, R. J. Trent, and K. J. Petersen, *Effective Global Sourcing and Supply for Superior Results*, (Tempe, AZ: CAPS Research, 2006): 13.
8. For access to the Boston Consulting Group's analysis, see *Made in America, Again: Why Manufacturing Will Return to the U.S.*, http://www.bcg .com/documents/file84471.pdf; *U.S. Manufacturing Nears the Tipping Point: Which Industries, Why, and How Much?* http://doingwhatmatters .cccco.edu/portals/6/docs/US%20Mfg%20Nears%20Tipping%20Point .pdf; and *The U.S. as One of the Developed World's Lowest-Cost Manufacturers* https://www.bcgperspectives.com/content/articles/lean_manufacturing _sourcing_procurement_behind_american_export_surge/#chapter1.
9. "Made in America," *Consumer Reports*, May 21, 2015, retrieved from https://www.consumerreports.org/cro/magazine/2015/05/made-in -america/index.htm.
10. M. Ma., "For Kangol Hats, a Costly Move to the U.S.," *The Wall Street Journal*, September 29, 2017, B5.
11. ibid.
12. R. M. Monczka, P. L. Carter, W. J. Markham, K. J. Petersen, R. J. Trent, and E. L. Nichols, "Emerging Global Supply Strategies," (Tempe, AZ: CAPS Research, 2014): 26.
13. "Made in America," *Consumer Reports*, May 21, 2015, retrieved from https://www.consumerreports.org/cro/magazine/2015/05/made-in -america/index.htm.
14. S. Clifford, "That Made in U.S.A. Premium," *The New York Times*, November 30, 2013, retrieved from http://www.nytimes.com/2013/12/01/ business/that-made-in-usa-premium.html.
15. R. M. Monczka, P. L. Carter, W. J. Markham, K. J. Petersen, R. J. Trent, and E. L. Nichols, "Emerging Global Supply Strategies," 51.

14

THE PROCESS-CENTRIC ORGANIZATION

Imagine working for a company where a focus on functional groups and activities is the norm. Imagine further that your CEO has announced a major restructuring—a restructuring that is sure to involve significant changes. She has asked you to visualize an organizational model that features the widespread sharing of information, a flattened decision-making hierarchy, vastly different performance measures and, perhaps most important, a model that is centered around processes that create this thing called value. In short, imagine being part of an organization that is about to be turned upside down.

One result from this scenario should be the identification of those processes that will have the greatest impact on supply chain performance. This, unfortunately, is not as easy as it sounds. A second outcome should be the realization that the changes that are required by this transformation will support attention to few rather than many processes. The late Michael Hammer once observed that hardly any company can manage more than ten or so principle processes.[1] If organizations are in fact moving toward a process-centric orientation, and there is evidence that suggests this is the case, the challenge becomes one of identifying those processes that are the most likely to create value. But what are those processes?

The time has come to focus on specific processes that create unique kinds of value. The following sections discuss a shift toward a process-centric organization and identify a set of value-creating supply and supply chain processes, along with the characteristics that define process excellence. The purpose of this chapter is to instill an appreciation that supply managers must be process thinkers, which Chapter 3 already touched upon.

THE SHIFT TOWARD PROCESS-CENTRIC THINKING

While the idea of a process-centric organization can be confusing, the reality is that processes, at least conceptually, are relatively straightforward. An organizational or business process consists of a set of interrelated steps, tasks, or activities designed to achieve a desired outcome or objective. These outcomes could include fulfilling customer orders, developing new products or services, or compiling financial reports. If we know our key objectives, then we begin to know the processes that must be in place.

What makes processes confusing to many is they can be tangible and intangible. Tangible or physical processes can be touched and measured relatively easily. They produce physical output, such as a process that produces semiconductor chips. Organizational or business processes, while still producing output, are not as tangible or physical. For example, what does the process that is responsible for developing new products actually look like? Our focus here is on business processes that are essential to supply chain success. Recall from Chapter 1 that strategic supply management is a process.

Organizing work around processes makes sense for a number of reasons. Because processes create the output that should lead to desired outcomes, it makes intuitive sense to focus on the process steps and activities that create that output. Furthermore, well-developed and understood processes accelerate learning as participants become experienced in applying a defined framework. Processes can also build in best practices and consistency that enhance the likelihood of success. And perhaps most importantly, organizations can document, measure, illustrate, and continuously improve their processes.

Taking a process view also helps manage the conflicts and trade-offs that occur as work inevitably crosses functional boundaries. (A trade-off is a balancing of factors, all of which are not attainable simultaneously.) Left unattended, these crossing points can easily lead to conflict, competition, and inefficiency. A process orientation, supported by performance measures that are broadly rather than narrowly defined, should promote the seamless movement of work and information across groups.

Some indications suggest a growing shift toward process-centric thinking, particularly through organizational design changes. A study by Deloitte revealed that many companies have already moved away from functional structures. That study found that only 38% of all companies and 24% of large companies (more than 50,000 employees) are organized functionally today. Over 80% of respondents say that their organization is undergoing a restructuring or have recently completed the process.[2]

Even with this shift, it is unlikely that corporations will ever completely disband their functional structures. The need to maintain a critical mass of functional knowledge ensures that some functional structure, albeit a diminished one, will remain in place. The dramatic changes in organizational design, measurement, and information that surround a shift from a functional to a process-centric organization also ensures that any changes will be gradual.

FOUR VALUE-CREATING PROCESSES

Figure 14.1 presents a supply chain model superimposed with four value-creating processes that illustrate the logic behind performing certain processes well. Michael Porter, who first articulated the value chain concept, argued that a firm's value chain is comprised of primary and support activities that can lead to competitive advantage when configured properly. Notice that purchasing and supply management is predominantly represented as a support activity. To reflect current thinking, this figure also includes those enterprises that reside upstream and downstream from the focal organization, a concept referred to as the extended enterprise.

If we agree that organizations can benefit from taking a process-centric view, then the challenge becomes one of identifying those processes that are the source points for the creation of value. The processes presented here are source points for four unique types of value that are essential for achieving differential advantage. And, as we will see, supply management plays a role within these processes, both directly and indirectly. While hundreds of processes and

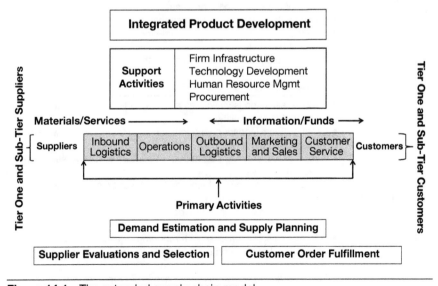

Figure 14.1 The extended supply chain model

subprocesses populate complex organizations, the proposition is put forth here that integrated product development, supplier evaluation and selection, demand estimation and supply planning, and customer order fulfillment should rise to the top of almost everyone's importance list, especially for industrial companies. Service companies may perceive a different set of value-creating processes.

Table 14.1 summarizes the best practices associated with each process. Something that must underlie every major process is the presence of well-defined process steps, activities, practices, and measures.

Integrated Product Development

It is widely accepted that the successful development of products and services is an important part of what differentiates one firm from the next. In fact, a large body of literature has identified product development as a core process

Table 14.1   Process best-practice characteristics

Process	Best-Practice Characteristics
New Product and Process Development	• Cross-functional teams focus on developing products and their required physical processes concurrently • Early involvement of customers and suppliers is part of the development process • Product development participants have access to a wide range of software applications • The research and development (R&D) process is formally linked to the product development process • Participants develop target prices that are market driven • Development teams are accountable for meeting stringent concept-to-customer cycle times • Management practices subtle control throughout the development process • Development teams practice *Design for "X"*
Supplier Evaluation and Selection	• Supplier selection is viewed as an organizational rather than functional responsibility • Organizational leaders continuously search for innovative ways to reduce selection time • A higher-level steering committee is responsible for overseeing the selection process • A segmentation process helps identify the appropriate rigor to apply to the selection decision • Cross-functional teams are responsible for making critical selection decisions • A formal selection process with reporting milestones is followed • International purchasing offices support selection tasks in different geographic regions • The selection process serves the needs of corporate and other functional groups

Demand and Supply Planning	• Planning leaders rely extensively on systems and practices that help balance demand and supply, including sales and operations planning (S&OP) and collaborative planning, forecasting, and replenishment (CPFR) • Various organizational design features are in place that support planning capabilities • An executive or executive committee has accountability for forecasting success • Regular reviews of forecast accuracy and detailed assessment of the root causes of forecast error take place • Supply chain planners recognize that different forecasting models fit different products • Rigorous mathematical models identify the forecasting approach that best fits a historical demand pattern or product requirement • Demand management techniques are used effectively to influence demand
Customer Order Fulfillment	• Organizations take a broader rather than narrower view of customer order fulfillment • Supply chain leaders understand the relationship between the quality of demand planning and the ability to satisfy customer orders • The removal of time from the fulfillment process is a relentless pursuit • Lean principles are applied extensively when improving the fulfillment process • A wide array of e-systems supports fulfillment and the removal of transactions costs • The important linkage between inventory control and satisfying customer orders is well understood • Customer lead times are the result of cooperative discussions with the customer • Accounts receivables is considered an important part of the fulfillment process • A complete set of measures, including the perfect order, support order fulfillment

playing a major role that supports innovation and competitiveness. The process of discovery, development, and commercialization of products and services is a major source for innovation and growth. It's difficult to read respected business publications without hearing about the importance of innovation.

A well-designed development process can lead to many benefits, including shorter development times that market leaders rely on to capture market share or create barriers to entry. While an analysis conducted by *Industry Week* revealed hundreds of ways to develop products and services faster, better, cheaper, and smarter, experience with leading companies suggests that the biggest improvements are the result of a set of specific practices. The following subsections summarize these practices.

Concurrent Product and Process Development

The concept of concurrency during product development has two major dimensions. The first is the simultaneous development of products and the physical processes required to produce them. The second dimension involves the simultaneous rather than sequential involvement of functional groups. Sequential development features a handing off of work from one functional group to another, something that requires a time-consuming learning period after each hand off. It also results in far too much work being handed back for revision when later groups receive a design or some output they find to be unworkable.

What is it about a concurrent approach with cross-functional teams that is attractive? A concurrent approach requires cross-functional agreement throughout the development process, something that minimizes time-consuming and costly design changes at later development stages. This approach also features the interaction of competent professionals, which hopefully leads to better decisions. Furthermore, concurrency offers opportunities for early customer and supplier involvement, accelerated learning as team members learn simultaneously, and the establishment of organizational rather than functional product development goals. Good reasons exist to pursue a concurrent approach to product and process development.

Early Involvement of Suppliers and Customers

Leading firms recognize that external involvement during product and service development is an idea whose time has come.[3] Most executive leaders recognize the importance of increased external involvement during product development, and they further recognize the need to involve suppliers and customers earlier rather than later in the process.

A powerful relationship exists between supplier involvement on product development teams and a variety of desirable outcomes. Teams that involve suppliers, either as formal or informal participants, report greater average satisfaction with the exchange of buyer-seller information compared with teams that did not include suppliers. These teams also report fewer problems coordinating external work and had a higher reliance on suppliers to support the team's goals. Perhaps most important, external evaluators rate teams that involve suppliers as more effective with greater effort put forth toward their assignments compared with teams where supplier involvement is lacking.

While early involvement with suppliers sounds easy, widespread implementation can be a different matter. Confidentiality of information continues to be a major concern when involving external organizations in something as important as product development. Other concerns include not knowing how to pursue early involvement, maintaining too many suppliers for a given requirement, or relationships that are adversarial rather than cooperative. Given the expected growth in new product teams that involve suppliers and even customers, overcoming any barriers to early involvement must become a priority. Fortunately, none of these concerns violates the laws of physics.

Information Technology (IT)

Effective product development relies extensively on software applications to accelerate and improve the development process. Chapter 6 described some IT applications that support new product and process development.

Linking R&D and Product Development

This characteristic involves the direct linkage between R&D and product development. Far too often, worthwhile innovations from the laboratory are not commercialized. Best-in-class companies have in place a process to develop and validate new technology and then link that technology to the product development process. While not all new technology emanating from R&D labs will be commercially viable, the linkage of one process to another ensures that market-ready technology can be designed quickly into new products. When this comes together it can create a difficult barrier for less effective competitors to overcome.

Target Pricing

Most product development efforts would benefit from target pricing (sometimes called target costing). With a traditional approach to product development, selling price is arrived at by combining product costs and adding a profit margin. Unfortunately, this approach often overstates the price a marketplace will bear or ignores what competitors are doing. It is an inwardly focused approach that usually does not consider the voice of the customer. Traditional pricing also tends to minimize the importance of cost management during product design.

Target pricing is a complete reversal of traditional pricing. Under a target approach, product development teams—often with marketing taking a lead role—identify the price that customers are willing to pay for a product or service. After identifying a target price, profits margins are backed out to arrive at a product's allowable costs. If allowable costs are below current cost levels, then the design team must identify ways to remove or lower costs (or accept a lower profit margin). With target pricing, costs are something to manage rather than take for granted.

Cycle Time Measures

Product development will benefit from an important metric called concept-to-customer (C-to-C) cycle time. This metric reflects the importance of the time it takes to develop products and their processes as well as acting as a superordinate target that no single functional group can attain by itself. Surprisingly, many companies do not measure their internal cycle times, making the development of a C-to-C cycle time measure an attractive opportunity. Holding functional groups accountable for attaining this measure sends a powerful message about the importance of collaboration during the development process.

Subtle Control

Years ago Taguchi and Nonaka identified some salient features of successful product launches.[4] One of these features is something they termed *subtle control*, a powerful concept that executive leaders should routinely practice, particularly when using teams to develop new products. Simply stated, subtle control is a delicate balancing act that seeks to ensure that teams and processes proceed as expected but without blatant control or micro management by executive leaders.

Executives have many ways to practice subtle control. They can identify which products to develop, select leaders and members for development teams, create and manage the development process that teams will follow, require performance updates at regular intervals or milestones, and establish broad performance targets that teams use when establishing specific goals. Subtle control recognizes that while empowerment can be an attractive notion, relinquishing control of the product development process may not be so attractive.

Design for "X"

A final practice mentioned here is something called *Design for "X."* Industry leaders appreciate the power of the product development process to satisfy some important aspirations or objectives. The term "X" represents different aspirations the development teams consider even before beginning design work. *Design for "X"* aspirations can involve design for quality, reliability, serviceability, sustainability, end-of-life recycling, target price, assembly, cycle time, and postponement. This is a powerful concept because it ensures that important objectives are considered at the onset of product development.

We know that integrated product development is a major source point for innovation and growth. We also know that companies that are leaders in product development endorse certain practices that differentiate them from those that are not leaders.

Supplier Evaluation and Selection

Supplier evaluation and selection is probably not what comes to mind for nonprocurement professionals when thinking about an essential set of value-creating processes.[5] As a result, supplier selection has often been performed by buyers who are measured more by their ability to obtain a low price rather than the lowest total cost or highest value. While not equally true at all organizations, supplier evaluation and selection is increasingly becoming the major source point for the inputs that define important capabilities of a buying company, including quality, cost, responsiveness, flexibility, and cycle-time performance. We have also known for some time that industrial buyers are relying on their suppliers as a source of technology and innovation.

Executive leaders have historically viewed suppliers and the process that selects them with relative indifference. However, a strategic focus on core capabilities and competencies, which often results in the outsourcing of noncore (but still essential) requirements, along with a reliance on fewer suppliers makes supplier selection a critical process. When external suppliers typically receive over half of a buying firm's total revenue, the logic behind developing a world-class selection process becomes clear from a financial perspective. Furthermore, a continuing reliance on suppliers to act as systems integrators within an original equipment manufacturer's supply chain magnifies the importance of the selection process.

The way that firms evaluate and select suppliers can be a source of competitive advantage, particularly since many suppliers assume some demanding responsibilities on behalf of the buyer. Particularly when sourcing critical and high-value goods and services, best-practice firms evaluate a supplier's financial stability, capacity, logistics capability, labor relations, logistical networks, design capability, supply management practices, process capability, environmental compliance, willingness to work with the buyer, design capability, flexibility, ability to act as a systems integrator, and technology innovation. The selection process also allows a buying company to use its first-tier suppliers to gain insights into its second-tier and even third-tier suppliers. Figure 14.2 illustrates how supplier selection fits into the strategic supply management process.

While not always the case, many supplier evaluation and selection decisions occur because of product development. Given that development times for new products and services are declining, sometimes at a dramatic rate, it seems intuitive that the cycle times for any supporting processes must also decline. Figure 14.3 identifies ways to accelerate the evaluation and selection process, ideally without sacrificing process effectiveness. This figure also illustrates a generic process for evaluating and selecting suppliers. Gone are the days when supply managers are afforded the luxury of spending months to evaluate, select, and negotiate agreements with suppliers. Selection decisions often have to occur in weeks, perhaps even days.

Similar to new product development, important selection decisions are now made by cross-functional teams that report directly to corporate executives. The use of selection teams that are comprised of members from purchasing,

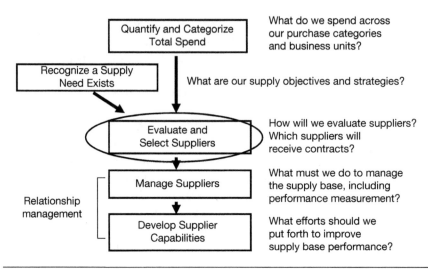

Figure 14.2 Supplier selection and the supply management process

operations, finance, and engineering reflects the organizational rather than functional nature of supply management decisions.

Supplier selection takes on added risk when international suppliers are part of the process. Best-practice companies recognize the importance of having access to local resources to represent their interests. To that end, many firms have established international purchasing offices (IPOs) that are responsible for, among other things, identifying and evaluating suppliers. Overwhelming consensus exists regarding the importance of IPOs. One study found that over 85% of companies that maintain IPOs say these offices are extremely important to their international success while 10% say IPOs are moderately important.[6] Using IPOs to support supplier selection is clearly a best practice.

Supplier selection is not practiced in isolation from corporate strategy or other functional groups. Supply executives should never forget their role as a support activity, which means they have internal customers. If engineering requires a supplier that is on the cutting edge of a certain type of technology, then the selection team needs to factor this into its search. If the corporate strategy calls for a supply chain that is highly responsive to changing requirements, then selected suppliers must be responsive and flexible. And if a stated corporate objective is to be environmentally aware, then selection teams will want to stress working with suppliers with strong environmental records. Leading supply organizations know how to link their selection process with the needs of internal customers.

Evaluation and Selection Process Steps	Time Reduction Activities
Recognize the Supplier Selection Need	Participate on product teams; provide users with e-systems to forward requirements; develop a system that provides early warning to expiring contracts; pre-qualify suppliers in anticipation of future needs
Identify Supply Requirements	Develop templates for users to forward requirements electronically; supply representatives work concurrently with product designers to identify requirements
Determine Supply Strategy	Develop commodity and part numbering schemes and place purchase requirements into categories; identify selection requirements and supply strategies using a portfolio matrix approach
Identify Potential Sources	Develop a preferred supplier list; use internal and external databases to identify potential sources; send requests for information (RFIs) to collect data about new sources
Reduce Suppliers in Selection Pool	Perform supplier financial analyses using third-party data; develop minimum performance thresholds before the search; pre-qualify or reject suppliers using electronic request for quotes and proposals
Conduct a Formal Evaluation	Visit suppliers directly; use international purchasing offices to evaluate foreign suppliers; join consortiums that collect supplier data; use third-party data or other support; develop company-wide assessment templates and tools
Select Supplier and Negotiate Agreement	Develop pre-approved contract language; use "cut and paste" contract clauses during negotiation, consider electronic negotiations

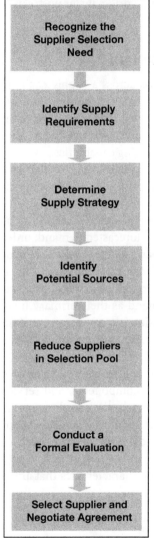

Figure 14.3 Reducing supplier evaluation and selection cycle time

Few leaders could reasonably argue that the inputs received from upstream suppliers do not affect their company's downstream customers. We know that producers are afforded minimal forgiveness when they fail their end customers. Developing a world class supply base, with supplier selection as a key process, demands attention to the inputs and relationships that originate far upstream in the supply chain.

Demand Estimation and Supply Planning

Perhaps the most important information that flows across a supply chain are estimates of customer demand. Best-practice companies understand well the need to have a demand planning process that identifies the future claims on their output. And these companies know they must seamlessly link their demand planning capabilities with their supply planning capabilities.

If demand and supply planning is important, it makes sense to step back and explain what is meant by these terms. Demand planning includes the steps taken to arrive at the most vital information that moves across a supply chain—estimates of anticipated demand. Demand estimates include all the claims on a company's output for a particular period, including forecasted demand, orders for which commitments are already made, spare parts requirements to support aftermarket needs, product recalls that require replacement, promotional items, and adjustments resulting from changes in inventory policies. It is almost startling how many systems rely on estimates of demand as their primary input. One could argue persuasively that demand estimation is a company's most important planning process. (The terms demand estimation and demand planning are used interchangeably here.)

The counterpart to demand planning is supply planning, which involves the steps taken to ensure that suppliers, materials, components, and services are available to support the demand plan. Unfortunately, the coordination and hand off of information between the demand and supply sides of the supply chain, not to mention the trust between these two sides has sometimes been less than stellar.

Best-practice companies demonstrate four major characteristics that are related to demand and supply planning:

1. They have business processes and systems that promote the sharing of demand and supply information;
2. They have in place organizational design features that bring together the demand and supply sides of the supply chain;
3. They are relentless in pursuing better forecasts and forecasting techniques; and
4. They make demand management a fundamental part of demand planning.

Systems to Balance Demand and Supply

The first characteristic involves ways to balance demand and supply across a supply chain. Two such systems for aligning demand and supply are sales and operations planning (S&OP) and collaborative planning, forecasting, and replenishment (CPFR).

S&OP is a cross-functional process that creates a three- to 18-month production schedule for product categories and families. The objective of S&OP is to develop an output plan that minimizes total costs, given a specific demand level. Understanding that cost minimization is a major objective of S&OP, finance must play a major role in any planning exercise. This system, which is conceptually similar to aggregate planning, routinely reviews customer demand and supply resources and updates plans across a rolling time horizon.

CPFR follows a defined framework that combines the intelligence of multiple trading partners in the planning and fulfillment of customer demand. It has the stated objective of increasing product availability to customers while reducing inventory, transportation, and logistics costs.[7] A key part of CPFR involves collaborative forecasting, which is the process of collecting and reconciling information within and outside of the organization to come up with a single projection of demand. Demand and supply plan leaders routinely practice these more advanced planning techniques.

Organizational Design Features

A second characteristic of effective planners is that they stress organizational features that support their planning capabilities. For example, a planning group at a leading chemical company has responsibility for all of the activities that are associated with demand and supply planning and execution, except production. Using sophisticated algorithms, planners have responsibility for managing the flow of a product's material and information from suppliers all the way through to customers. No hand off of information between demand and supply planning is necessary, creating clear responsibility for demand planning, supply planning, and customer service.

Another innovative feature is to make a single executive responsible for demand and supply planning activities. A leading U.S. company has created the position of vice president of supply chain management and charged that executive with responsibility for worldwide supply planning and replenishment, demand and finished good forecasting, inventory planning, primary customer order fulfillment and logistics, and integrating supply chain activities with operational positions. The primary objective is to create a single point of accountability to satisfy customer requirements at the lowest total cost.

Pursuit of Improved Forecasts

A third characteristic of planning leaders is a relentless pursuit to improve forecasts and forecasting techniques. While many practices are associated with companies that excel at forecasting, the following are usually part of their portfolio.

Perhaps first and foremost, best-practice companies hold an individual or group accountable for forecasting accuracy as well as the continuous improvement of the process. It is difficult to overstate the important linkage between accountability and forecasting effectiveness.

Forecast leaders also regularly measure forecast accuracy across their different product lines. One survey revealed that fully two-thirds of respondents reported forecast accuracy of between 50 and 80%, indicating room for improvement. Forecast accuracy, which is an important supply chain metric, should be calculated regularly and compared against preestablished benchmarks.

A major part of the continuous improvement process involves regular reviews to identify the root causes of forecasting error. Review teams should determine if errors are randomly distributed, if forecasts are consistently too high or too low, or if other techniques might produce better forecasts. Best practice companies apply Six Sigma and other improvement techniques when evaluating forecast error. Instead of improving the quality of a tangible product, they work to improve the quality of the information that is the output of a business process.

Insightful leaders recognize that different forecasting models fit different scenarios. A *one-size-fits-all* approach is usually not the best way to forecast demand. Forecasting leaders also rely on quantitative systems to identify the forecasting algorithms and models that best fit their historical demand. These forecasts are updated frequently, often daily, as new information becomes available.

Research suggests that quantitative models are generally more accurate than qualitative or managerial forecasting techniques. This does not mean that managerial inputs to forecasts are not considered when managers have contextual knowledge that is difficult to quantify or when managers are domain experts. On the other hand, best-practice companies are careful to avoid using salesperson estimates to drive their planning efforts given the gamesmanship that often surrounds the setting of sales quotas. Knowing when and how to apply rigorous analytical techniques is a forecasting necessity.

Influencing Demand

A fourth characteristic of planning leaders is they do not simply react to changes in demand patterns—they influence these patterns by managing demand. Demand management attempts to influence customer orders while trying to reduce the uncertainty of when those orders will occur. Most observers would agree that even though a forecast is a projection into the future, most techniques rely on history as the basis of that projection. Demand management moves beyond demand estimation or planning by trying to influence when demand will occur. This is often done to smooth the demand pattern by removing the volatility that often comes with customer demand.

The bottom line is that life is good when you have a solid idea of your demand. Life gets even better when demand planners work well with supply planners. Effective supply and demand planning also makes the execution part of the supply chain that much easier.

Customer Order Fulfillment

The three previous processes create unique sources of value that are essential for competitive success; however, none create any revenue. This brings us to customer order fulfillment, a process that can be viewed narrowly or broadly. The fulfillment process is too often a saga of broken promises—the seller seduces the customer, the sale is made, the order is transmitted—but where is the product or service? Even when a producer establishes a promise date, that date often reflects the producer's convenience rather than the customer's requirement. Best-practice companies know this does not have to be the case.

When viewed narrowly, order fulfillment primarily includes the acts of distribution and logistics. Those who take a narrow view will focus extensively on operational tactics to improve the pick, pack, ship, and return elements of fulfillment. Materials handling, storage, facility layout and flow, and picking and sorting technology will be prime topics of conversation.

When viewed broadly, fulfillment includes the steps and activities from the sales inquiry through the receipt of the payment from the customer; it even includes the return of the final product or service. This broader view involves order preparation, transmission, entry, filling (which includes production and purchasing), accounts receivable, shipping, tracking, and returns. Each of these subprocesses has its own set of steps and outputs. Some might even include after-sale service within the customer order fulfillment process, although this is usually treated as a separate process.

Whether a narrower or broader view of customer order fulfillment is taken, the ultimate objective of order fulfillment is to satisfy a promised delivery date at the right quantity and condition while managing total costs. While demand estimation stresses planning, customer order fulfillment stresses execution.

Companies that take a broader view of order fulfillment often make order-to-cash cycle time a key performance indicator. This stresses the financial aspects of the fulfillment process by not viewing the process as complete until customer payment is received.

Discussing customer order fulfillment is not nearly as easy as it may appear. One reason is that fulfillment is a broad process. Instead of identifying which groups are involved with fulfillment, it might be easier to identify the groups that are not involved. Second, companies practice a wide variety of order fulfillment models, including make-to-stock, make-to-order, assemble-to-order, and engineer-to-order. Each of these approach order fulfillment differently. To complicate matters even further, the fulfillment process is usually different in business-to-business versus business-to-consumer environments. While no standard fulfillment model exists, there are some characteristics that help make order fulfillment a value-creating process.

One characteristic is recognition of the relationship between effective demand planning and the ability to satisfy customer orders. Fulfillment is the part of the supply chain where planning and execution meet directly. Performing demand and supply planning well makes customer order fulfillment that much easier.

Customer order fulfillment, like supplier selection and new product development, is a process that, if performed faster and more responsively, can lead to competitive advantage. A maker of beverage and ice dispensers on the East Coast forecasts and builds a base product in anticipation of customer orders. Final product configuration occurs only after receiving actual orders, something that is called *form postponement*. Final configuration takes only three days versus four to six weeks for competitors—providing a decided market advantage. Restaurants and other customers, such as cruise ships and institutions, purchase beverage dispensers because they have every intention of using them. In another example, high-end U.S. furniture makers that saw their market share steadily taken by Chinese imports responded by slashing customer order cycle times for custom-ordered furniture, something that furniture arriving via ocean carrier cannot match. They are also offering customers a wider selection of product varieties and colors. These companies see their future linked to speed, responsiveness, and product variety. Companies that excel at customer order fulfillment rigorously apply lean principles as they improve their fulfillment process. In particular, they attack wasteful and non-value-adding activities through process redesign. A small cable and wiring company began to see its customers migrating toward foreign competitors. Instead of moving its production to China (the immediate reaction of many U.S. companies), this company concluded that providing customers with volume flexibility (see Chapter 12), a high quality product, and shorter lead times offered the best opportunity to challenge new competitors. By redesigning its fulfillment process, the company reduced its order lead time from 20 days to 12 days, or a 40 percent reduction, with further improvements expected. Customers responded favorably because a shorter lead time allowed them to shorten their planning horizons. Shorter planning horizons reduce supply chain uncertainty.

In addition to redesigning their fulfillment process, leading companies rely extensively on electronic systems to support fulfillment efforts. A sample of these systems include electronic data interchange with suppliers and customers, on-line ordering systems up and down the supply chain, extensive use of advance shipping notices and electronic funds transfers, and point-of-sale data to trigger upstream replenishment requests. Additionally, sales personnel who work directly with customers should have visibility into production scheduling systems. This allows sales representatives to work directly with customers when scheduling sales commitments. E-systems are ideal for removing time and transaction costs from the fulfillment process.

Any company that excels in order fulfillment will appreciate the importance of inventory control. And, at the center of inventory control is something called *record integrity*. Record integrity is the result of activities and procedures that help ensure the amount of physical material on hand (POH) is equal to the computerized record of material on hand (ROH). Any difference between POH and ROH represents an error that can affect costs and customer service. In short, record integrity exists when the physical inventory equals the electronic record, regardless of the quantity of inventory. (Inventory management is concerned with determining the right mix and amount of inventory to maintain.) Record integrity helps ensure that customer orders are not delayed due to inventory record inaccuracies. During supplier selection, it is a good idea to request record integrity data from perspective suppliers.

Order fulfillment leaders rarely assume that a single lead-time applies to all customers. At times, it becomes necessary to arrive at a promise date after consulting closely with internal participants and the customer. Leading companies know that the methods used to establish lead times and promise dates can be a way to offer flexibility to customers, enhance business-to-business relationships, and more closely align internal capabilities with external commitments. A rigid lead time policy that works to the benefit of internal operations may not be the lead time policy that benefits the customer base.

Order fulfillment leaders also appreciate the importance of reporting a set of fulfillment-related measures. Indicators such as the perfect customer order, order fill rate, order cycle time, on-time delivery, inventory accuracy, and order-to-cash cycle time all provide revealing insights into the fulfillment process.

The perfect customer order is a comprehensive measure of fulfillment capability that highlights the deficiencies in a company's operations. Figure 14.4 illustrates the perfect order measure—a humbling measure that too few companies calculate. In this figure, the perfect order figure is arrived at by multiplying $.93 \times .95 \times .97 \times .96 \times .97$. The probability that a customer will receive a perfect order is just under 80%, which is about a 200,000 parts per million defect level. What does supply management have to do with this measure? The answer

A perfect order is an order that is delivered complete, on time, in perfect condition, and with accurate and complete documentation.

"Perfect orders":

– Orders received on time	┄┄┄┄┄┄┄┄┄→ **93%**
– Orders received complete	┄┄┄┄┄┄┄┄┄→ **95%**
– Orders received damage free	┄┄┄┄┄┄┄┄┄→ **97%**
– Orders filled accurately	┄┄┄┄┄┄┄┄┄→ **96%**
– Orders billed accurately	┄┄┄┄┄┄┄┄┄→ <u>**97%**</u>

$$\text{Perfect Order} = 79.8\%$$

Figure 14.4   The perfect order measure

is quite a bit. Suppliers represent the source that impacts a firm's ability to satisfy end customers. The ability to provide a perfect order does not originate only with the immediate seller.

CREATING THE FOUNDATION FOR PROCESS EXCELLENCE

Gaining performance advantages from the processes presented here is not simply a matter of hoping good things will happen once we buy into the importance of processes. A process orientation cannot become a reality until competency is achieved within the four enabling areas that were presented in Chapters 3–6.

The Right Performance Measures

Adopting performance measures that are customer and process focused is one way to send a message that an organization is serious about taking a process perspective. When thinking about customer order fulfillment, no other measures can send this message better than the perfect customer order and order-to-cash cycle time. Within product development, the tracking of C-to-C cycle time becomes essential, while measures of forecast accuracy will provide insights into the quality of the demand planning process. Measures of supplier performance will help validate the effectiveness of the supplier evaluation and selection process. For an overall perspective of supply chain performance, it is hard to beat the total cost of ownership and return-on-assets measures. Each process presented here should feature measures that emphasize process rather than functional excellence.

The Right People

The knowledge and skills that are required to excel within a process environment are vastly different from those required in a functional environment. Effective process management requires close collaboration and coordination between engineering, procurement, operations, logistics, marketing, suppliers, and customers to coordinate material and information flows across the supply chain. A process focus also requires individuals who understand their company's business model, who can assume a holistic rather than narrow supply chain perspective, and who can manage critical internal and external relationships. An ongoing challenge centers on the ability of functional personnel to fit within a process environment.

The Right Systems

Regardless of the technology platform or software used, information systems should capture and share information across functional groups and organizational boundaries in a real-time or near real-time basis. IT is rapidly becoming the great enabler behind the process-centric organization.

The Right Design

Design features that support process-centric thinking include collocating support personnel with internal customers, cross-functional product development teams that include supply personnel and suppliers, full-time process management teams, sales and operations planning groups, full-time teams assigned to manage critical processes, and buyer-supplier councils that feature executive to executive interaction. Leading companies are often quite creative when it comes to designing a process-driven organization.

Advanced process thinking requires a foundation that supports a new way of operating. And that means building a foundation that has the right measures, people, systems, and design. Failing to build this foundation will make it painfully clear why organizations often struggle with process-centric thinking.

CONCLUDING THOUGHTS

It would be naïve to suggest that a singular focus on the processes presented here guarantees market success. It would be even more naïve to discount other processes that must be performed at world-class levels, including those that support financial, marketing, and human resource needs. In addition, principal processes such as the four presented here require hundreds of supporting processes and thousands of distinct process variants, all of which require some level of management.[8]

With that said, it is hard to imagine being successful as we move forward without paying close attention to those processes that are the source points for the kinds of value that help differentiate one company from the next. In today's hyper-competitive markets, any opportunity to differentiate oneself should be taken seriously. Supply management is an integral part of this effort.

REFERENCES

1. H. Smith and P. Fingar, *Business Process Management: The Third Wave*, (Tampa, FL: Meghan-Kiffer Press, 2003): 52.
2. T. McDowell, D. Agarwal, D. Miller, T. Okamoto, and T. Page, *Organizational Design: The Rise of Teams*, February 29, 2016, retrieved from https://dupress.deloitte.com/dup-us-en/focus/human-capital-trends/2016/organizational-models-network-of-teams.html.
3. For a more detailed discussion of this topic, see Robert J. Trent, *Strategic Supply Management*, Chapter 13, 221–235.
4. H. Takeuchi and I. Nonaka, "The New New Product Development Game," *Harvard Business Review*, 64, no. 1 (January/February, 1986): 137.
5. For a more detailed discussion of this topic, see Robert J. Trent, *Strategic Supply Management*, Chapter 10, 163–178.
6. R. M. Monczka, R. J. Trent, and K. J. Petersen, *Effective Global Sourcing and Supply for Superior Results*, (Tempe, Arizona: CAPS Research, 2006): 59.
7. From www.scm.ncsu.edu/public/cpfr/index.html.
8. Smith and Fingar, 52.

15

BATTLING COMPLEXITY— AND WINNING

A revealing way to appreciate how supply chains have changed over time is to visit a supermarket.[1] During your visit be sure to stop by the Mediterranean bar, the florist, the bakery, the pharmacy, and the organic and gluten-free foods sections. Don't forget to visit the parts of the store that feature fruits, vegetables, and seafood brought in daily from around the world, the premade and gourmet meals section, and the products targeted to the Hispanic, Asian, and Kosher community. Do you need toothpaste? One analysis found that consumers can choose from over 350 different stock keeping units (SKUs) of toothpaste. And, any parent knows that a trip down the diaper aisle with its dozens of choices can be a daunting experience. Supermarkets today typically stock 40,000–50,000 items, up from around 15,000 in the 1980s. Welcome to the world of supply chain complexity, a condition that affects virtually all industries, not just retail supermarkets.

Why should anyone be concerned with complexity? The short answer is that most CEOs expect the internal and external complexity that their organizations face to increase. A study by the *IBM Institute for Business Value* revealed that 60% of CEOs say their organization currently experiences high or very high levels of complexity. Almost 80% say they expect to see high or very high complexity as they look out over a five-year horizon. A second finding is that more than half of CEO's express concerns about their company's ability to manage increased complexity.

This chapter addresses the increasingly important topic of complexity by defining the concept, describing why it can be a problem, and explaining why we have business complexity. The chapter also presents strategies for addressing an emerging topic that supply and supply chain professionals must confront, whether they recognize the need or not.

WHAT IS COMPLEXITY?

Let's agree on something important before we define complexity. Few rational people wake up in the morning and say, "My goal today is to make my organization unnecessarily complex!" Things usually do not work that way. But yet, we often find ourselves consumed by unhealthy levels and kinds of complexity.

What, then, is complexity? While we can define business and supply chain complexity in a variety of ways, a general perspective views something as complex if it is hard to separate, analyze, or solve. Another perspective views complexity as something with many parts in an intricate arrangement. Perhaps more revealing are the synonyms that describe the word complex. These descriptors include complicated, intricate, and involved. While there are academics and consultants who have attempted to define this concept, the word complexity, at least conceptually, should not be that complex.[2] It is often something that we know it when we see it. The following list provides a diverse set of examples that shows the many faces of complexity. Unfortunately, there is usually no shortage of examples to illustrate this concept:

- A simple sounding proposal to begin collecting state sales tax on online purchases is not all that simple. At Overstock.com it took a team of 20–30 experienced information technology (IT) professionals 9,142 hours over a period of five months to install, test, and integrate the software that let the company properly calculate use tax in one additional state.[3]
- The merger between United and Continental Airlines still presented challenges years after it was announced. In technology alone, the two carriers had 1,400 separate systems, programs, and protocols. Workers were also represented by different unions with dissimilar work rules. It required almost a year of study to arrive at a single brand of coffee to serve on the combined airline.[4]
- A study of overlapping and duplicative U.S. federal programs revealed that the U.S. government has 15 different agencies overseeing food safety laws, more than 20 separate programs to help the homeless, 80 programs for economic development, 82 programs to improve teacher quality, 47 programs for job training and employment, and 56 programs to help people understand their finances.[5]
- Spire, a data tracking service, reported in 2011 that U.S. consumers could select from 352 distinct types and sizes of toothpaste at retail outlets. The good news is that this figure is down from 412 in 2008.
- At one point 3M's picture hanging hooks, a relatively simple product made of plastic and strips of sticky foam, were part of a production process that, over a period of 100 days, meandered more than 1,300 miles through four factories in four states. 3M's former CEO referred to these convoluted travels as *hairballs*.[6]

- Hostess, the now out-of-business maker of Wonder Bread and Twinkies, made its final trip into bankruptcy in 2012. The heavily unionized company ended life with 36 plants and more than 500 distribution centers across the U.S., 372 collective-bargaining agreements, a dozen separate unions, several billion dollars in unfunded pension liabilities, 5,500 sometimes duplicative delivery routes, and 40 multi-employer pension plans.[7]
- After a fire destroyed the sole Japanese supplier that provided a critical P-valve brake part to Toyota, engineers came to realize that over time they had designed 200 P-valve variations, many of which had complex tapered orifices that required highly customized jigs and drills. This made the recovery from the fire even more challenging.
- Harvard University announced plans to outsource the management of most of its endowment assets and lay off roughly half of the staff at the university's Harvard Management Company. The university could no longer justify the organizational complexity and resources that were required to support the investing activities of the portfolios that comprise the university's $26 billion endowment.[8]
- The City of Los Angeles passed new rules that require developers to include affordable housing in new projects. The rules require up to 25% of units in rental properties and up to 40% in for-sale projects meet affordability guidelines. Developers must also pay construction wages on par with those required for public works projects, such as a carpenter making $55 per hour; hire 30% of the workforce from within the city limits; set aside 10% of jobs for certain disadvantaged workers who were living within five miles of the project, and ensure that 60% of the workers have experience on par with graduates of a union apprenticeship program. Developers contend that these new requirements will prevent new projects from even being started in Los Angeles.[9] Welcome to La-La Land!

The issue is not necessarily whether something is complex but rather, at what point does something cross a threshold and become excessively complex? A comparison to cholesterol is one way to think about this topic. The human body has good and bad cholesterol, and even the bad cholesterol is tolerable until it reaches a certain level. Complexity is much the same way. Companies that understand how to manage certain kinds of complexity can use it to gain competitive advantage. Others are simply overwhelmed by it.

Types of Complexity

McKinsey researchers have studied the topic of complexity probably as much as anybody. They have concluded that two broad categories of complexity exist. The first category, *institutional* complexity, stems from strategic choices, the external context (such as regulations), and from major choices about organizational and operating systems.[10] The second major category is *individual* complexity. Individual complexity deals with how hard it is for employees to perform their jobs. Employee role ambiguity, conflict, administrative burdens, duplicate roles, and ill-defined tasks and processes all contribute to individual complexity. More specific types of complexity can characterize industries and organizations:

- *Designed* complexity—this results from choices about where the business operates, what it sells, how it sells, to whom its sells, and so on
- *Inherent* complexity—this is intrinsic to the business and can only be removed by exiting a portion of the business
- *Imposed* complexity—this includes laws, industry regulations, and interventions by external organizations
- *Unnecessary* complexity—this results from a misalignment between the needs of an organization and the processes in place to support it—this is probably the easiest complexity to address

Organizations that learn how to manage and exploit complexity should generate additional sources of profit and gain competitive advantage. When managed well, complexity can also increase corporate resilience by enhancing the ability to adapt to change. On the individual side, McKinsey research has determined that companies that are reporting the lowest levels of individual complexity have higher returns on capital employed and returns on invested capital.[11]

An example of managing complexity comes from the retail world, where something called omni-channels has suddenly become big news. Major retailers are turning their stores into order-fulfillment centers where workers pick, pack, and ship online consumer orders—part of a complicated plan to grow their business. While filling online orders from stores instead of distribution or fulfillment centers adds channel complexity, these retailers expect to gain a competitive edge over online-only rivals by providing customers with greater ordering flexibility and service while offering the retailer an opportunity to better manage its inventory, service levels, and order delivery times. Perhaps most important, these retailers hope to stay relevant to consumers.

One of the challenges with complexity is that we do not have measures or tools to arrive at a complexity score. Within quality management, if a process-proving study reveals that a process has a capability index (Cpk) of .8, we know that process is not capable of producing output that conforms to requirements on a consistent basis. In fact, the Cpk value can even be used to estimate the parts per million (ppm) defect level for that process. Fact-based tools and methodologies are readily available and known. No such tools, at least at this time, specifically score complexity, making it difficult to operationalize this concept.

WHY COMPLEXITY IS (OFTEN) BAD

An overly complex product or business process usually brings with it an impressive list of less than desirable outcomes. Consider how an overdesigned product, for example, can affect product quality. The case against product complexity during product design is a strong one, since it can be shown mathematically that overly complex designs affect product quality levels. Let's illustrate this with an example.

Assume a design team creates a product with seven components, each with an average reliability of 99%. The overall reliability of this product is $.99^7$, or 93%. This corresponds to a 70,000 ppm defect level (7% defects per one million opportunities). Next, a design simplification project eliminates the need for two of the components, making the overall reliability $.99^5$, or 95%. A new predicted defect level of 50,000 ppm defects represents almost a 30% reduction from the original defect level. Further assume that another improvement project increases the average reliability of each component to .995. The overall reliability now becomes $.995^5$, or 97.5%. This further reduces the ppm defect level to 25,000 ppm. These numbers, which are nowhere near Six Sigma levels, are used to show how complexity in product design leads to higher predicted defect levels. More components, which results in not only more defects but also more suppliers and greater supply chain complexity, create more opportunities for error.

Few would argue with the notion that complexity usually increases business costs. A cost that is associated with complexity—and one that is rarely calculated—is complexity's opportunity cost. Employees who deal with the effects of complexity simply are not able to focus their attention toward more productive pursuits. Unfortunately, economists have yet to develop a way to calculate a *complexity tax*. And, it is somewhat futile to argue that cost accounting systems provide much help here. As mentioned, we have yet to see any key indicators that address business complexity well.

Complexity often works against speed and flexibility—two attributes that increasingly define world-class companies. Without question, the way that companies compete today is different than it was just a few years ago. Characteristics such as speed and flexibility (what some call dexterity) are becoming as important to competitive success as quality and cost capabilities. It should be somewhat intuitive that excessive complexity inhibits these important capabilities.

Even after conceding that certain types of complexity are a natural part of the business landscape, it is safe to conclude that other types of complexity should not be welcome. The one perspective we should all share is that at some point unwelcome complexity increases costs and affects organizational performance, often with no corresponding return. And, higher costs and diminished performance elevate the risk that a company will no longer remain competitive.

HOW ORGANIZATIONS BECOME COMPLEX

Most executives understand that complexity is not something that is in short supply. This is ironic given that no company has a stated objective or strategy of becoming unnecessarily complex. For a variety of reasons, however, it is often the state in which we find ourselves. It is often the cumulative result of many small actions and decisions taken over time.

Complexity often evolves at a pace that ensures it does not draw any unusual attention. The tendency to become more complex over time represents something we will call *complexity creep*. At some point, the realization sets in that steps have to be taken to regain control, or else the risk of being consumed by complexity becomes very real. The causes of complexity are widespread.

Marketers Gone Wild

Product proliferation has resulted in a large increase in the number of SKUs moving through supply chains. With product proliferation, a company has made a conscious decision to extend its brand offerings or develop entirely new products to retain or attract customers. While new products and product extensions hopefully create market excitement and growth, there is no question they also lead to greater business complexity. In reality, SKU proliferation occurs for a variety of general reasons. These include:[12]

- Nimble, responsive companies are striving to meet ever-changing market opportunities and competitor demands
- Businesses that create excessive amounts of new products are chasing an impossible dream of being all things to all people
- Companies have ineffective product exit strategies
- Organizations use an innovation metric that rewards SKU proliferation as proof of innovation

Engineers Gone Wild

One of the most visible sources of complexity involves products that are overdesigned by engineers. Overdesign may mean that a product has too many components, more features than what the customer wants or can use, or are overly complex to produce or distribute. Failing to check whether a previous component is available for reuse during product design, using custom designed components when standard components are available, or failing to leverage commonalities across product platforms can also contribute to excessive product and supply chain complexity. It is not that engineers necessarily endorse complexity; they simply tend to treat product designs as an opportunity to create the next Mona Lisa.

More Efficient Product Development Processes

Although it may seem counterintuitive, complexity can be a consequence of faster and more efficient product development processes. While shorter development times, on average, are a good thing, an interesting consequence of improved development processes is the ability to introduce more new products using fewer, if any, additional resources. And, more new products mean additional complexity. As product development processes become more efficient, the complexity related to product proliferation often increases.

Lack of Process Thinkers and Ill-Defined Processes

As presented in Chapter 14, a process is a set of interrelated tasks or activities designed to achieve a specific objective or outcome. Even though this is a straightforward idea, organizations often suffer from a shortage of process thinkers because most individuals are trained to think functionally or to focus on specific tasks. Unfortunately, organizational processes almost always cross functional boundaries. Complexity arises when individuals try to optimize their work within a process they do not understand or cannot conceptualize. Even those individuals who understand processes sometimes fall into the same trap as engineers—they tend to over-engineer a process rather than simplify it.

Strategic Choices

Some organizations choose to be complex. They make strategic choices about introducing new product lines or expanding into new geographic regions. No one would dispute that FedEx is a more complex organization today compared to when it served only the U.S. market. Expansion brings complexity, and that's the way it will always be. Successful companies learn how to manage the institutional complexity that results from strategic choices.

Continuous Reorganizations and New Programs

Continuously reorganizing governance structures or introducing new programs are often seen as a way to show visible progress toward some real or perceived challenge. Continuous reorganizations, however, also can lead to chaos, confusion, and complexity. The same is true about new programs. It seems like every challenge can be overcome with a program that has a clever acronym, often with a new position assigned to it. Programs to improve quality, reduce costs, improve customer satisfaction, enhance supplier relationships, promote diversity, or improve employee morale and retention are constantly being added, revised, and sometimes deleted. A constant churning of programs breeds not only complexity—it also breeds cynicism.

Bureaucracy

Bureaucracies are systems of administration characterized by red tape and a proliferation of rules, procedures, and positions. It would be hard to argue that bureaucracies are not complex. They stifle innovation, lengthen decision-making times, and erect barriers to change. Being referred to as a bureaucrat, at least in most circles, is not a compliment. While we often think that bureaucracy relates to government, corporate structure and governance—particularly at larger corporations—can rival some of the worst public bureaucracies.

Most individuals find that bureaucracies stifle their individual goals. Tim Cook, the CEO of Apple summarized clearly his views regarding bureaucracy when he said,

> "No bureaucracy. We want a fast-moving, agile company where there are no politics, no agenda. When you do that, things become pretty simple. You don't have all of these things that companies generally worry about. You don't have silos built up where everybody is trying to optimize their silo and figuring out how to grab turf. It makes all of our jobs easier so we're freed up to focus on the things that truly matter."[13]

Mergers and Acquisitions

Probably the quickest way to create complexity, not to mention anxiety and role confusion, is through mergers and acquisitions (M&A). The M&A process almost always features a complex set of legal and financial issues. After the ink is dry on an agreement, it becomes evident how much duplication, overlap, and even conflict exists between the combined entities, a complexity that does not go away simply because the legal part of the process is complete. When brought together, organizations bring different cultures, systems, policies, procedures, suppliers, customers, employee contracts, and part numbering schemes. Some companies, such as Oracle, have created a competitive advantage by assimilating newly acquired companies quickly into the corporate portfolio. Mastering the complexity brought about by M&As is an example where managing complexity creates a business advantage.

Increased Government Oversight and Regulation

New laws and regulations such as Dodd-Frank, conflict mineral rules, the Food Safety Modernization Act, assorted transportation anti-terror acts, anti-slavery laws, new regulations resulting from catastrophes (such as the Gulf of Mexico oil explosion), and rulings by entities such as the National Labor Relations Board and the Environmental Protection Agency have combined to make business much more complicated. It is safe to say that those who make these new regulations are not the ones who have to live by them.

Has the tendency of governments to issue thousands of regulations year after year had an effect on business? A survey published annually by The World Bank ranks countries according to their ease of doing business. In 2009, the U.S. ranked third in the overall ranking in terms of the ease of doing business. In 2016, the U.S. had slipped to 8th place. Each year *Forbes* conducts an analysis to identify the best and worst countries to conduct business. In 2007, the U.S. was ranked as the most business-friendly nation. By 2016, the U.S. had slipped to 23rd, hardly a proud achievement.[14] In 2009, it required 40 days on average to get a construction permit in the U.S., now it requires 81 days; it took 300 days on average to enforce a contract, now it is 420 days; and the cost to register property was .5% of the property's value, now it is 2.4%.[15] It is safe to conclude that the cumulative effect of these regulations has created a burden on business. The U.S. alone issued well over 20,000 new regulations in the period from 2009 to 2016.[16] The U.S. Association of American Railroads estimated that in 2015, paperwork costs to comply with safety regulations issued by the Federal Railroad Administration required 25 million labor hours (over 5% of all labor hours worked in the industry) and $1.5 billion in costs.[17]

Some experts have concluded that regulatory burdens and regulations that have been placed on U.S. businesses are a primary reason that the U.S. economic expansion after the Great Recession of 2008 was so tepid. A line in a Rob Thomas song sums up well the feeling that many have when faced with thousands of new regulations each year. Excusing the somewhat awkward English in the song, the singer asks, "Why do you got to go and make it so hard on me?"[18]

Complexity Equals Job Security

It should come as no surprise that some individuals, and even organizations, have a vested interest in keeping complexity alive and well. Some will fight vigorously against anything that seeks to make life simpler. We all know someone who works hard to protect the status quo by resisting even the most reasonable change. These individuals may earn their living formulating or enforcing the many rules, policies, laws, and regulations that others must follow. Or perhaps they earn their living managing supply chains that probably should not be as complex as they have become. What would happen to accountants, lawyers, and IRS personnel if tax returns were simplified to one page? We have complexity because some people want complexity—they owe their livelihood to it.

Complacency

At some point, most organizations—particularly larger ones—commit a sin that brings forth a swift and painful outcome. That sin is complacency, which reflects a high level of self-satisfaction with the status quo, often with an unawareness of actual dangers or deficiencies. Complacent organizations have no idea of the costs or risks associated with being overly complex, nor do they probably care, at least in the short run. A lack of urgency leads these organizations to ignore the subject until it is far too late.

Let's Go Global

Statistics that show a steady growth in international commerce over the last 25 years are impossible to refute. While most international decisions likely reflect sound courses of action, something that is often overlooked is the impact these decisions have on supply networks. Figure 15.1 illustrates some of the supply chain issues that arise when doing business on a worldwide basis; issues that are not nearly as prevalent with domestic supply networks. Unfortunately, few companies fully account for total costs when making global decisions.

Other areas where complexity may arise due to worldwide supply chains include working across different cultures, language and communication barriers, different legal systems, time differences, unreliable information, countertrade demands, a total landed cost that never equals the unit cost of what is purchased,

• Longer pipelines in distance and time • Increased risk (damage, theft, etc.) • Different shipping terms (Inco terms versus U.C.C. terms) • Increased use of agents and other third parties • Delivery variability • Managing different currencies
• Extensive documentation requirements • Reduced ability to plan due to longer cycle times • Increase in supply chain "touch" points and handlers • Multiple modes of transportation • More challenging to identify the true total cost of ownership • Greater supply chain risk management requirements

Figure 15.1   International logistics and business complexity

and increased risk management requirements—particularly regarding the protection of intellectual property and currency fluctuations. Globalization brings with it no shortage of issues to manage, which increases complexity. Some observers argue that a fair portion of the increased risk and complexity faced by businesses today are largely a result of globalization.

WAYS TO BATTLE COMPLEXITY

In some ways the battle against complexity is a logical progression after applying lean principles, which is a mature concept that is often applied narrowly in the battle against waste. Most sources address complexity by putting forth general rather than specific ways for tackling this issue. While these approaches are well and good, they are rarely specific enough for really understanding how to battle complexity. Complexity management should focus on eliminating bad complexity while exploiting the kinds of complexity that can lead to competitive advantage.

The first step in this battle is recognizing that complexity exists and that it must be managed. Fortunately, some powerful ways exist for addressing complexity once a firm moves beyond the awareness stage.

Simplify Product Designs

Simplified product designs offer one of the fastest ways to reduce business complexity and risk. Besides the many supply chain benefits that accrue from simplified product designs, the bottom line is that customers appreciate simplicity. Although it has been an electronic eternity since Apple introduced the iPhone, the iPhone has remained a hot-selling item. Besides being cool, some analysts attribute part of the product's success to the simplicity of its design and use.

Product design is the time to think about simplification. Industry leaders understand the power of the product development process to satisfy some important objectives. Predesign objectives can involve setting targets for quality, reliability, serviceability, sustainability, end-of-life recycling, target cost, assembly, cycle time, and simplicity of design and use. The concept phase of product development is also the time to think about how to tackle overly complex designs and production processes.

An interesting example of simplification of a service offering involves FedEx. FedEx Freight has launched a simpler way to use less than truckload (LTL) shipping based on dimension and distance. The shipment includes a flat rate up to 1,200 pounds regardless of what the customer ships within the box. The system is being marketed to customers who normally do not use LTL. The new system is easier for customers to understand from a rate perspective compared with the more complex National Motor Freight Classification system.[19] Indications are the new freight system is a success as customers enjoy the simplicity of not having to rely on the more complex freight classification system. As one FedEx manager stated, "I want it to be so simple that my 9-year-old can do it."[20]

Standardize and Reuse Components

Few supply managers would dispute the notion that custom-designed components almost always cost more than standardized components. And, customized components are often not as readily available when demand patterns shift. They are usually provided by a limited number of suppliers (often one) that may be unable to respond when market conditions change. Related to the idea of standardized components is the reuse of components. Reuse means using a component that is available from a previous use or design.

A way to address any complexity that comes with over-customization is to make standardization and reuse key objectives during product design. A word of caution, however, is required here. Excessive use of standard and reused components creates a risk that customers will not be able to differentiate a new product from a previous product, or one product line from another. As an automotive design engineer noted during a research interview, "If a customer feels it, touches it, sees it, or smells it, then it better look new and improved. And it better not look like what we have already designed or look like our other models." Some companies rely on reuse engineers and supply management personnel as a check and balance to ensure that designs are not over-engineered, resulting in excessive customization when a standard or reuse item would work just as well.

Become Rational

Rationalization is the process of determining the right mix and number of something to maintain. It is a powerful concept that has wide application across every part of a supply chain. It is also a concept that offers one of the best ways to battle complexity. While rationalization should be ongoing, it is usually of the most interest when executive leaders finally realize they have too many of something. A number of years ago, Procter and Gamble announced its desire to eliminate 20,000 suppliers from its worldwide supply base and reduce the number of distribution centers it maintains from 400 to 200.[21] At some point the marginal cost of one more of something outweighs the marginal contribution of that next something.

Areas where companies should continuously evaluate the right mix and number of something to maintain include the supply base, component SKUs, product lines and product features, customers, contracts, retail outlets, distribution centers, production sites, and engineering centers. Figure 15.2 identifies

- Fewer contracts to negotiate or purchase orders to write
- Fewer material releases to suppliers
- Less effort expended to process fewer material receipts
- Easier material traceability
- Better communication and relationships with suppliers, thereby offering the possibility of greater trust
- More attention given to supplier selection, thereby improving the effectiveness of that process

- Lower purchase prices due to leveraging of volumes with fewer suppliers
- Fewer supplier performance reports or scorecards to issue
- Fewer supplier performance review meetings
- Improved supply base performance as lower performers are removed from the base
- Fewer accounts payable transactions
- Easier to identify early involvement candidates

Figure 15.2 Benefits of fewer suppliers

a range of benefits from maintaining a supply base that has been rationalized to a manageable level. The rationalization process almost always offers benefits that reduce complexity, many of which were never even considered beforehand as benefits.

Recently, General Motors (GM) has decided to rationalize its portfolio of countries and regions where it conducts business. In 2017, GM sold its European operations to Peugeot—and, more markets and countries could eventually exit the GM portfolio. Why did GM sell its European operations? A combination of factors, including buyers with fickle tastes and new government regulations, convinced executive management that Europe would not be a profitable market for the foreseeable future. The CEO of GM said, "Our overall philosophy is that every country, every market segment has to earn its cost of capital."

Standardize and Redesign Processes

Process design and redesign efforts should have the removal of waste and complexity as a primary objective. Process modeling using American National Standards Institute symbols and value stream icons are two recommended approaches when designing and redesigning work processes. Once an organization is able to conceptualize itself in terms of its core processes, steps can be taken to ensure that those processes are efficient, effective, and consistent (i.e., standardized) across operating units.

A center-led group should assume responsibility for designing processes that build in best practices and eliminate duplicate effort. It is hard to justify having every work center essentially develop its own set of processes. The complexity that results from suboptimal processes and duplication should not be a source of pride. Unfortunately, some interpret this to mean that every location or group must conform to a narrowly defined process with no deviation or flexibility allowed. Standard processes should provide a best-practice framework or platform that allows modifications where necessary, particularly when working across different geographic locations.

Use Information Technology

We often take for granted the use of information technology (IT) to make life less complex. Whether we bank online, use ATM machines to get cash, renew library books, shop for the holidays, renew prescriptions, or rely on powerful search engines to find information in a fraction of a second, the use of IT grows daily. Amazon's one-click feature is an example of removing transaction complexity from the online buying experience.

Whether stated or not, most IT applications are designed to remove, simplify, and streamline transactions. They also make the transfer of data from one system to another seamless while making information more transparent. Given that IT is a complexity killer, organizations will continue to be relentless in their search for applications that simplify the supply chain and the transactions that flow across it. IT supports something called complexity transfer. The systems rather than the users assume the complexity.

Streamline the Legal Review Process

If your legal department is a source of frustration and complexity, welcome to a group that has quite a few members. This frustration is often the result of a contract review process that can take months rather than days. For whatever reason, the legal review process for contracts is often excessively complex. Supply managers at a major logistics company were dismayed to find the longer term agreements they negotiated with suppliers required months to work their way through the legal review process. They were even more dismayed to see many months of contract benefits unrealized as original contract terms remained in place.

Streamlining the review process can happen in several ways. One way is to create contracts that are not overly complex. Most suppliers do not appreciate 50-page contractual agreements. While he was at IBM, the late Gene Richter reduced contracts from 40 pages on average to six pages. Another approach involves the use of preapproved contract language. Instead of reviewing an entire contract, lawyers review and initial only the changes that are made during contract negotiations. The legal department can also designate a representative to review contracts, presumably resulting in better response times. Finally, metrics can be compiled that track review times. The point here is that ways exist to take complexity out of the legal review process.

Modify the Organizational Design

We often overlook the fact that the features that comprise an organization's design can directly reduce organizational complexity. Research findings are clear that early supplier involvement on product design teams helps avoid complex rework as products move through the design process. Collocation models simplify patterns of communication as support personnel work in close proximity to their internal and sometimes external customers. And, cross-functional teams bring different perspectives together to make important decisions, usually enhancing the quality of the decision-making process.

An example of using organizational design to address complexity can be found at Boeing. The company has 9,000 employees outside of the United States, based in 70 countries that face challenges daily involving the laws, regulations, and customs of individual countries and jurisdictions.[22] Boeing has created five regional teams to support individual sites and business units. The purpose of these teams is to serve as *one-stop shops* to support Boeing business units as they operate internationally. Previously, each site or unit was forced to navigate some very complex issues on its own. Now, regional teams, acting much like centers of excellence, provide expert support to these locations, most of which are involved with different kinds of programs. Boeing is using its organizational design to minimize the complexities of international business.

Survey Stakeholders

One way to identify where complexity exists is to ask stakeholders directly. Try asking suppliers, customers, and employees directly whether or not your company is doing anything that makes their life unnecessarily complex. With online survey technology readily available, the barriers to using these surveys are low. Is it possible that your material planners change release quantities to suppliers right up to their delivery due date? Does your company have an online ordering system that confuses customers? Are employees frustrated over how to enroll in a benefits program? A survey of suppliers conducted on behalf of two original equipment manufacturers (OEMs) asked suppliers what these OEMs were doing to make their relationship overly complex. Suppliers provided dozens of responses that offered specific ways to reduce business complexity. If suppliers, customers, and employees take the time to provide feedback, then the requestor must ensure that feedback is reviewed and acted upon.

Develop Simple Rules

A body of research is emerging that counters the notion that complex algorithms and models are always more effective than simple rules of thumb or guidelines when making organizational decisions. Furthermore, a hypothesis put forward is that complex situations create so many possible courses of action that individuals become confounded, often to the point where they delay decisions, default to the safest option, or avoid making choices altogether. Research suggests that simple rules equal (and at times exceed) the effectiveness of more complicated analyses across a range of decision areas. Simple rules are most useful when the challenge is not to perform a process repeatedly and efficiently, but rather when a need exists to adapt quickly to changing circumstances.[23] While the analysis and data that lead to the rules may be sophisticated, and at times will even be complex, the resulting rules should be elegant in their simplicity as they provide guidance to users.

An example of simple rules involves the retailer Zara, a company that is synonymous with fast fashion. Since its inception the company's founder has insisted that the retailer always follow two simple rules—inventory at stores must be replenished twice a week and stores must receive their orders within 48 hours.[24] These simple rules are adhered to even as the retailer expands globally, thereby influencing the design and placement of Zara's production facilities.

Empower Employees

Recall from Chapter 2 that to empower means to give an individual or team decision-making authority. What most managers fail to recognize is that a failure to empower a team or individual to perform basic tasks or make decisions (up to a point) usually leads to individual complexity. A newly hired MBA at a global manufacturer was surprised to find that he could not organize a meeting without going through a cumbersome process to obtain a manager's signature. Unauthorized meetings of non-managers violated company policy.[25] Treating competent adults like untrustworthy children likely ensures that these individuals will not stay very long. Chapter 2 addressed various types of authority that apply to organizational work teams.

The ideas put forth here for battling complexity are varied and specific. While the first part of addressing any problem is recognizing that a problem exists, the other part involves dealing with the problem. Fortunately, relatively low-cost ways are available to address complexity.

CONCLUDING THOUGHTS

Complexity is not something that magically goes away by itself. Unfortunately, we often fail to grasp the extent or seriousness of complexity on supply chain performance. This is due partly to accounting systems that are incapable of capturing the true costs and impact of complexity. Complexity costs are scattered across different entities and buried within dozens of overhead accounts. Organizations that are serious about battling complexity will put forth a concerted effort to attack it wherever it exists.

While it is often an inevitable outcome of business decisions, and there is no question that firms that learn how to manage certain kinds of complexity can gain an advantage over their less competent competitors, unnecessary complexity should not be an accepted part of your business structure. If this is true, why is bad complexity a way of life at so many organizations?

REFERENCES

1. This chapter is adapted from R. Rudzki and R. J. Trent, *Next Level Supply Management Excellence*, (St. Lucie: FL: J. Ross Publishing, 2011), Chapter 13.

2. B. Kogut, "Introduction to Complexity: Emergence, Graphs and Management Studies," *European Management Review*, 4, no. 2 (2007): 67–72; M. Milgate, "Supply Chain Complexity and Delivery Performance: An International Exploratory Study," *Supply Chain Management*, 6, no. 3 (2001): 106–118.

3. P. M. Byrne and J. E. Johnson, "The Rights and Wrongs of Taxing Internet Retailers," *The Wall Street Journal*, July 23, 2012, from http://www.wsj.com.

4. M. J. Credeur, "Making United and Continental Fly in Formation," *Bloomberg Business Week*, (July 1, 2011): 23–24.

5. D. Paletta, "Billions in Bloat Uncovered in Beltway" *The Wall Street Journal*, March 2, 2011, retrieved from http://www.wsj.com.

6. J.R. Hagertry, "3M Begins Untangling its Hairballs," May 16, 2012, *The Wall Street Journal*, from http://www.wsj.com.

7. D. A. Kaplan, "Hostess is Bankrupt . . . Again," *Fortune*, 166, no. 3 (July 2, 2012): 63.

8. J. Chung and D. Lim, "Harvard Outsources Endowment," *The Wall Street Journal*, January 26, 2017, B1.

9. C. Kirkman, "Builders Balk at New Rule," *The Wall Street Journal*, November 18, 2016, A3.

10. S. Haywood, J. Spungin, and D. Turnbull, "Cracking the Complexity Code," *The McKinsey Quarterly*, (May 2007): 86.

11. J. Birkinshaw and S. Heywood, "Putting Organizational Complexity in its Place," *The McKinsey Quarterly*, (May 2012): 2.

12. J. Thatcher, "Managing a Rising Tide of SKUs," apics.org/magazine, (March/April 2017): 16.

13. J. Tyrangiel, "Tim Cook's Freshman Year," *Business Week*, (December 10–16, 2012): 69.

14. "Forbes Leader Board: The Best Countries for Business," *Forbes*, (February 28, 2017): 22. For the complete rankings of 139 countries, go to forbes.com/best-countries-for-business.

15. B. Stephens, "Doomed to Stagnate?" *The Wall Street Journal*, December 20, 2016, A21.

16. B. Stephens, A21.

17. E. Hamberger, "Freight Railroads Are Braking for Regulatory Creep," *The Wall Street Journal*, June 15, 2016, retrieved from https://www.wsj.com/articles/freight-railroads-are-braking-for-regulatory-creep-1465943599.

18. Rob Thomas from *This is How a Heart Breaks*.

19. Ari Ashe, FedEx Freight Adds Pricing Option Based on Distance, Dimensions, *Transport Topics*, (July 18, 2016): 3.

20. A. Ashe, "FedEx Pleased with Response to Freight Box for LTL Pricing," Transport Topics," (April 10, 2017): 6.

21. P. Teague, "P&G is King of Collaboration," *Purchasing*, 137, no. 9 (2008): 46.

22. B. Seil, "Excellence without Borders," *Boeing Frontiers*, 11, no. 8 (2012): 40–41.

23. D. Sull and K. Eisenhardt, "Simple Rules for a Complex World," *Harvard Business Review*, 90, no. 9 (2012): 69–74.

24. V. Walt, "Meet the Third-Richest Man in the World," *Fortune*, 167, no. 1 (January 14, 2013): 74–79.

25. L. Ryan, "5 Ways to Ensure Mediocrity in Your Organization," (May 17, 2010), from www.finance.yahoo.com/career-work/article.

EPILOGUE

Thriving in an era of rapid change and disruption requires an expansive and holistic view of the world. This view should lead to the realization that the past may not be as good a predictor of the future as we once thought. The great New York Yankees catcher Yogi Berra once commented that *the future ain't what it used to be.* He could easily have been talking about a world that is fraught with political, economic, and social changes that are increasingly complex and uncertain.

When thinking about the future, it would be wise to consider a set of megatrends that are affecting businesses of all kinds. These trends will continue to impact not only supply management, but also supply chains and even entire corporations. Ignorance of these trends can have a profound and lasting effect that is not at all positive. What are these megatrends, many of which will affect global supply networks and supply chains?

- Overall risk is increasing rather than decreasing, partly due to globally extended supply chains
- Demand is increasing for green, organic, and sustainable products and services
- New entrants are intensifying the level of competition within many industries
- Changing demographics are altering the composition of the workforce
- Volatile demand and supply pressures are affecting commodity markets
- Political and social unrest are affecting established social structures, including voter disillusionment with political parties
- Customer value expectations are increasing rapidly
- Faster technology changes and shorter product life cycles are disrupting established products and brands
- Stakeholder demands of all kinds are increasing
- Pressure to modify trade agreements and trading blocs is upsetting well-established systems (NAFTA and the European Union, for example)

- Easy access to data and information is shifting supply chain power from sellers to buyers on the consumer side and from buyers to sellers on the industrial side
- Industry acquisitions and consolidation (for example, in the air, railroad, and aerospace industries) are providing buyers with fewer choices

Even after taking these megatrends into account, there is no telling what wildcards are just waiting to break loose. Examples include confrontation with North Korea; global pandemics such as the Zika virus; an attack on the electrical grid; massive computer hacking; Iran closing the Strait of Hormuz; currency manipulation; conflict in the China sea; and natural disasters such as earthquakes, wildfires, volcanoes, and hurricanes. There is no shortage of topics that keep supply managers up at night.

While many of the problems that businesses face are self-inflicted, others are external to the organization. What we hope is that there is at least an awareness regarding what is happening around us. Being ignorant is not an ideal way for supply managers to go through life. Supply managers must create a supply network that is anticipatory, responsive, flexible, and resilient. If your supply network lacks these traits, well, good luck.

The purpose here is not to run around like Chicken Little screaming the sky is falling. It is about supply managers doing their part to enable their organizations to compete in an era of change and disruption. This means:

- Understanding the pressures that internal customers face and then supporting those customers;
- Anticipating disruptive events whenever possible and then working to manage their impact;
- Recruiting and retaining talent who have the skills and abilities to thrive in an uncertain world;
- Developing supply strategies that are innovative and leading edge;
- Appreciating the megatrends that are prevalent now and in the future; and
- Never having to say you are sorry because your supply management group was not up to the task.

The book, *Strategic Supply Management*, presented a framework and body of knowledge that is still relevant today. This book extends that knowledge by introducing a set of supply management topics that are an integral part of competing in an era of rapid change and disruption.

Let the journey continue.

INDEX

Page numbers followed by "f" indicate figures;
and those followed by "t" indicate tables.